Latinas in
American Politics

LATINOS AND AMERICAN POLITICS

Series Editor: Henry Flores
Advisory Board: Tony Affigne, Edwina Barvosa,
Benjamin Marquez, and Rodolfo Torres

Latinos and American Politics is concerned with the role Latinos, of all national origins and races, play in the American political process. Latinos are the largest minority group in the United States and have become the single most important group in presidential politics. This series, interdisciplinary in nature, seeks to advance the knowledge of Latino politics in the academy. The series includes works that focus on racial identities and their impact on intra-Latino relations and politics, Latina politics broadly defined to include the politics of gender, institutional and identity politics, electoral politics, community level politics and activism, the shifting types of politics Latinos have played in order to have their agendas entertained by political institutions, the behavior of Latina/o politicians, and the effects of the Civil Rights Acts on the political participation of Latinos. Contributors are encouraged to submit book-length manuscripts that encompass besides the above-named topics those focusing on gender, identity, racial politics, and all areas of public policy.

Titles in this Series

Latinas in American Politics: Changing and Embracing Political Tradition, edited by Sharon A. Navarro, Samantha L. Hernandez, and Leslie A. Navarro, 2016

Latinas in American Politics

Changing and Embracing Political Tradition

Edited by
Sharon A. Navarro,
Samantha L. Hernandez,
and Leslie A. Navarro

Foreword by Carol Hardy-Fanta

LEXINGTON BOOKS
Lanham • Boulder • New York • London

Published by Lexington Books
An imprint of The Rowman & Littlefield Publishing Group, Inc.
4501 Forbes Boulevard, Suite 200, Lanham, Maryland 20706
www.rowman.com

Unit A, Whitacre Mews, 26-34 Stannary Street, London SE11 4AB

British Library Cataloguing in Publication Information Available

Library of Congress Cataloging-in-Publication Data

Names: Navarro, Sharon Ann, editor, author. | Hernandez, Samantha L., editor, author. | Navarro, Leslie A., editor.
Title: Latinas in American politics : changing and embracing political tradition / edited by Sharon A. Navarro, Samantha L. Hernandez, and Leslie A. Navarro ; foreword by Carol Hardy-Fanta.
Description: Lanham : Lexington Books, 2016. | Includes bibliographical references and index.
Identifiers: LCCN 2016010021 (print) | LCCN 2016014910 (ebook) | ISBN 9781498533355 (cloth : alk. paper) | ISBN 9781498533362 (Electronic)
Subjects: LCSH: Hispanic American women—Political activity. | Hispanic Americans—Political activity. | Hispanic American women legislators. | Hispanic American legislators. | Women politicians—United States. | United States—Ethnic relations—Political aspects.
Classification: LCC E184.S75 L349 2016 (print) | LCC E184.S75 (ebook) | DDC 305.48/868073—dc23
LC record available at http://lccn.loc.gov/2016010021

∞™ The paper used in this publication meets the minimum requirements of American National Standard for Information Sciences—Permanence of Paper for Printed Library Materials, ANSI/NISO Z39.48-1992.

Printed in the United States of America

Contents

PART 2. STATE ELECTIONS: POLITICAL ASCENSION, CAMPAIGNS, COMMUNICATION, AND GOVERNING

Foreword

Carol Hardy-Fanta

"I've seen changes. . ."

—New Mexico woman leader (Prindeville 2003)

Twenty-five years ago, the literature in the fields of political science and women in politics was virtually silent on Latino politics—and Latinas had received even less attention. As I wrote at that time (Hardy-Fanta 1991), Latina women's leadership—whether in the formal sphere as candidates and elected officials, or as community activists—had been rendered invisible.

In listening to the women and men talking about politics when conducting the research that culminated in *Latina Politics, Latino Politics: Gender, Culture and Political Participation in Boston* (Hardy-Fanta 1993), I heard differences: Latino men talked about politics almost exclusively in terms of elections and positions. Latinas, in contrast, talked about making a change, making a difference, even as they combined electoral successes with their community-based efforts. I heard differences, but, because in the late 1980s there was no literature focusing on Latinas in politics, or, for that matter, on gender differences by race, I felt alone in the wilderness of a field occupied by White men. I would turn to my colleagues for validation that what I was uncovering was important, even as it challenged existing scholarship.

Such scholarship that existed on Latinos when I began my research was also based on flawed premises, showed limited understanding of the sociopolitical histories of Latino politics, and simply left Latinas out of the picture. I found, for example, those who claimed that Puerto Ricans and Dominicans came from a "weak participant culture" (Nelson 1979, 1037) and Latinos suffered from political apathy (see, for example, Kernstock

1972). Furthermore, even though Browning, Marshall and Tabb (1984) included "Hispanics" in the subtitle to their award-winning book, *Protest is Not Enough*, they paid only lip service to Latino politics; left out the political activism around bilingual education and the efforts of Dolores Huerta and Cesar Chávez of the United Farm Workers (in a study of cities in northern California, no less); and included nothing on gender or Latina women. Women rarely appear in the indices of major works such as *Latinos in the Political System* (Hero 1992); Pachon and DeSipio (1992) included only a single paragraph on gender in their analysis of Hispanic elected officials (p. 215).

Since then we have seen a burgeoning interest and increasing amount of research. In the ten years following publication of *Latina Politics, Latino Politics*, numerous journal articles were published on the political experiences, activism, and careers of Latinas (see, for example, Takash 1993; Sierra and Sosa-Riddell 1994; Hardy-Fanta 1995, 1997, 2002; Pardo 1998; Montoya et al. 2000; García and Marquez 2001; Fraga et al. 2006). More recently, researchers have continued to add to the scholarship (see, for example, Fraga and Navaro 2007; Fraga et al., 2008; Sierra 2009), including a number of full-length books on the subject. Sharon Navarro, co-editor of the current volume, authored *Latina Legislator: Leticia Van de Putte and the Road to Leadership* (Navarro 2008) and co-authored *Políticas: Latina Public Officials in Texas* (García et al. 2008); others include, for example, Bejarano's (2013) *The Latina Advantage*. And scholars in the relatively new field of intersectionality regularly include Latinas in their gender race analysis (Lien et al. 2007; Hardy-Fanta et al. 2006; Hardy-Fanta et al. 2016).

So, like the woman leader quoted above from Diane-Michele Prindeville's (2003) study on the political efficacy of American Indian and Hispanic women leaders, *I've seen changes*. It has been particularly heartening to see changes in political science, where women of color have increasingly moved from the "margins to the center" of new research.

With this history and a sense of change in the air, *Latinas in American Politics: Changing and Embracing Political Tradition*, co-edited by Sharon Navarro, Samantha Hernandez, and Leslie Navarro, is a welcome addition to the "new Latina scholarship" in political science. This volume includes chapters by newer scholars, as well as by senior scholars such as John Garcia, Jessica Lavariega Monforti, Christine Sierra, Tony Affigne, as well as, of course, Sharon Navarro.

In this volume we see researchers apply a variety of methods to a range of topics, including Latinas as candidates, how stereotypes affect Latinas, and the various campaign strategies that Latinas employ. Further, the scholars in this volume examine political ascension, communication, and legislative action that Latinas take once in office.

The contributors to *Latinas in American Politics* continue the tradition of contributing new insights through case studies based in discrete geographical areas: Hellwege and Sierra (New Mexico), Sharon Navarro (Texas), and Gonzalez and Affigne (Rhode Island). At the same time, the volume should be commended as it branches out into the new relatively uncharted arenas of research using new media and experimental design: José Marichal, for example, explores the Twitter accounts of Latina state legislators; in the chapter by Samantha Hernandez we also see analysis of Twitter accounts, this time of congressional candidates. Cargile, Merolla, and Shroedel's study is innovative not only because they fielded an Internet survey by YouGov, but also because of their experimental design; political science would do well to test theories and assumptions by such experiments. Lavariega Monforti and Gershon's chapter is also noteworthy due to its use of a survey experiment to study the viability of Latina candidates.

This volume also contributes to the state of knowledge through López's mixed-method study and Wilson and Urbano's close analysis of the substantive policy effects of the growth in Latinas in Congress over two decades. The chapter by John Garcia is important because, in the field of political science, large-scale, national surveys have the potential to yield generalizable results.

So, yes, like the woman leader quoted above, "I've seen changes" since first examining Latina politics more twenty-five years ago—and the publication of a volume such as this is evidence of these changes. With its rich content and strong scholarship, the chapters bring to light a deeper understanding of one of the most important groups in American politics today: Latina women—in all their varied roles, as candidates, elected officials, and political activists.

Acknowledgments

We would like to thank our contributors to this edited volume. Without them, this project could not have been possible. We especially thank Dr. Carol Hardy-Fanta for writing the foreword to this edited volume. It is our hope that we have succeeded in carrying on her work of examining the changing political landscape of the Latina political actor. I also thank my coeditors, Samantha and Leslie. I have known Samantha for quite some time as a very talented graduate student and now as a budding scholar. She is on her way to being a prolific scholar. I also thank Leslie for her inspiration and contribution to this project. She was the youngest Latina college president in the country and walked away from it all to inspire a new generation of Latina leaders. There are others we thank, our parents, Hope, Vidal, Fred, Suzie, and other family and friends, especially M. M. Pennington, who patiently stood by us as we completed this project. We thank reviewers and scholars who pointed out key items at the American Political Science Association Conference. We would like to thank the Latino Caucus for support of this project. She would also like to thank Sharon for her constant belief and support. We dedicate this book to Juan G. Perez.

Introduction

It has been said that the growth in the number of Latino elected officials in the United States is one sign of the Latino population's political progress. This progress is partly due to the ability of the Latino community to translate its population growth into increased political participation. Nearly three-quarters or 68 percent of all current Latino elected officials are male and 32 percent are female. The level of representation of Latinas who serve the United States in higher offices is greater than the level of all other female officeholders (NALEO 2015). For example, although 16.8 percent of all U.S. representatives are female, 26.1 percent of the Latinos in the House are women (NALEO 2015). According to the Center for American Women and Politics at Rutgers University, women hold 22.0 percent of the nation's state senate seats and 25.4 percent of the state lower house seats. In comparison, Latinas comprise 34.9 percent of the Latino state senators and 27.9 percent of the Latino state lower house members. As of 2015, nine Latina women serve in the 114th Congress, according to the Center for American Women and Politics. Of the seventy-nine women serving in statewide elective executive office, four are Latina. Eighty-six women out of the 1,789 women state legislators who are serving nationwide are Latina, and three of the 100 largest American cities have a Latina mayor (CAWP 2015). Despite this growth, Latinas in the political sphere receive little attention from the media, the public, and the academy.

We know that race can compound the challenges that women face as political candidates. In the case of Latinas, stereotypes as well as national media coverage and the labeling of "Latino" issues create a potential electoral burden for Latina candidates at the local, state, and national levels. The intersection of race and gender is complicated and often generates more questions than it answers. How are Latinas elected? Does this complex identity serve Latinas or hinder them? How does the intersection of gender and ethnicity in descriptive representation contribute to patterns of substantive representation?

This edited volume attempts to address these questions by examining the stereotypes Latinas face when making the decision to run for political office. Voters' perceptions on Latina candidate ideological standings, their clothing choices, campaign materials, and policy preferences provide insight as to with what party they are identified, how seriously they are taken as candidates, and how Latinas might use this insight to their advantage. The images that Latinas present and how they interact with voters via social media establishes a new dynamic in campaigning and allows for theory building in the areas of race, gender, and electability. Aside from campaigning, party identification creates a different type of barrier. How do Latinas bridge this? In this book, case studies of four prominent Latina officials are examined to understand the contexts and conditions in which Latinas as candidates and as elected officials experience intersectionality as an advantage and a disadvantage. We argue that the research on Latinas in politics has been generally under-studied and/or under-appreciated. Using qualitative and quantitative techniques, this timely volume aims to cover a range of essential topics that highlight Latinas as political players in an ever-changing landscape.

METHODOLOGY

In addition to content analysis and statistical modeling, the case studies include experimental methods in two forms: a survey experiment using a general population sample and a traditional experiment within minority-majority locations. The use of two forms of experiments allows the volume to explore perceptions of Latinas and how they would fare in elections without the traditional criticisms of experimental methods. Meaning, the two chapters present limitations, but the findings in each help the volume provide a more complete picture. The methodological diversity provides a thorough explanation of the Latina identity and how it is leveraged to achieve a successful campaign. Further, the case study analysis approach allows for an examination of the intersection of race, gender, and party identification. Although a different area of concern, Latina identity and party identification creates an interesting binary that merits further exploration.

Using interviews and secondary sources, authors Tony Affigne, Lizeth Gonzalez, Julia Marin Hellwege, Christine Marie Sierra, Sharon A. Navarro, and Patricia López compare the experiences of various Latinas who have run running as candidates and become policy-makers. When possible, the authors conducted face-to-face and follow-up interviews. While limitations exist in a qualitative analysis, a case study approach enables the interviewer to delve more deeply into the lives of subjects. Because these studies were conducted in states with a majority-minority Latino population, the analyses may be broadly applicable.

LOOKING AHEAD

We divide this edited volume into two parts. Part one explores Latinas and national elections. We begin the analysis with John Garcia's chapter, "Is there a Gender Divide: Exploring Latinas' Political Worlds and Intersectional Dimensions." While more attention has been directed to Latinas' (and Latinos') civic and political engagement, less attention has been paid to "internal variations" under this pan-ethnic umbrella. Important distinctions include national origin, nativity, social class, age, and gender. In the case of the latter, gender differences have been primarily focused upon participation levels and more recently on Latinas as office seekers and office holders. This study tries to expand the scope of participation (i.e., in both the range of politically related activities as well as civic engagement) in order to more fully understand the participatory worlds of Latino/as. In addition, the study identifies salient factors affecting Latinas' participatory spheres and incorporates the intersectional factors of marital status, nativity, gender roles, participatory orientations, and linked fate. While some research has highlighted differences in policy preferences and the saliency of policy areas, it is the antecedent attitudes and statuses that can affect Latina/os in different ways in terms of political participation and to what extent.

Garcia uses data from the *Election 2008 and Beyond Survey* (under the auspices of the Black Youth Project at the University of Chicago) as the vehicle to explore these relationships. Using Knowledge Networks (KN), an online computer methodology, he draws from a random population sample of U.S. households. The *Election 2008 and Beyond Survey* is a nationally representative panel survey that includes over-samples of Blacks, Latinos, Asians, and young people from 18–35. One-third of the Latino respondents came from Spanish-language dominant homes and received the questionnaire in Spanish. The Latino portion of the survey had 931 Latino/a respondents and over 500 Latinas. The data explore the attitudes and behaviors of different demographic groups, including those who are eligible to vote vs. those who are not. In addition, batteries of items on the survey tap media sources, language of media, and trust and reliance on media sources. The over-sample of 18- to 35-year-olds also allows us to explore cross-cutting influences among Latinas.

In chapter 2, Jessica Lavariega Monforti and Sarah Allen Gershon begin
with the argument put forth by Christina Bejarano in her book, *The Latina
Advantage: Gender, Race, and Political Success*. Bejarano explores evidence
that women of color may be helped rather than hurt by the way in which
the intersection of gender and ethno-racial identities influences U.S. voters. Using data from the American National Election Studies (ANES) from
1992 to 2009, Bejarano demonstrates that Anglo voters are more likely to
support a female (vs. male) candidate of color. Fellow minority voters are
also more likely to support the candidate. She argues that gender softens
the perception of ethno-racial differences. In other words, rather than
facing the double disadvantage of being a woman and a member of a minority, a Latina candidate for political office benefits from her "multiple
identity advantage." Bejarano also demonstrates that because Latinas
gather more qualifications in anticipation of potential electoral obstacles,
they are more successful candidates. Using original data from a survey
experiment with over 900 respondents in two minority-majority localities,
we simulated races to test Bejarano's theory in which a Latina candidate
runs not only against another Latina, but also against a Latino, an African
American male and female, and an Anglo male and female. Monforti
and Gershon examine the foundation of support for Latina candidates.
They focus on the differences in participants' willingness to vote for a
candidate and perceptions of character traits and issue positions while
considering the impact of voters' identities, the level of political interest,
ideologies, and political knowledge. They conclude by discussing the implications of our results for Latinas seeking elective office.

In chapter 3, Ivy A.M. Cargile, Jennifer L. Merolla, and Jean Reith
Schroedel explore stereotypes of female candidates and how these
stereotypes influence women's electoral prospects. The scholarship on
stereotypes of minority candidates is comparatively sparse, especially
with respect to Latino and Latina candidates. Although existing scholarship shows that Latino candidates are perceived as more compassionate,
liberal, pro-immigration reform, and less competent, Cargile, Merolla,
and Schroedel explore a broad range of perceived traits and issue competencies. Furthermore, experts know very little about the intersection
of gender and ethnicity as it pertains to Latina candidates. This study
is designed to provide answers to these important issues of stereotypes
(or lack thereof) with regards to Latino and Latina candidates. Cargile,
Merolla, and Schroedel conduct a survey experiment using YouGov in
which respondents were randomly assigned to evaluate hypothetical
candidates on a battery of trait and issue-competency measures, as well
as ideological placement. Their results suggest that Latino candidates
are stereotyped very similarly to female candidates on traits and issue
competencies relative to male candidates and white candidates. However, Latina candidates appear to be doubly disadvantaged by sex and

ethnicity in trait and issue-competency ratings: not only do they not receive a boost when both characteristics reinforce positive stereotypes; they also receive the lowest evaluations when both characteristics reinforce negative stereotypes.

In chapter 4, Walter Clark Wilson and Juan Luis Urbano examine Latina representation at the congressional level. A record nine Latinas won election to the U.S. House of Representatives in November 2012. Although the numbers remain small, clear progress has been made with regard to the descriptive representation of Latinas since Ileana Ros-Lehtinen became the first Latina U.S. Representative in 1989. Along with increasing Latina electoral success come obvious questions regarding how this growing group of representatives impacts the legislative process. In this study, Wilson and Urbano examine legislative agenda settings of Latina members of Congress between 1989 and 2008 in an effort to better understand what types of policies Latinas have championed as U.S. representatives. They explore whether Latinas have brought policies to the congressional agenda that have set them apart from other representatives and ask what we might expect by increasing Latina representation in Congress to shape future policy agendas. Using data from the *Congressional Bills Project*, Wilson and Urbano's analysis considers the content of more than 250 bills sponsored by Latina representatives during the period in question, and compares their agenda-setting behaviors with those of other, similarly situated representatives. Wilson and Urbano's findings yield insights into how and whether the intersection of gender and ethnicity in descriptive representation contributes to patterns of substantive representation and suggests that increasing Latina representation in the halls of Congress may substantively alter Congressional priorities.

In chapter 5, Samantha L. Hernandez's research focuses on the intersections of race, gender, and social media. Profiles that candidates create on social media enable a continuous connection with constituents—a major difference from past campaigns and elections. Blurring the lines of direct and indirect communication, how candidates come across on Twitter, Facebook, and personal websites is a critical component of a campaign. Hernandez compares the social media sites of congressional candidates and more specifically, uncovers the differences between Latina candidates' social media usage during the 2014 elections. Although held within different states, these races capture unique aspects, such as the comparison of Latina candidates to their male and female non-Latina counterparts, the development of social media usage, the messages that candidates perceive to be important to convey to constituents, and the importance of using new campaign techniques while still following traditional methods. In addition, the different pathways that lead these women to run for office, their age, educational attainment and physical traits that are usually discussed about female candidates and how candidates highlight their histories via their social media. Hernandez finds that the rate of tweets increases as an election draws near. Moreover, the types of images these candidates project on Facebook and Twitter often depict a blend of the "iron lady" and "loving mother" personae found in gender and politics. This mixed methods approach adds to the study of women in politics, media, and politics, as well as to new changes in campaigns and politics.

The second part of the book, which begins with chapter 6, focuses on state elections. José Marichal's "Networked Representation: Latina Legislators on Twitter," explores how Latina state legislators use Twitter to engage with their constituents. Little scholarship has been conducted on how social media changes the constituent/representative relationship. Marichal analyzes sixty-one Latina state legislator Twitter accounts. Although Twitter has become a significant mode of communication for a vast majority of the American public, politicians are only beginning to adopt the technology and political scientists have yet to look deeply at differences in use. In this chapter, Marichal seeks to test a number of theories regarding representation through Twitter. He uses grounded theory and constant comparative analysis (Glaser and Strauss 1967) to compare posts and patterns in Tweets. From this analysis, Marichal develops a theory of *networked representation* that highlights the novel ways in which Latina legislators use social media tools as part of their governing style. He groups the legislators' Twitter behavior online into three distinct elements: virtual home style, intra-party network building, and personalization.

In chapter 7, Julia Marin Hellwege and Christine Marie Sierra analyze the election of the country's first Latina governor, Susana Martinez, in 2010, which was an important moment for several reasons. First, Martinez's election marked a significant advancement for women in reaching executive leadership positions—to date, only thirty-seven women have held a gubernatorial position in any U.S. state. In addition, it marked only the third time in history that two women competed for governor, as Martinez ran against Democratic nominee and former New Mexico Lieutenant Governor Diane Denish. Martinez's election, as a Latina Republican, also posed an interesting question for Latino partisanship in a time when immigration was (and still is) a highly divisive issue. Finally, her election presents an interesting contrast and point of comparison to Michelle Lujan Grisham, the first female Democrat and the first Latina to win congressional office (CD1) since its creation in 1969. Lujan Grisham won her seat—the largest urban area in the state—in the 2012 election. Examining the elections and time in office of both Martinez and Grisham provides an opportunity to assess through a qualitative analysis whether Latinas are disadvantaged (Githens and Prestage 1977; Fraga and Navarro 2007) or advantaged (Scola 2013; Bejarano 2013; Fraga et al. 2008) as candidates and officeholders in electoral politics.

Marin Hellwege and Sierra propose an examination of the Latina identity in electoral politics and within partisan and institutional contexts. They use existing theory and empirical evidence to understand how Latinas as candidates and as elected officials will experience the advantages or disadvantages of intersectionality. Marin Hellwege and Sierra also examine the partisanship of Latina descriptive representatives and how Latina elected officials seek to mobilize and respond to a more divided partisan Latino electorate. To hone in on the causal mechanisms of the complex relationship between identity, partisanship, and institutions, they present case studies of New Mexico Latina elected officials, Governor Susana Martinez, and U.S. Congresswoman Michelle Lujan Grisham. Martinez and Grisham have each reached significant leadership positions and their choices pose interesting contrasts in terms of branch (executive/legislative), party (Republican/Democrat), level of government (federal/state), and size of district (state-wide/congressional district).

In chapter 8, Sharon A. Navarro analyzes the Texas lieutenant governor's race between state Democratic Senator Leticia Van de Putte and Republican state Senator Dan Patrick. Senator Patrick reportedly spent close to $10 million on media—a historic amount in Texas—and won. Van de Putte was the first viable, competitive Latina candidate to run for the state's most powerful statewide office. Although the second-highest office in the state, the lieutenant governor's office is constitutionally more powerful than the office of governor. Van de Putte set out to do what no Democrat had done in twenty years—win a statewide office. The demographics of the state are changing from Anglo majority to Hispanic majority. By all accounts, Van de Putte, as a Latina, was the perfect demographic. She entered Texas politics when few women and even fewer Latinos were elected to office. She has deep roots in the state as a sixth-generation Texan, or *Tejana,* and both her maternal and paternal grandmothers are from Mexico. Was she the candidate to turn the state from red to purple? How did she utilize her identity to her advantage? Did she utilize her identity strategically? This case study examines how campaign television ads managed to nullify Leticia Van de Putte's strategic ability to use race, ethnicity, or gender to win the Texas lieutenant governor's office.

Lizeth Gonzalez and Tony Affigne, in chapter 9, explore political challenges, electoral conditions, and future prospects for Latina political leaders in the state of Rhode Island. Based on interviews with candidates, state legislators, city and town councilors, school committee members, and political appointees, our findings depict patterns of recruitment and exclusion, ambition, opportunity, and constraint that confront Latinas who aspire to elective office and political leadership in the state.

Rhode Island Latinos appear on the cusp of significant empowerment. While just a fraction of the broader electorate, Latino voters in

2010 nonetheless provided slim margins of victory for Governor Lincoln Chafee, 1st District Congressman David Cicilline, and Secretary of State Ralph Mollis. A Latino mayor was elected in Providence the same year. Now, after the 2014 elections, Latinos and Latinas hold sixteen elected offices and numerous board, commission, and administrative posts in state and local government.

Among this group, it is the *female* office holders—Latinas—who predominate, having been elected to the state house of representatives and municipal councils in Providence, Pawtucket, Central Falls, and Smithfield. Of the state's Latino elected officials, nine are women and seven are men. The women hail from Hispanic origins in Puerto Rico, Colombia, Guatemala, Panama, and the Dominican Republic. Thus, although Latina officials in Rhode Island represent only a small portion of the Latina population in the country, they are distinctive. Many of them present as leaders from commonly underrepresented Latin American countries.

Gonzalez and Affigne's chapter explores their experiences and their roles in politics through qualitative research in the form of confidential interviews. Our subjects respond to a series of questions and provide additional personal and descriptive narratives about their experiences as Latinas in politics. The scope of questions draws on experiences that took place both before and after being elected or appointed. Gonzalez and Affigne find evidence, for example, of Latinas' uncertain reception in the political sphere, an emphasis on role modeling, and obstacles to leading an "independent" lifestyle in regards to the family. They also find that changing conditions over time have altered outsiders' perception of Latinas and consequently in the way Latinas are received in government.

In chapter 10, Patricia D. López examines Latina intersectionality and race-gendering in Texas' legislative process. She begins by asking: what if more Latinas held political office? This question has become a driving force behind growing efforts to increase the representation of Latinas in politics. While scholars have long noted the significance of Latinas as political actors, their trajectories and ascent into politics, and the need to uncover the multiple dimensions of their political experiences, a dearth of scholarship remains in regards to Latinas' political practices once they hold decision-making positions, particularly in state legislatures. This chapter draws from a larger ethnographic study that examines the political actors and forms of agency informing education policymaking during the 81st, 82nd, and 83rd legislative sessions of the Texas State Legislature. Using the theoretical concept of race gendering as a political process that silences, stereotypes, and challenges the epistemic authority of women of color, López examines how one Latina legislator navigates the race-gendered context of Texas' legislative process. This analysis of political agency reveals the possibilities and double-edged sword of Latinas in state-level politics.

ONE

NATIONAL ELECTIONS: BELIEFS, CAMPAIGN STRATEGIES, ELECTABILITY, AND LEGISLATIVE STRENGTH

ONE

Are There Gender Differences Among Latina/os?

Exploring Participatory Orientations

John García

Most of the extant research on gender and politics has examined the effects of gender on the world of politics. A significant amount of this research has focused on the gender gap, which has tried to assess any patterns of variations between male and female members to see if they have differential levels of political engagement (Burns et al. 2001; Inglehart and Norris 2000). For example, the concept of the triple oppressions (the intersection of race, class or cultural traditions, and gender) can compound access to opportunity structures, or diminish activism and political engagement, or heighten concerns about social justice and equality (Hardy-Fanta 2007; García Bedolla 2007). Research on gender equality (or the limitations of it) has suggested that structural or institutional factors, gender-biased socialization, socioeconomic status, and gender roles are important contributors to understand the political, behavioral, and attitudinal domains for males and females (Sapiro 1983; Verba et al. 1997). This chapter examines Latino/as and their participatory orientations. Participatory orientations such as political trust, efficacy, and interest serve as antecedent cognitive assessments that can facilitate and motivate individuals to become engaged politically (Montoya et al. 2000). While previous studies have examined a variety of participatory activities that may be differentiated by gender and its contributing factors, this chapter studies important attitudes that can facilitate and motivate individuals to become politically engaged.

LATINO/A POLITICAL PARTICIPATION

There has been growing attention to the political involvements of Latino/as in the American political system. Earlier research portrayed the

Mexican-origin population as the "sleeping giant" whose potential was driven by a fast growing and youthful population and its regional concentration in the southwest; but the actualization fell far short (García Bedolla 2005; García 2011). Several decades forward, the pan-ethnic "aggregation" of Latinos continues to press the themes of a fast growing community, increasing political capital, and increased attention by political parties, mass media, and political institutions (Espiritu 1992; Gonzalez 2008). Our discussion of participation continues to assess the political development of Latinos as a political force with more focus on voting (turnout and registration), party affiliation and support, identifying salient political issues and attitudes. The overall research findings indicate identifiable progress by Latinos in terms of expanding its proportion of the active electorate and crystalizing policy concerns and priorities; while, at the same time (Fraga et al., 2010; García 2010), Latinos still lagged in terms of voter registration and turnout, mobilization efforts, and obtaining statewide and national offices. While socio-economic factors, a younger population, and an appreciable non-naturalized foreign-born segment continue to be contributors of lower electoral participation "rates," more recently, institutional and policy actions such as voter identification laws, anti-immigration policies and attitudes, unresponsive educational systems limit and/or depress Latino political participation.

For our purposes, I will provide some backdrop about Latinos' political engagement and the impact of Latinas on political participation. A long-standing theme of Latino/as boarding a rising wave of influence and impact on the American political landscape has seen some recent evidence of that development (Fraga et al. 2006). Electorally, among racial/ethnic groups, Latinos have experienced the greater registration increases, especially in key electoral states (i.e., California, Texas, New York, and Florida). While Latinos still demonstrate turnout gaps with White and African American Voters (usually 10–15 percent), directionally it is closing slowly. Partisan-wise, Latinos still maintain a proclivity to affiliate and support the Democratic Party and its candidates. Overall, the Democratic Party enjoys a 2.5:1 advantage over Latinos who identify with the Republican Party (García 2015). A continuing partisan-related issue is the substantial percentage of Latinos who do not identify with either party (as no preference or independent). In addition, among Latino Democrats, the percentage of moderate or weakly identified partisans is noteworthy (García and Sanchez 2007).

In addition to partisanship (Box-Steffensmeier et al. 2004; Cain et al. 1991), Latinos' political ideology reflects similarity with much of the general electorate, by falling more into the moderate ranges between extreme conservative and extreme liberal continuum. They are not as conservative as the press and partisan officials posit. On social and economic issues and supportive participation of government, Latinos score higher than their white counterparts (Erskine 1971; Hood and Morris 1997). On moral issues, while there is a tendency to be on more of the conservative "side," their "distribution" leans more to the middle. The other aspect of Latino political engagement lies with the mobilization process. For political parties, the catch-22 scenario has been lower rates of registration and turnout with a growing population base. So the calculus has been the ratio of the expended resources to activate Latinos vs. the expected returns in terms of levels of electoral support (Verba et al. 1995; Wolbrecht 2000). One of the consequences of this ambivalent or benign neglect has been the relatively infrequent incorporation of campaign mobilization to target Latinos for mobilization. More recent research has examined mobilization efforts in the Latino community and the effectiveness of using co-ethnics as the contacting persons and identifying salient issues. In addition, several media-oriented studies demonstrate how Spanish language media serves as informational source and catalytic impetus for political actions (Abrajano and Panagopoulos 2011; Eshbaugh-Soha 2014; Kerevel 2011).

Within the broad scope of political participation have been the concepts of civic engagement and participatory orientations. In the case of the former, civic engagement refers to activities that can position and enhance an individual to have "political interface" with the political process and system. Belonging to civic and/or neighborhood organizations or active involvement in their children's schools can inform the individual, acquire important skills and experiences, and seek redress from political decision-making units (i.e., school boards, city councils, state legislatures, and so forth. (Leighley 2001; Lien 1998). Thus participation in these civic "arenas" brings the individual closer to becoming politically engaged as well as developing important organizational skills and political knowledge. Participatory orientations represent a set of cognitive attitudes that "establish" a person's attachment, support, and belief system toward the polity, its values and basic tenets. More specifically, efficacy (sense that one's actions can make a difference), trust (belief in the processes and responsiveness of government and its officials will be fair and just), and belief in democratic principles and institutions can serve as building blocks to impact policy-making and support for candidates. Conversely, cynicism leads to distrust and possible contempt for political institutions, officials and lack of confidence of a fair and equitable political process. Such a disposition could lead to apathy, withdrawal, or engaging in non-conventional political activities (García 2011). While I have tried to outline and discuss, briefly, the scope of Latino political participation, I will now discuss what are major contributors to the patterns of Latino political participation.

Political science has concentrated much of its intellectual energy on the connection of the "citizenry" and its government. Interactions between these two segments represent who governs, what government does or does not do, and levels and types of political engagement by individuals and groups (Tolbert and Hero 1996; Fraga et al. 2010). Identifiable and active communities of interests place demands and preferences for public policies and representation. In the case of Latinos, many of the national origin groups (i.e., Mexican origin, Cubans, Dominicans, Puerto Ricans, etc.) have been politically active on behalf of their community's needs and status (Itzigsohn and Dore-Cabral 2000; Pardo 1990). Besides, socio-economically based issues, and, more recently, immigration, Latinos' political agenda has included basic concerns about social justice, equal rights, equal opportunities and representation, and equal protection (Hood et al. 1997; Jones-Correa 1998). Advocacy and political engagement have been organized around group status and commonalities of cultural, historical, and experiences in the United States. As a result, group identity and consciousness along racial/ethnic lines is a foundational element for Latino political behaviors and attitudes. Not only does group identity and consciousness define community and "boundaries," they serve to establish connections for collective action and policy agendas (Masouka 2006; Lawless and Fox 2005).

Most studies of political participation focused upon an individual's attributes and experiences to examine the accumulation of resources and experiences that are transferrable to the political world. Early socialization can serve to inculcate participatory roles and interest and exposure to adult participatory actions. The familial setting is affected by the race/ethnicity of the household, gender role differentiation, and class status. In these situations, minority households, especially low income and being female, affects their levels of political engagement (usually lower) (Fraga et al. 2006; Beltran 2010). The prevailing explanatory participation model is the resource model (Verba et al. 1997). That is, time, money, and civic skills help to develop communication and organizational skills that are critical for political activity. For the most part, Latinos, other minorities, and women have been at the lower end of such resources. Our earlier discussion of group consciousness has been incorporated into models of participation such that salient group consciousness (Sanchez 2006; Stokes 2003) can compensate for lower socioeconomic status to affect greater levels of political engagement (Verba et al. 1995).

While the individual has been the focus of determining their political behaviors and attitudes, the influence of one's environmental context, institutional practices, and legal status also play a significant part. For communities of color, discriminatory practices, prior and past legislation that limits their involvement, exclusionary policies (Schlesinger and Heldman

2003), and differential and unfair treatment influence these group political patterns (Bennett and Bennett 1999; Clark and Clark 1986). Minority group status has been a struggle to be politically active as well as the motivation to seek change and redress through the political system (Hancock 2007). This differential status and treatment has a gender dimension as women of color have been characterized as experiencing "triple oppression or triple bind constraints" in which the combination of gender, race/ethnicity, and class creates significant obstacles for full political engagement (Carter et al. 2002; Crenshaw 1989; Simien 2007). Gender roles that perpetuate subordinate status and public and private spheres (i.e., women "take on" certain roles in the home and "assume" different ones in public) are reflected in their patterns of civic and political engagement. Research on Latinas focuses on the added elements of traditional cultural values and patterns around gender and expected roles. Interestingly, recent studies have shown that the "pervasive" machismo culture attributed to Latinos is not reflected as strongly in stated attitudes (Jaramillo 2010; Pardo 1997). Added dimensions deal with immigration status and legal standing, as well as English language proficiency. For the most part, being foreign-born, limited English language proficiency, and lesser familiarity with the American political system represent obstacles for Latino/a political participation.

On the whole, the comparisons of Latina versus Latino political engagement have produced mixed results (García Bedolla et al. 2007; Montoya 1996; Norrander 1999). For example, explorations of the gender gap in terms of levels of participation, group identity, and voting and registration show little difference. The saliency of policy areas has a slight gender "bias" indicating that Latinas have stronger levels of support and priorization for social welfare and family-oriented policy areas (Hancock 2007; García Bedolla 2007). Latinas are more engaged civically in their communities and schools than their Latino counterparts.

In the areas of conventional political participation, (i.e., electoral) Latino/as are making gains but gender has not marked any major differences. In addition, a recent study about Latino/a group identity shows that Latinas are less likely to identify as American than Latino men (Silber Mohamed 2015). At the same time, Latino men express a greater desire to blend into the United States while Latinas are more likely to want to maintain a distinct Hispanic culture. However, consistent with intersectionality theory, which emphasizes the interaction between race/ethnicity, gender, and class; these differences disappear once a certain socioeconomic status is reached. Silber Mohamed (2015) also demonstrated a stronger relationship between an American identity and political participation for Latino men than for Latinas.

Overall, examination of gender and any "gaps" that may exist between Latinas and Latinos has received mixed results. That is, in many areas of conventional political engagement, little or no statistical significance was evident. At the same time, areas of policy salience and civic involvement in community organizations indicate that Latinas are different from their Latino counterparts. In dealing with gender, the interactions of class in addition to being a Latina provides a fuller and a more complex set of relationships (Montoya et al. 2000; Scholzman et al. 1999). As I indicated at the offset of this chapter, my focus on gender among Latinos is focused on the participatory orientations that can serve as precursors to a variety of political behaviors and policy preferences. The vehicle for this investigation is the Election 2008 and Beyond project organized and directed by the National Black Youth Project at the University of Chicago.

ELECTION 2008 AND BEYOND SURVEY: DESIGN AND IMPLEMENTATION

The Election 2008 and Beyond is a nationally representative panel survey that includes over samples of Blacks, Latinos, Asians, and young people ages 18–35. One-third of the Latino respondents come from Spanish language dominant homes and received the questionnaire in Spanish. The survey's purpose was to explore the attitudes and behaviors of different groups of people, including eligible voters. Knowledge Networks conducted three waves of this study focusing on attitudes, knowledge, and behaviors of U.S. adults leading up to, and following, the November 2008 general election. The Wave 1 survey was fielded between October 17 and November 3, 2008. The survey was available in both English and Spanish, depending on respondent preference. Information on the initial and resulting sample sizes, by age/race-ethnicity and overall and resulting completion rates are provided in Table A1.1 (see appendix A for chapter 1).

Knowledge Networks has recruited the first online research panel—KnowledgePanel—that is representative of the entire U.S. population. Panel members are randomly recruited by telephone and households are provided with access to the Internet and hardware if needed. Knowledge Networks surveys are based on a sampling frame, which includes both listed and unlisted numbers, and is not limited to current Web users or computer owners. Knowledge Networks selects households using random digit dialing (RDD). Once a person is recruited to the panel, they can be contacted by e-mail (instead of by phone or mail). This permits surveys to be fielded very quickly and economically.

Knowledge Networks' panel recruitment methodology uses the quality standards established by selected RDD surveys Knowledge Networks utilizes list-assisted RDD sampling techniques on the sample frame consisting of the entire United States residential telephone population and excludes only those banks of telephone numbers (consisting of 100 telephone numbers) that have zero directory-listed phone numbers. Two strata are defined using 2000 Census Decennial Census data that has been appended to all telephone exchanges. The first stratum has a higher concentration of Black and Hispanic households and the second stratum has a lower concentration relative to the national estimates. Telephone numbers for which Knowledge Networks is able to recover a valid postal address is about 60–70 percent. In May 2007 subsampling was resumed at a rate of 0.75 of non-address households.[1]

LATINO PANEL RECRUITMENT

The Latino panel sample is recruited by a hybrid telephone recruitment design based on random-digit dial (RDD) probability-based landline sample of U.S. Latinos and Hispanic-surname sample. It is a geographically balanced sample that covers areas that, when aggregated, encompass approximately 93 percent of the nation's 45.5 million Latinos. The Latino Panel covers the entire United States—fifty states and the District of Columbia. National coverage of Latinos is obtained via bi-lingual telephone recruitment using the KnowledgePanel RDD-based probability sampling. The KnowledgePanel recruitment, therefore, captures the full spectrum of assimilated and unassimilated Latinos, including Latinos whose primary language is English and others for whom it is Spanish. To increase the sample size of Latinos that are less assimilated or so-called "unassimilated," use of oversampling of Latinos residing in seventy United States Designated marte areas (DMAs) that have relatively large Latino populations was implemented. The DMA-oversampling approach is dedicated to the recruitment of Spanish- Language-Dominant adults that are categorized as "unassimilated" on the basis of Hispanic self-identification, Spanish-language TV viewing frequency, and primary spoken language.[2]

LATINO/AS IN WAVE I: ELECTION 2008 AND BEYOND

The foci of this survey project were to examine the various dimensions of attitudes and behaviors among the diverse populations comprising the American political landscape. Extensive attention was directed to a wide range of political and civic activities, media sources and use, political variables (i.e., ideology, party identification, candidate assessment, etc.) and general political attitudes and policy preferences. This chapter extracts the Latino segment of Wave 1 to explore their participatory orientations and whether any gender differences are evident. In addition, given the established research literature on the role of socio-economic and gender roles as well as forms of group consciousness, a multivariate analysis is conducted to determine the contributing factors for the selected participatory orientations.

ANALYSIS AND DISCUSSION

As indicated in the Election 2008 and Beyond (E08B) description, the nationally diverse sample enables this researcher to extract the Latinos from the Wave 1 file with sufficient numbers to conduct this inquiry. The demographic narrative in table 1.1 provides some general information, primarily socio-demographic among the Latino/a respondents. Some noteworthy distinction based upon gender includes educational attainment. A higher percentage of Latinas have some college experience and college degrees. In addition, the traditional mode of Latinos as head of the house-

Table 1.1. Demographic Characteristics of Latino/as in Election 2008 and Beyond

Demographic Characteristics	Latinas	Latinos	Total
Educational Attainment			
Less than High School	111(11.9)	65 (7.0)	176
High School Grad	131 (14.0)	99 (10.6)	230
Some College	190 (20.4)	109 (11.7)	299
BA and beyond	138 (14.8)	90 (9.6)	228
Head of Household *			
Yes	181 (19.4)	389 (41.7)	570
No	267 (28.6)	96 (10.3)	363
Marital Status			
Married	293 (31.4)	188 (20.2)	481
Widowed	9 (.1)	19 (2.0)	28
Divorced/Separated	66 (7.1)	48 (5.1)	114
Not Married	113 (12.1)	80 (8.6)	193
Cohabitating	79 (8.5)	38 (4.1)	117
Age*			
18–29	160 (17.1)	63 (6.8)	223
30–44	255 (27.3)	167 (17.9)	422
45–59	101 (10.8)	93 (10.0)	194
60+	40 (4.3)	54 (5.8)	95
Employment Status *			
Work for Pay	264 (34.5)	238 (31.1)	502
Self-Employed	49 (6.4)	29 (3.8)	78
Not working	6 (.8)	5 (.7)	11
Not Looking for Work	83 (10.8)	32 (4.2)	115
Retired	34 (4.4)	26 (3.4)	60
Total N			933

*Significant @ .05 level

hold is reflected by the distribution on this status by gender (i.e., more males as heads of households). Age-wise, the grouping of thirty- to forty-four-year-olds is more the case for Latinas. Even though both Latinas and Latinos have similar percentages as employed, a higher percentage of Latinas are not looking for work.

The findings in table 1.2 represent some political dimensions in which to compare Latinas and Latinos. The political items included party identification, ideology, and voter registration status. Overall, Latinos are clearly more Democratic by a ratio of 3:1. That is, if one combines strong and not so strong partisans, then Latinos are more likely Democrats. In terms of political ideology, Latinos tend to fall in the middle range on the liberal to conservative continuum. Yet there are some gender differences as Latinas are more likely to be situated in the moderate to liberal end of the continuum. On the other hand, percentage-wise, Latinos are more evident in the conservative and extremely conservative end. There are also some differences in extent of registration status. Latinas are more likely to be registered voters than their Latino counterparts. The results of these political dimensions do suggest there are indicators of gender differences. In the case of voter registration, the Current Population Voting and Registration survey in November (even number years) has shown not only gains in Latinos as registered voters, but more so among Latinas.

Table 1.2. Politically Related Characteristics of Latina/os in Election 2008 and Beyond

Politically Related Characteristics	Latinas	Latinos	Total
Party Identification			
Strong Republican	37 (4.0)	18 (2.0)	55
Not so Strong Republican	37 (4.0)	37 (4.0)	74
Leaning Republican	68 (7.4)	58 (6.3)	126
Undecided	25 (2.7)	14 (1.5)	39
Leaning Democrat	151 (16.5)	96 (10.5)	247
Not so Strong Democrat	82 (8.9)	50 (5.5)	132
Strong Democrat	149 (16.2)	95 (10.4)	244
Political Ideology*			
Extremely Liberal	19 (2.1)	15 (1.6)	34
Liberal	97 (10.6)	63 (6.9)	160
Somewhat Liberal	58 (6.3)	45 (4.9)	103
Moderate	221 (24.1)	130 (14.2)	351
Somewhat Conservative	79 (8.6)	40 (4.4)	119
Conservative	7 (.8)	56 (6.1)	63
Extremely Conservative	14 (1.5)	72 (7.9)	86
Registered to Vote			
Yes	384 (41.5)	234 (25.3)	618
No	183 (19.8)	124 (13.4)	307
Total			933

Significant @ .05 level

As our focus lies with the "precursors" of political behaviors—partici-patory orientations, we present three such measures that are the results of created scales. The first one is referenced as "political efficacy." The two items (on a strongly agree to strongly disagree continuum) deal with feeling that by participating, one can make a difference. The other item is the respondent's assessment that they have the "necessary skills" to par-ticipate politically. The Cronbach alpha score was .67. The range of sum-mated scores was presented in low to high clusters. There were relatively little gender differences as most of the Latino/as fell into the medium to high range. This distribution would suggest that Latino/as are inclined to see their roles in American politics as active participants. At the same time, there is evidence that countervailing attitudes and structural condi-tions can depress or create obstacles to realize political efficacy orienta-tions into political actions.

The second participatory orientation can be characterized as political trust or its converse—cynicism. The two items included feeling that politi-cal leaders care about "people like themselves" and whether government is run more by big interests. Again a Cronbach alpha of .779 was produced. We constructed to scale to directionally indicate higher combined scores as representing high levels of cynicism about government and its leadership representing the interest of the people at large. There were gender differ-ences as Latinas were more likely to hold less trusting views of govern-ment than their Latino counterparts. If such an orientation is more evident among Latinas, this could result in a more reluctant disposition to use one's skills to impact political arenas. Another possible interpretation is that La-tino/as could differentiate levels of government such that one's views of the national government can be more positive (or negative) than local or state government. Our federalist system means that the citizenry interacts with many different governments most of the time.

Finally our last participatory orientation can be characterized as system beliefs about the American democratic system. That is, a series of four items constitute this participatory cluster. They include: (1) everyone in America has an equal chance to succeed; (2) the American legal system treats everyone equally; (3) people have a fair chance to succeed in this economic system; and (4) belief in the fundamentals of our Constitution. The Cronbach alpha for these items was .758. Latinas scored more in the medium range on this cluster of items, and slightly more on the lower end than their Latino counterparts.

Not unlike examination of gender differences in the realm of political behaviors, our initial examination of participatory orientations had some similar results. Yet, the contributing factors to these orientations may be influence by gender and other established factors. The next step in this chapter is a series of multivariate analyses. We will use each of the three scaled participatory orientations as the dependent variables. Our independent variables represent a combination of socio-demographic variables (i.e., age, income, religious affiliation, marital status, language use, educational attainment, and employment status). Two additional independent variables were gender and a "double-bind affinity." In the case of the latter variable, the Election 2008 and Beyond had a series of questions that tapped a sense of group affinity and connectedness. The battery included connections with other Latino national origin groups, with other minority groups, and with other women. The three-item battery on Latinos being connected linguistically, culturally, and interests did not scale together. However the items that indicated connectedness with other women and other minority groups did produced a Cronbach alpha of .749. As I had indicated earlier, much of the literature on gender focuses on the intersectionality of gender, class, and race/ethnicity. This variable can be described as the double bind component in which Latino/as evidence affinities beyond their own ethnic group background. This result affords an opportunity to empirically incorporate a measure of this intersection. Finally, the dependent variables are ordered whereas the levels of agreement represent the upper end of the summated scores. Or for interpretation purposes, efficacy, trust, political cynicism, and system beliefs are on the higher end of the scale values.

Table 1.3. Participatory Orientations and Attitude Clusters Among Latino/as in 2008 Election and Beyond

Participatory Orientations	Latinas	Latinos	Total
Political Efficacy[1]			
Low	53 (5.8)	29 (3.2)	82
Medium	271 (29.5)	139 (15.1)	410
High	234 (25.5)	193 (21.0)	402
Political Cynicism[2]			
Low	54 (5.9)	29 (2.8)	83
Medium	281 (30.6)	162 (17.7)	443
High	223 (24.3)	168 (18.3)	391
American Belief System[3]			
Low	143 (15.6%)	91 (9.9)	243
Medium	322 (35.2)	189 (20.7)	602
High	91 (9.9)	79 (8.6)	170

1. Q42 I believe that by participating in politics I can make a difference. Would you say you... : Q43 I have the skills and knowledge necessary to participate in politics? Do you... (Str. Disagree to Str. Agree)
2. Q44 The leaders in government care very little about people like me. Do you... : Q45 The government is pretty much run by a few big interests looking out for themselves and their friends. Would you say you... Str. Disagree to Str. Agree).
3. Q47 How much of the time do you think you can trust the government in Washington to do the right thing? Q48 "In the United States, everyone has an equal chance to succeed." ; Q49 Generally the American legal system treats all groups equally ; Q50 "In the American economic system, everyone has a fair chance." : Q 51 I believe in the fundamentals of our political system like the Constitution. (Str. Disagree to Str. Agree)

The results of the multivariate analysis reveal some interesting results. Since many of the socio-demographic variables were categorical variables, the use of dummy variables was implemented. Employment status, homeowner, and gender are dichotomous with being employed, a homeowner and female with values of one. The religious affiliation variables were a series of dummies (i.e., Catholic, Protestant, other religious affiliations, and no religious affiliation) and being Catholic as the reference variable. Language use was measured by English speaking, bilinguals, and Spanish speakers with Spanish speakers as the reference group. Finally, income categories were clustered into four income levels and the lowest income category was the reference group. Educational attainment was measured by years of schooling.

The first dependent variable analyzed was political efficacy. For the most part, several socio-demographic variables proved to have significant B's. They were language proficiency (bilinguals and English speakers), and those with greater number of years of schooling. Relative to Spanish speakers, those Latino/as who have greater facility with English had higher levels of political efficacy. While these factors had a positive effect to enhance efficacy, the one negative and significant factor was gender. In this case, an inverse relationship indicated that Latinos exhibited higher levels of efficacy. Interestingly, other socio-demographic factors associated with participation did not produce significant results (i.e., home ownership, income, religious affiliation, and employment status). Our "double bind" variable produced a positive coefficient, but not a significant coefficient. As political efficacy serves as a valuable resource for political engage, the gender results could be an intervening factorment in possible participatory gender gaps.

The second dependent variable examined dealt with perceptions about governmental responsiveness and class interest biases. Directionally, the higher score represented perceptions that government favored special interests rather than general public interest or those at the middle to lower end of the economic spectrum. Our gender variables (i.e., gender and minority/gender) produced significant coefficients, but in different directions. Whereas Latinas indicated a noticeable tendency to evaluate government and its leadership as less biased to the "people's" interest, those that identified with other minorities as well as with women's tended to see government as more responsive to "big interests." On the other hand, Latino/as who identified as "born again Christians" did not feel that government did not have a class bias. Similar patterns existed for all of the income clusters relative to the lowest income category. This was truest for the middle-income categories as opposed to those Latino/as the higher income levels. None of the other traditional socio-demographic

Table 1.4.   Multivariate Analysis of Participatory Orientations Among Latino/as Using Socio-Demographic and Group Identity Variables

Independent Variables	Political Efficacy (B)	Political Efficacy (Std. Error)	Political Cynicism (B)	Political Cynicism (Std. Error)	Belief in American Political System (B)	Belief in American Political System (Std. Error)
Gender/Minority Identity	.150	.049	.174*	.050	-.443*	.113
Homeowner	.061	.136	.139	.140	.494	.318
Born-Again Christian	.145	.170	-.359*	.174	.506	.398
Gender	-.426*	.130	-.432*	.133	-.143	.304
Never Married	-.262	.159	.015	.162	-1.062*	.370
Widowed, Separated, Divorced	.101	.180	.025	.185	-.409	.421
Income 20K-34.9K	-.265	.188	-.533*	.192	-.352	.436
Income 35K-84.99K	-.258	.196	-.570*	.201	-.718	.458
85K and higher	.189	.244	-.575	.250	-.434	.570
Protestant	-.101	.192	.272	.197	-.392	.449
Other Religions	.023	.264	.083	.270	-.768	.616
No Religion	-.219	.184	.167	.188	-1.129*	.428
Bilinguals	.563*	.189	.167	.193	.159	.441
English speaker	.385*	.155	.134	.158	-.651	.360
Employment status	-.154	.130	-.138	.133	.387	.303
Years of Schooling	.069*	.027	.023	.027	.056	.062
Constant	6.225	.320	6.864	.274	16.287	.748

*statistically significant at the < .05 level

variables proved to have significant coefficients. Another interesting outcome is the significant role of income, which for Latino/as, has not been as strong a predictor for political attitudes and behaviors as has been the case for other population groups.

The final dependent variable represents Latino/as beliefs in many of the democratic principles embedded in the American political value system—that is, fairness, equality of opportunity, equal treatment, and the like. Again the higher scores on the dependent variable indicate stronger degrees of belief in America's democratic principles. Among the factors that reflect less of a belief that the American system operates consistent with democratic principles are those Latino/as who have an affinity with other minorities and women (B = −.443). The gender variable also has a negative coefficient and is statistically significant. This pattern is also found among Latino/as who are not religiously affiliated and have never been married. The latter two significant variables pose a challenge for an interpretation. Perhaps no religious affiliation and being single might suggest being on the margins and "consistent" with atypical American norms. Again, with the two gender variables as significant can place Latinas as internalizing the beliefs of the American democratic system and processes that will have a depressing effect on political engagement with accompanying attitudes of systemic biases toward the upper stratum of society.

Our exploration of participatory orientations would suggest that while Latinas have positive orientation about having the necessary skills and motivation to be politically engaged, and exhibit lower levels of political cynicism, they have less "faith" in America's political system operating consistent with its democratic principles. An additional insight into the political world of Latina/os is reflected by some other types of political activities that most people are less likely to be involved with. In table 1.5, I start with the traditional registration status in which no gender differences are found. The other activities include "giving money," volunteering for a campaign, signing a petition, part of protest rally, convincing family/friends to be politically engaged, and being part of political organizations. As I indicated, these particular political activities are not as common as registering and voting. The overall percentages of Latino/as answering affirmatively on any of these activities only exceed eleven percent once. Even though, these are not common activities, we do have some significant gender gaps. Latinos are more likely to donate money to campaigns and belong to a political organization. Although not significant statistically, the proportion of Latino/as who discuss "things political" with family members and friends exceeds 75 percent. This brief look at a broader range of political activities adds to the challenge for Latinos to continue their positive trajectory of greater levels of political engage-

Table 1.5.   Indicators of Political Participation by Latinos and Latinas

Types of Political Participation	Latinos	% Latinos	Latinas	% Latinas
Registered to Vote				
Yes	215/233	92.3	315/381	82.7
Give Money for candidate, political party, etc.*				
Yes	45/359	12.5	38/565	6.8
Volunteered on a campaign				
Yes	29/360	8.1	31/567	5.5
Signed a petition				
Yes	42/360	11.7	63/567	11.1
Taken part in protest or rally				
Yes	21/363	5.8	31/566	5.5
Tried to involve others by engage in vote contact				
Yes	46/361	12.7	57/563	10.1
Been active or joined political party, organization, or club*				
Yes	32/328	9.6	27/539	5.0
Talked to family, friends about political issue, candidates?				
Yes	280/361	77.6	438/567	77.2

*statistically significant at the < .05 level

ment, building upon voter registration and turnout growth. Part of that responsibility lies within the Latino communities, the various segments (i.e., national origin, Latina/os, class, etc.)

LATINO/AS, GENDER AND POLITICAL ORIENTATION: DISCUSSION AND CONCLUSION

Our introduction to the focus on Latina/os and political engagement is a continuation of the research examination of patterns and contributors of Latino/as as participatory segments of the American populace. Over the past two decades there has been a major expansion of systematic investigation about the nature, extent, and contributing factors associated with their political participation. While most of that research has been directed to the electoral arena, the resurgence of protest activities, especially immigration reform efforts, the scope of examination has now included non-electoral activities as well as involvement by non-citizens and undocumented persons. Included in these areas of research has been the exploration of variations among segments of the Latino communities—that is, non-citizens, legal status, national origin, generations' distance from immigration, and gender. In the case of the latter, questions about the existence of a gender gap in terms of participation levels, types of civic and political engagements, and contributory factors to explain any inter-group variations.

The examination of gender differences is also grounded in the structural and societal effects of how women are socialized, treated, and expectations as to their behaviors, goals, and ambitions. For the most part, gender differences have been noted, in terms of political recruitment and leadership training/experience. Latinas as political candidates and office holders come more from civic engagement venues and are less recruited by political organizations and parties. Latinas' policy "maps" place greater saliency on social welfare issues and policies affecting children and families. On the other hand, significant differences in the electoral arena are much less evident. Finally, the influence of traditional gender roles, familial responsibilities and participation in the work force or not, and group and gender consciousness have played a role in the types and levels of political engagement.

In this chapter, I made an effort to add to the extant literature on Latina/os by focusing on participatory orientation. The cognitive link to political engagement lies with a range of attitudes about government, its leaders and institutions, and the connection of its citizenry to the political system. More specifically, the orientations examined were political efficacy, belief in the democratic principles associated with the American political system, and responsiveness of political leaders to the public interest or special interest. The query was to determine if gender differences occurred between Latinas and Latinos; and if so, are the established contributing factors (i.e., socio-demographic, economic, and attitudinal variables) affecting these orientations? Two of the three participatory orientations produced some significant gender differences. Latinas felt less efficacious about becoming politically engaged and less cynical about governmental representatives primarily advocating on behalf of "big interests." Both Latina/os were skeptical about the actual "implementation" of democratic practices/processes of fairness, equal treatment, and opportunities, although the gender coefficient was not statistically significant.

Our examination of the contributing factors, with the inclusion of socio-demographic and attitudinal factors, did not eliminate gender as a significant factor. The introduction of a "double bind" variable (i.e., sense of connectedness with other minority groups and women) proved to be significant with the political cynicism orientation. Whereas, gender demonstrated a less cynical view of class biases by elected officials, the "double bind" variable contributed to a more cynical view that officials look out for the "big interests" more. Language skills (being primarily English speakers or bilinguals) contributed to higher levels of political efficacy. Of the "big" three socio-economic variables (income, education, and employment status) only income proved to be significant and that was limited to the political cynicism orientation. Gains in years of schooling were important for heightening levels of political efficacy. Rather that repeat the finding from the earlier section, it is important to note that socio-economic factors do not have the same, more or less uniform effects on political participation and attitudes for Latina/os as with other groups. Whether it increases Latina labor force participation and changes in attitudes about women in the workforce, gender effects due to employment status are not a significant factor. Marital status and children in the household have gender implications, yet single status was the only significant factor regarding negative assessments about the actualization of democratic principles in the American political system.

The notion of intersectionality has a clear theoretical relevance in any examination of the role of gender and politics. It appears that the challenge is to capture, measurement-wise, in order to operationalize valid measures. Interaction terms to group persons based upon their race/ethnicity, gender, and class require sufficient numbers of respondents and reasonable distributions along these combined permutations. The socialization effects on males and females regarding opportunities, status attainment, group types of identifications (multiple identities), and "societal" interactions/experiences of Latino/as will provide the inter-play of being Latino/as and male-female that is relational and institutional. In other words, the understanding how, whether, and what contributes to Latino/as' patterns of political engagement extends beyond an individual's skills, resources, knowledge, and motivations as contextual, institutional, and in relation to other groups in American society are important dimensions. Participatory orientations are part of the participation equation as this dimension provides the evaluative and cognitive aspect of motivating and incentive bases to become more engaged in the political processes. The identification of relevant aspects of Latina/os' experiences, key "characteristics, and/or statuses" are critical elements to differentiate within the larger Latino cluster in order understand the complexities and variability of this community and their intersection with the American political system.

NOTES

1. Following the mailing, the telephone recruitment process begins for all sampled phone numbers. Cases sent to telephone interviewers are dialed up to 90 days, with at least 10 dial attempts on cases where no one answers the phone, and on phone numbers known to be associated with households. Extensive refusal conversion is also performed. Experienced interviewers conduct all recruitment

interviews. The recruitment interview, which typically requires about 10 minutes, begins with the interviewer informing the household member that they have been selected to join KnowledgePanel. If the household does not have a PC and access to the Internet, they are told that in return for completing a short survey weekly, the household will be given a WebTV set-top box and free monthly Internet access. All members in the household are then enumerated, and some initial demographic variables and background information of prior computer and Internet usage are collected.

2. The 70 DMAs are grouped into 5 regions (Northeast, West, Midwest, Southeast, and Southwest). Each region is further divided into two groupings of census tracts, those that have a "high density" Latino population and the balance made up of all the "low-density" census tracts. The threshold percent for "high density" varies by region. The 5 regions each divided into 2 density groups constitute 10 unique sample frames (5 × 2).

Using a geographic targeting approach, an RDD landline sample is generated to cover the high-density census tracts within each region. Due to the inaccuracy of telephone exchange coverage, there is some spillage outside these tracts and some smaller degree of non-coverage within these tracts. About 32 percent of the Latino population across these five regions is theoretically covered with this targeted RDD landline sample. All the numbers generated are screened to locate a Latino household.

The remaining 68 percent of the Latinos in these five regions are addressed with a listed-surname sample. Listed surnames only include households where the telephone subscriber has a surname that has been pre-identified to likely be a Latino name. It is important to note that excluded from this low-density listed sample frame are: (a) the mixed Latino/non-Latino households where the subscriber does not have a Latino surname, and (b) all the unlisted landline Latino households.

The percent of listed vs. unlisted varies widely at the DMA level. The use of the listed surname is intended to lower screening costs to locate a Latino household in these low-density areas since the rate of finding a Latino household from this list although not 100 percent is still very high. Finding Latino households only means that the households are qualified (i.e., they have one or more Latino residents) but this does not yet mean that the household is eligible for DMA-based oversample of Spanish-Language-Dominant Latino Panel. To be eligible for the panel, the household member(s) must pass two screening tests. First, they need to speak Spanish in their home at one of three response levels: All the time, Most of the time, Equally with English.

Next, they need to be able to read Spanish since all our communications and online surveys require a Spanish-reading ability. It is a complex task to identify eligible persons in households with multiple adults and especially in households where English and Spanish are spoken equally. In the latter case, for a household to further be eligible, that household must watch Spanish language television for 5 or more hours per week.

This screening is designed to achieve a panel of Spanish-speaking and Spanish-reading Latinos who are a subset of all Latinos but who are unique due to the dominance of Spanish language as their mode of communication in their home environment. English-speaking Latinos are recruited by the existing RDD-based KnowledgePanel recruitment. Based on the hybrid sample design of RDD and surname-listed sample and on the eligibility screening criteria, the DMA-based recruited sample is not 100 percent precisely representative of the Spanish-speaking Latino population (a most difficult standard to achieve under any design), but it is an excellent approximation of this population with good geographic balance across the nation.

Two

Una Ventaja?[1]

A Survey Experiment of the Viability of Latina Candidates

Jessica Lavariega Monforti
and Sarah Allen Gershon

Two major trends are evident in U.S. society and politics in contemporary times: an increase in the number of women being elected and increasing attention to growing Latino populations. For example, in 1970 there was just one woman elected to serve in the U.S. Senate and 25 women in the U.S. House of Representatives; in 2012 there were 18 women elected to the U.S. Senate and 166 in the U.S. House (plus 4 delegates). This represents about a 30 percentage point increase over the four decades.[2] Similarly, the number of women elected to serve in state legislatures has more than doubled over about the same period of time, growing from 1,125 in 1974 to 2,445 in 2012. There is a significant body of literature that has examined these trends (Wilcox 1994; Dolan 1998; Sanbonmatsu 2006; Dolan and Lynch 2014; Thomas and Wilcox 2014).

The second trend focuses on Latino population growth and political influence. According to the most recent U.S. Census Bureau data,[3] the Hispanic[4] population grew to 53 million in 2012, a 50 percent increase since 2000 and nearly six times the population that was counted in 1970.[5] Increases in the number of Latinos elected to public office have accompanied this population's growth. An early study by Lemus (1973) focused on six states with significant Latino populations and found 1,280 "Spanish-surnamed elected officials." Since 1985, the National Association of Latino Elected and Appointed Officials (NALEO) has been regularly collecting and reporting such data. According to their latest figures, the total number of Latino elected officials now stands at approximately 5,928.[6] The number of federal and state legislators steadily grew from 129 in 1985 to 292 in 2014 or by 126 percent. The number of county and municipal officials grew from 1,316 to 2,293 or by 74 percent. According to Hardy-Fanta, et al. (2005), between 1990 and 2000 Latino officials experienced a higher rate of growth (30 percent) than that of Blacks (23 percent) and Asian Americans (4 percent). While the authors reported that reliable statistics for American Indians were only available at the state legislative level, they found that in 1997–1999, 28 American Indian/including Alaskan natives) served in 8 states. In 2003–2004, 42 were found to serve in 12 states. But what about those people who are located at the intersection of these major societal trends—what do these trends mean for Latinas in politics, particularly given that Hispanic population growth trends are expected to continue? Using an intersectional approach, we examine this question.

INTERSECTIONALITY

Women face multiple challenges when seeking elective office. Women face greater fundraising challenges, and are considered less serious candidates by both male and female voters (Carroll 1994; Burrell 1995 and 1998; Fiber and Fox 2005; Lawless and Fox 2008 and 2011; Dolan 2008; Ford 2010; Norris and Inglehart 2008; Sanbonmatsu 2013). Beyond these gender-based challenges are the additional challenges faced by women of color. They are marginalized by both their ethnorace and their gender. Latinas, in particular, often have to contend with machismo[7] within their communities and therefore choosing to seek elective office can generate hostility and backlash among Latino voters (Hardy-Fanta 1993; Petersen, et al. 2005; García et al. 2008). García and Marquez (2001, 112) have argued that "Chicanas and Latinas approach mainstream political participation differently than do their white female counterparts because of their unique experiences and political history as minority women."

The concept of intersectionality, therefore, refers to the ways in which a person's process of identification can link to, overlap with, and operate through the other possible identifications available in a given context. Therefore, the political context faced by Latina candidates and elected officials is impacted by their ethnic identities, their gender identities, as well as their specific immigration status (and legacy) and language identities.

LA VENTAJA DE LATINA ELECTED OFFICIALS

In recent years, Latinas[8] have enjoyed growing success in politics and leadership roles. Of the 104 women serving in the 114th Congress, nine are Latina—up from just one in 1990. Of the 78 women serving in statewide elective executive offices in 2015, four are Latina.[9] Of the 1,786 women state legislators serving nationwide, 87 are Latina. This is certainly an increase since 1930 when two Latinas, Fedelina Lucero Gallegos (R) and Porfirria Hidalgo Saiz (D), were elected to the New Mexico House of Representatives, the first Latina state legislators.[10] Of the 100 largest cities, two have a Latina mayor: Corpus Christi, TX, and Chula Vista, CA.[11] Despite the trends and their political implications, previous studies of minorities or women in politics have failed to include Latina officeholders.

Latinas have enjoyed relatively higher election rates than their Latino male counterparts (Sierra 2009). Sierra's (2009) work shows that, between 1996 and 2009, the number of Latina elected officials grew more quickly than the number for Latino males; the total number of Latina officials doubled (100 percent increase) compared to a 36 percent increase for Latinos. Local offices are an important entry point for Latinas in politics, and we find about 42 percent of Latina officeholders here. Bejarano (2013) even finds that Latinas have an advantage at the local level. We find few Latinas in national-level offices, however.

In her new book, *The Latina Advantage: Gender, Race, and Political Success,* Bejarano (2013) explores evidence that women of color may be helped rather than hurt by how the intersection of their gender and ethnoracial identities influence voters in the U.S. Using ANES data from 1992 to 2009 Bejarano demonstrates that Anglo voters are more likely to support a candidate of color if she is a woman, along with fellow minority voters. She argues that gender softens the perception of ethnoracial differences. In other words, rather than facing the double disadvantage of being a woman and minority, a Latina candidate for political office benefits from her "multiple identity advantage." She shows that they are also more successful candidates due to their increased qualifications for political office, which they tend to gather in anticipation of potential electoral obstacles.

One shortcoming of this work is that Bejarano cannot directly examine the intersectional identities of Latina candidates or their opponents, and the impact they may have on voter choice. Utilizing original data from a survey experiment with over 700 respondents in two minority-majority localities, we simulate races where a Latina candidate runs against another Latina, as well as Latino, African American male and female, and Anglo male and female candidates to test Bejarano's theory. We examine the foundation of support for Latina candidates, focusing on the differences in participants' willingness of vote for her, their perceptions of her character traits and issue positions while considering the impact of voters' identities, as well as their level of political interest, ideology, political knowledge, and the like. We conclude by discussing the implications of our results for Latinas seeking elective office.

CANDIDATE IDENTITY AND WINABILITY

Racial, ethnic, and gender identity often inform attitudes about others, shaping expectations regarding group characteristics and behaviors

(Ghavami and Peplau 2012; Madon et al. 2001). Candidate identity across ethnorace and gender may result in different voter perceptions of candidates' expertise and qualifications for office, ultimately shaping their chances at the polls (Fox and Smith 1998; Kahn 1996; Sapiro 1981). Scholars have found that voters use gender and race stereotypes as cues or shortcuts when evaluating candidates' traits or competence in various policy domains (Sapiro 1981/82), particularly in low-information elections (Alexander and Anderson 1993; McDermott 1997 and 1998).

Existing literature on women of color suggests that they face assumptions and stereotypes about the intersection of their racial and gender identities that accumulate and harm their chances of electoral success; this is the idea behind the double bind or multiple marginalities theory. Gay and Tate (1998) have argued that it in fact isn't a matter of deciding between these identities—they argued that black women are doubly bound, that gender matters as much as racial identity. They demonstrate that black women identify as strongly on the basis of their gender as their race, and that these gender and racial identities are mutually reinforcing. Theory and research has acknowledged that women have myriad parts of their identities, and terms such as triple disadvantage or multiple marginalities have been used to describe this concept. It means that individuals do not experience belonging to multiple categories of identity such as race, ethnicity, gender, and the like, in a cumulative manner that can be explained away by simply listing the effects produced by each of the categories (Hancock 2007; McCall 2005; Simien 2007; Stewart and McDermott 2004; West and Fenstermaker 1995). In other words, the concept of intersectionality refers to the ways in which a person's process of identification can link to, overlap with and operate through the other possible identifications available in a given context. Therefore, the political context faced by Latina members of Congress is impacted by their ethnic identities, their gender identities, as well as their specific immigration status (and legacy) and language identities. In the final analysis, however, the number of identities women choose is not our central focus—the effect(s) that their identities may have or be associated with is. According to Mirza (2008), "ethnic minority women are caught up in a collision of invisibility and visibility that means they slip through the cracks of everyday policy and politics" (5).

However, Bejarano (2013) argues that women of color may be aided rather than hurt by how the intersection of their racial and gender identities influence American voters. She argues that women of color, as candidates, can secure more public support by appealing to a wider array of communities and voter coalitions—women and minority communities. She points out that these women are often better prepared for office holding and they are perceived as less threatening than their male counterparts by white voters.

This study is exploratory in nature; however, the literature outlined above gives us reason to expect that the combination of ethnic and gender identities of Latina candidates will lead to substantively different voter evaluations of them when running for office. We ask, under what conditions are Latina candidates likely to be successful? Do contexts such as demographic composition of potential voters, assumptions about issue positions, or the intersectional identities of opponents impact Latina chances for electoral victory? If so, how?

Before turning to answer these questions, it is essential to point out that the underrepresentation of people of color, and in this research—Latinas, in elected office is an important reflection of the health of our democracy, with real-world implications for both descriptive and substantive representation. Descriptive representation refers to the form of individuals who mirror certain social characteristics of their constituents along the lines of factors such as race, class, or sex; substantive representation refers to the ability of the representative to act for the interests of the represented (Pitkin 1967).

First, in terms of descriptive representation, proportional representation of Latinas (and other major subgroups) serves as a measure of the strength and health of a representative democracy, indicating the capacity of all citizens to participate in governance in meaningful ways. If the political voice of any group that exists within a society is muted or silenced, then representation, and ultimately democracy, fades. Moreover, Mansbridge argues that minority and women representatives engender feelings of trust and legitimacy on the part of people of color in cases where a history of discrimination exists, as well as represent the views of that group at the policymaking table—bringing new issues to the forefront. Minority and women representatives can advocate, speaking with moral authority as group members, and serve as role models for others (1999). Swain (1995) also argues that descriptive representation increases minority trust in government. Burrell (1995, 6) notes that, "When citizens can identify with their representatives they become less alienated and more involved in the political system."

Second, turning to substantive representation, Fraga et al. (2005) and Jaramillo (2007) posit that the Latinas have a distinctive style of politics as a result of their intersectional identities as women and Hispanics. That is to say that it is their intersecting identities of ethnorace and gender, along with other socio-political identities such as language and immigration status/history, that contour their political worldviews. The lack of parity between constituencies and the demographics of the members of elected governmental institutions such as the U.S. Congress raise doubts about the representativeness of the policies they adopt. This representation gap is likely to increase given the dramatically changing demographics and Latino population growth in the United States, particularly in the southwest. In other words, representation, and democracy itself, is threatened when governance is not inclusive (Thomas and Welch 1991; Tate 2003; Swers and Larson 2005) and Latinas play an essential role in broadening the scope of voices making policy for the country, just as been the case for other cross-sections of the population. Previous research has shown that the race, ethnicity and gender of elected officials can affect substantive policy outcomes (Pinney and Serra 1999). Now we turn to our data.

DATA AND METHODS

To examine the foundations of voter support for Latina candidates, we rely on a survey experiment conducted at two universities. While examining the willingness of voters to support Latina candidates during real-world campaigns is ideal, a non-experimental setting would include a number of campaign, district, and individual-level variables that likely shape voter attitudes, limiting the our ability to isolate the impact of voter identity and perceptions on support for Latina candidates. We are also able to control the characteristics of the campaign, exploring the role of opponent identity in shaping voters' willingness to support Latinas running for office. Finally, through the use of a survey experiment online, respondents in this study were exposed to the stimulus in a more natural environment, which may improve the external validity of the findings.

The data utilized in this research is part of a broader study conducted at two large metropolitan universities. The students included in the sample were recruited largely from political science classes, and provide for a nice cross-section of the student population at each institution (see appendix for a description of the sample). As the table in the appendix demonstrates, both schools have large populations of color (one with over 80 percent Latinos and the other with over 40 percent African American respondents). While the racial and ethnic make-up of this sample limits the external validity of the experiment to some extent, it also allows us to examine the interaction between voters' and candidates' identity in a politically relevant way. Many candidates of color seeking seats in the U.S. Congress run in minority-majority districts, and as a result, we are particularly interested in how voters' own racial and ethnic identity shapes their perception of and willingness to vote for Latina candidates. Thus, it is necessary to have oversamples of minorities in our study.

Further, as briefly mentioned in our introduction, the United States is in the midst of major demographic change with a rapidly growing Hispanic population. For instance, from 1960 to 2010, the percentages of Americans identifying themselves as Black, Hispanic, Asian, or "other" increased from just 15 percent of the population to 36 percent of the population; Black: Increased from 10 to 12 percent, Hispanic: Increased from 4 to 15 percent, Asian: Increased from 1 to 5 percent, and "Other": Increased from 0 to 3 percent. According to U.S. Census Bureau estimates, in the next fifteen years, those numbers will jump again, with the Hispanic population alone increasing to 22 percent; by 2060, Hispanics will comprise 31 percent of the U.S. population. It is essential to note that communities of color are growing as a result of native U.S. births, not just immigration. Since 2000, the U.S.-born Latino population continued to grow at a faster rate than the immigrant population. As a result, the foreign-born share of Latinos is now in decline. Therefore, these Hispanics will not have the barriers of lack of citizenship to negotiate to become voters and/or candidates for elective office. Due to these demographic changes, it is now more important than ever to understand the attitudes of minority voters in the United States.

During the course of the experiment, participants answered a series of questions regarding their political attitudes and demographic characteristics. We then presented respondents with two similar candidates, varying only their ethnorace and gender. Thus, we are able to clearly identify the impact of candidate identity on subjects' willingness to vote for Latina candidates, holding other variables constant. The subjects were then shown pictures of two fictional candidates in a primary race for the U.S. House of Representatives and a short statement about each candidate. In an effort to understand voter support for Latina candidates in a variety of circumstances, our experiment relies on six conditions in which a Latina candidate faces six different candidates, including: a Latino, an Anglo woman, an Anglo man, an African American woman, an African American man and a Latina (the control condition).

The candidates used in the experiment each fit one of two similar profiles: 45 years old, a lawyer with previous experience as a school board member, married with two children OR 43 years old, small business owner with previous experience as a city council member, married with one child. Table 2.1 illustrates the conditions. To explore the impact of candidates' ethnorace and gender, we varied the candidates' pictures and names throughout the experiment.

As table 2.1 reveals, there are just under 700 respondents in this experiment, with each condition including between 94 and 133 subjects. Following exposure to the experimental treatment, subjects answered a

Table 2.1.   Experimental Design

Condition	Candidates	Sample Size
Condition 1	Latina vs Latino	133
Condition 2	Latina vs Latina	122
Condition 3	Latina vs White Female	113
Condition 4	Latina vs White Male	118
Condition 5	Latina vs African American Female	117
Condition 6	Latina vs African American Male	94

N=697

series of questions about the fictional candidates, including which candidate they would vote for and how well they thought the candidates would handle particular issues.

RESULTS

We begin by examining the descriptive differences in support for the Latina candidate across experimental conditions (results displayed in table 2.2). Our dependent variable is simply the percent of each condition who said they would vote for the Latina candidate or her opponent.

Table 2.2.   Vote for Latina by Experimental Condition

		Percent of Subjects Voting for Candidate
Condition 1		
	Latina	49
	Latino opponent	39
Condition 2		
	Latina	38
	Latina opponent	50
Condition 3		
	Latina	44
	White Female opponent	42
Condition 4		
	Latina	57
	White Male opponent	34
Condition 5		
	Latina	24
	African American Female opponent	65
Condition 6		
	Latina	26
	African American Male opponent	60

N=693

As the data in table 2.2 indicate, there were some substantive differences in support for the Latina candidate across conditions. The Latina received the highest levels of relative support when facing Anglo male and female opponents, as well as a Latino opponent. She received the lowest levels of support when facing African American male and female opponents.

The different levels of support for the Latina when facing Anglo and African American candidates may be due in part to the racial and ethnic context in the universities selected for analysis as well as the political context in the areas where the schools are located. As such, the demographic composition of the schools and their metropolitan areas bears greater discussion. The student samples utilized in this study differ from the average population in a few ways (see the appendix for a description of samples). School 1 is a Hispanic Serving Institution (HSI) in a mid-size metropolitan area in deep south Texas with a high concentration of Hispanic residents, mostly of Mexican origin. School 1's sample is majority Latino (76 percent). The sample is 20 percent White, 3 percent African American, 4 percent Asian American, and approximately 2 percent Native American and less than 1 percent Middle Eastern. School 2 is located in a large, majority African American southeastern city. The plurality of School 2's sample is African American (45 percent), and is 27 percent White, 13 percent Latino, 19 percent Asian, and 2 percent Native American and Middle Eastern. Furthermore, both schools are located in majority-minority cities with large numbers of Latino and African American elected officials. In fact, almost all of the major elected officials in these locations are held by people of color, therefore having African American and Latino candidates on the ballot is the norm for our participants. This may also lead participants to select black and brown candidates at higher rates than we might expect to see in the electorate, generally speaking (Wolfinger 1965; Parenti 1967; Leighley 2001; Baretto, Segura, and Woods 2004). We will examine the relative impact of school location in a multivariate analysis shortly, but first, we turn to an examination of subject identity and vote choice.

While the racial and ethnic context in the areas in which our samples are located may explain voter support for the Latina candidate in our experiment, we also expect that voter identities will shape vote choice. The literature indicates that a voter's own characteristics might affect their evaluations of different candidates. For example, women and minorities have been found to voice higher levels of support for female and minority candidates (Bejarano 2013; Bobo and Gilliam 1990; Burns, Schlozman, and Verba 2001; Dolan 1998; Philpot and Walton 2007; Terkildsen 1993; Sigelman and Welch 1984). In contrast, experimental research by Sigelman and Sigelman (1982) suggests that voters, White voters in particular, may react more negatively to minority women running for office compared with other candidates. Therefore, we anticipate that all else equal, women and minority subjects may express higher levels of support for candidates sharing their identities. As such, we expect Latinos and women (of all racial and ethnic backgrounds) to voice higher support for the Latina candidate, compared with their peers.

To examine the role of voter identity and attitudes in shaping support for Latina candidates, we rely on a series of difference of means tests. We examine the differences in levels of support by respondent *ethnorace* and *gender*, relying on binary variables for Whites, African Americans, Latinos and Asian Americans,[12] and men and women[13] (see appendix for a complete list of variables and measures). We also explored whether differences in respondents' party attachment, ideology, political interest, and knowledge shaped support for the Latina candidate. *Party attachment* is based on a question asking, "Generally speaking, do you usually think of yourself as a Republican, a Democrat, an Independent or what?" *Ideology* is based on a question asking "Generally speaking, in politics, do you consider yourself as conservative, liberal, middle of the road?" *Political Interest* relies on the following question: "Some people don't pay much attention to politics. How about you?" (Not at all interested=1, somewhat interested=2, very interested=3). Finally, *political knowledge* is measured using a four-point scale based on whether respondents correctly answered three questions asking about presidential term limits, which branch of government is responsible for deciding whether laws are constitutional, and who the speaker of the house is (0=no knowledge, 1=low knowledge, 2=moderate knowledge, 3=high knowledge).

The results of the difference of means tests are displayed in table 2.3. The data in the table reveal significant differences in support for the La-tina candidate across ethnoracial groups. As expected given previous re-search, Latinos support the Latina candidate—their co-ethnic—over her opponents at the highest rate (49 percent). 42 percent of Anglos in our sample supported the Latina candidate, followed by African Americans at 38 percent and Asian Americans at 30 percent. There may be some sup-port for Bejarano's work here because we see that there is also significant support for the Latina candidate among Anglo voters; the difference is statistically significant, so it is possible that Latinas have an advantage over other candidates among these two demographic groups. However, the percentage of support for the Latina candidate across all groups never surpasses 50 percent.

While there are no significant differences by gender, party attach-ment, or ideology, the data reveal that those on the high and low ends of the political interest and knowledge variables among the subjects ex-pressed significantly higher support for the Latina candidate, compared

Table 2.3. Percent Vote for Latina by Voter Identity and Attitudes

		Percent Vote For Latina
Race and Ethnicity**		
	Latinos	49
	Anglos	42
	African Americans	38
	Asian Americans	30
Gender		
	Men	38
	Women	41
Party Attachment		
	Republican	38
	Independent	37
	Democrat	42
Ideology		
	Conservative	39
	Independent	39
	Liberal	43
Political Interest†		
	Very Interested	50
	Somewhat Interested	38
	Not at all Interested	42
Political Knowledge*		
	No Knowledge	29
	Low Knowledge	43
	Moderate Knowledge	37
	High Knowledge	52
Total		40

N=648. Differences among all racial/ethnic groups statistically significant †p<.10 *p<.05 **p<.01

with their peers. As engagement in politics among voters increases, so does their willingness to support Latina candidates. One possible explanation for this finding is that the voters' views of politics are shaped by their level of interest and information. For example, low-information voters are less likely to vote, and when they do they generally vote for a candidate they find personally appealing. Researchers attribute this to low-information voters not having developed clear-cut ideological preferences (Walker 2008; Palfrey and Poole 1987; Lauderdale 2012). A 1992 study found that in the absence of other information, voters used candidates' physical attractiveness to draw inferences about their personal qualities and political ideology (Riggle, Ottai, Wyer, Kuklinski, and Schwarz 1992). A study using ANES data from 1986 through 1994 found that low-information voters tend to assume female and black candidates are more liberal than male and white candidates of the same party (McDermott 1998).

MULTIVARIATE MODEL

In order to examine the impact of voter identity and attitudes toward Latina candidates, controlling for alternative explanations, we rely on a multivariate model predicting vote choice (1=Latina candidate, 0=opponent).[14] In our multivariate analyses, we examined the voter identity and attitudes on the likelihood of voting for the Latina candidate in our experiment over her opponent. We rely on binary variables for Latino, African American, and Asian American subjects (Anglos are the excluded category). Gender is a binary variable (1=female, 0=male). We also include the same measures for political interest and knowledge described in the previous section. We controlled for party attachment (1=Democrat, 0=others) and ideology (1=conservative and 0=other) relying on binary codes. Finally, we controlled for several variables, including the ethnorace and gender of the opponent facing the Latina candidate. Specifically, we included binary variables capturing whether the opponent was a: *African American Female, White Female, African American Male, Latino,* or *White Male.* We excluded the "control" condition in which the candidate faced another Latina. We pooled the data from the two schools. While we control for many of the demographic differences in the samples (gender, partisanship, race, ethnicity, etc.), it is possible that the political context in which each school is located will shape attitudes about the candidates in the experiment.

To examine the impact of context on responses, we included a control variable for the school (0=HSI, 1=non-HSI). Finally, we control for subjects' assessments of how well the Latina candidate would handle different issues. In particular, we selected assessments of the candidate's ability to handle education, immigration, and the economy. Issue assessments are measured using a question that asks "Based on what you know about the candidates, how well do you think (the Latina candidate) would handle [Education/the Economy/Immigration]? (0=Not well at all, 1=not very well, 2=somewhat well, 3=very well). These particular topics are included in the analyses because these have been policy concerns rated the highest by Latinos over the last several years, and therefore can tell us something about the perceived ability of Latina candidates to address the issues highly associated with communities of color in recent times.[15]

To examine the dependent variables, we relied on logistic regression (results displayed in table 2.4). As demonstrated earlier, there are significant differences in support for Latina candidates among subjects of different racial and ethnic identities. However, the data presented here illustrate that once other variables are accounted for, subject identity does not significantly impact vote choice.

Table 2.4. Logistic Regressions Predicting Support for Female Candidates

	Coefficient (S. E.)	Min-Max
Subject Characteristics and Attitudes		
African American	−.127(.270)	−.030
Latino	−.104(.281)	−.025
Asian American	−.331(.317)	−.077
Democrat	.197(.191)	.047
Conservative	−.032(.184)	−.007
Female	.281(.192)	.066
Political Interest	.087(.163)	.041
Political Knowledge	.062(.117)	.044
School 2	−.405(.256)	−.098
Opponent Characteristics		
African American Female	−.733(.301)*	−.164
White Female	.331(.282)	.080
African American Male	−.638(.339)†	−.143
Latino	.510(.282)†	.125
White Male	.793(.284)**	.195
Issue Assessments		
Education	−.064(.125)	−.046
Economy	.213(.124)†	.149
Immigration	.226(.121)†	.157
Constant	−1.31(.620)*	
Chi-square	69.32	
N	628	

Note: (†p<.10, *p<.05, **p<.01, two-tailed).

Campaign context does significantly influence vote choice, in particular, the opponent's identity shaped support for the Latina candidate among subjects. Just as in the descriptive data reported earlier, facing an African American opponent (rather than a Latina) significantly decreased subjects' likelihood of supporting the Latina candidate and facing an African American female exerted a stronger relative impact on vote choice than facing an African American male. Alternatively, facing a Latino or Anglo male candidate, rather than a Latina opponent, significantly increased subjects' likelihood of voting for the Latina in our experiment. Interestingly, we find support for Bejarano's argument here—Latinas can win over support among Anglos voters in most match-ups. While we hypothesized that differences in support for the Latina candidates' opponent may be due in part to differences in the political context in the geographic region our samples are drawn from, this control variable exerts no significant impact in the model.

Finally, subjects' assessments of how well the Latina candidate would handle particular issues—the economy and immigration—significantly and positively impacted vote choice. As subjects' perceptions of the Latina candidate's ability to handle the economy and immigration improved, so did their likelihood of supporting the Latina candidate over her opponent.

DISCUSSION AND CONCLUSION

We set out to examine the idea that a Latina, as candidate for elective office, benefits from her "multiple identity advantage" rather than her identity disadvantaging her chances for victory. Bejarano (2013) argues that women of color, as candidates, can secure more public support by appealing to a wider array of communities and voter coalitions—women and minority communities. She points out that these women are often better prepared for office holding and they are perceived as less threatening than their male counterparts by white voters. We find support for her argument; Latinas with male and white opponents who run for office in racially diverse areas indeed benefit from the intersectional nature of their identities. It appears however, that Bejarano's broader argument that women of color may be aided rather than hurt by how the intersection of their racial and gender identities influence American voters extends beyond Latinas to African American women in our study.

NOTES

1. Translated: An Advantage?
2. http://www.cawp.rutgers.edu/fast_facts/elections/documents/can_hist sum.pdf.
3. https://www.census.gov/popest/data/national/asrh/2012/index.html.
4. The terms Hispanic and Latino will be used interchangeably to refer to the population of those who hail from Spanish-speaking countries and their descendants who currently live in the United States.
5. http://www.pewresearch.org/fact-tank/2014/02/26/the-u-s-hispanic -population-has-increased-sixfold-since-1970/.
6. http://www.naleo.org/downloads/2012_Directory.pdf.
7. The Spanish term *machismo* is a common reference to Latino masculinity, in particular, the gender construction of extreme traditional masculinity or of the characteristic of the "true" man ("macho") in Latin American and Caribbean societies. The term is commonly employed within Latina/o communities inside and outside of the USA to refer to such males or the behaviors associated with those males. It has been theorized as a form of masculinity derived from the Spanish conquistadores. For more on this see: http://link.springer.com/refere nceworkentry/10.1007%2F978-1-4419-5659-0_475. Here we use the term to refer to any form of sexism or attitudes that place males in a dominant position over females and other males.

8. The terms Latina and Hispanic woman will be used interchangeably throughout this work.

9. This includes Dianna Duran (R), Secretary of State in New Mexico; Nellie Gorbea (D), Secretary of State in Rhode Island; Susana Martinez (R), Governor of New Mexico; and Evelyn Sanguinetti (D), Lt. Governor of Illinois.

10. http://www.cawp.rutgers.edu/fast_facts/resources/Firsts.php.

11. Nelda Martinez in Texas and Mary Casillas Salas in California.

12. We choose to only examine differences in these four racial and ethnic groups because they comprised over 95 percent of both school samples. However, the inclusion of Native American and Middle Eastern subjects does not substantively alter the results presented here.

13. Data was pooled across all treatment categories.

14. In the survey from school 1, respondents were presented with an ordinal responses set for this question. Responses from school one were coded dichotomously (0=definitely or probably vote for the opponent, 1=definitely or probably vote for the candidate).

15. For more on this see: http://www.pewhispanic.org/2014/10/29/chapter-4-top-issues-in-this-years-election-for-hispanic-voters/. Also see Kendra King's 2010 African American Politics by Polity for information of African American preferences.

THREE

Intersectionality and Latino/a Candidate Evaluation[1]

Ivy A. M. Cargile, Jennifer L. Merolla, and Jean Reith Schroedel

A key element in assessing the legitimacy of a democratic government is the question of whether its elected officials are broadly representative of the underlying population. Although the United States for much of its history has fallen far short of this ideal, the nation has made enormous progress in addressing electoral inequities over the past half a century, much of this due to the passage of the 1965 Voting Rights Act and its 1975 and 1982 amendments (de la Garza and DeSipio 2006). For Latinos, the 1975 amendments that require voting registration and ballots be provided in minority languages and the 1982 amendments that allow challenges to electoral procedures that result in minorities having less opportunity to "participate in the political process and to elect representatives of their choice" even if discriminatory intent cannot be proven, have been particularly important in terms of increasing their representation in political office (Tucker 2009, 230–31).[2] In the past decade alone, the number of Latino elected officials has greatly increased, going from 4,853 in 2004 to 6,100 elected Latinos in 2014 (NALEO 2014). Additionally, we have witnessed Latina elected officials make history. For instance, Susana Martinez is the first Latina to be elected governor in the United States. Yet Latinos are still massively under-represented in electoral office. They comprise 17 percent of the overall population while only making up 4 percent of national elected officials (Ennis et al. 2010; NALEO 2014), and are projected to comprise nearly a third of all people in the United States by 2050 (Passel and Cohn 2008, 1).

Some scholars (Bullock 1984; McConnaughy et al. 2010) attribute the continuing under-representation of Latinos in office to racial stereotyping, such that voters are reluctant to cross over and vote for candidates of another race/ethnicity. While a large body of research has looked at stereotypes with respect to gender (e.g., Alexander and Andersen 1993; Huddy and Terkildsen 1993; Kahn 1994; McDermott 1998; Fox and Oxley 2003; Banwart 2010), there is less work on racial or ethnic stereotypes (Williams 1990; McDermott 1998; Sigelman et al. 1995; Schneider and Bos 2011; Jones 2013). Researchers have found that ideologically conservative white voters tend to stereotype Latino candidates as liberal (Sigelman et al. 1995; Sonenshein and Pinkus 2005; Jones 2013). Furthermore, voters presume Latino candidates favor immigration reform, even if untrue, which has been found to be harmful for their electoral chances (Austin and Middleton 2004; McConnaughy et al. 2010).

Although scholars have made some progress in understanding the impact of stereotyping on candidate evaluations, there are still many unanswered questions about how belief-, trait-, and issue-based stereotyping affects the viability of Latino and Latina candidates.[3] While there has been some research into belief-based stereotyping, there has been very little research into the attribution of trait characteristics to Latino candidates (Sigelman et al. 1995; Jones 2013). Aside from the aforementioned research showing that Latino candidates are perceived as being pro-immigration reform, we do not know what other, if any, issue-related stereotypes voters hold of Latino/a candidates. Moreover, we do not know about possible interactive effects between racial and gender stereotypes.

This study is designed to provide answers to these very important questions. More specifically, we seek to assess the content of voter stereotypes of Latino and Latina candidates. We conducted a survey experiment using YouGov where respondents were randomly assigned to evaluate one of five hypothetical candidates on a battery of trait and issue competency measures. The experiment included hypothetical candidates with different combinations of race/ethnicity (white or Hispanic) and biological sex (male or female) so that interactive effects could also be evaluated. Understanding the trait, belief, and issue stereotypes that voters have of Latino and Latina candidates will provide insight into how these candidates and their campaigns can try to mitigate the effects of stereotypes that disadvantage them and at the same time use positive stereotypes to enhance their electoral prospects. This chapter is divided into three sections. We begin by examining the gender and racial stereotyping literature in more detail, and draw upon that in developing expectations about Latino and Latina candidates. In the next section, we discuss our methodology and the results of the experiments. In the final section, we consider the implications of this study on the prospects of future Latino and Latina candidates.

HOW STEREOTYPES AFFECT FEMALE
CANDIDATES AND CANDIDATES OF COLOR

With the increasing number of electoral races, where at least one of the candidates is female and/or non-white, it is imperative that scholars fully explore the prevalence of racial and gender stereotyping in American politics, and the extent to which they help or harm candidates. As noted above, there has been limited research into the belief, trait, and issue stereotypes that individuals may hold of Latino and Latina candidates, so we will begin by summarizing the key points of that extant research and then turn to the more substantive scholarship on gender stereotyping.

Early work on racial stereotypes focused on differences between African American and white candidates. Using experimental designs where individuals were presented with hypothetical candidates who were similar on all dimensions except race, studies have found that African American politicians are perceived as more compassionate, less competent, and more liberal relative to white candidates, and as having competence in issue areas such as poverty, aid to minorities, and civil rights (Sears et al. 1987; Williams 1990; Sigelman et al. 1995; McDermott 1998; Jones 2013).[4] While these studies point to many positive attributes, the work of Callaghan and Terkildsen (2002) also shows that in comparison to white politicians, voters perceive African American politicians as possessing more negative personality traits and work-related behaviors, such as aggressiveness, laziness, and being irresponsible.

Of the handful of studies exploring the relationship between the race/ethnicity of Latino candidates and their chances for electoral success (Sigelman et al. 1995; Matson and Fine 2006; Barreto 2007; Casellas 2011; Bejarano 2013) only two (Sigelman et al. 1995; Jones 2013) assess stereotypes of Latino candidates. Both Sigelman et al. (1995) and Jones (2013) find that white voters classified conservative Latinos running for office as moderate or even liberal (Sigelman et al. 1995; Jones 2013). Sigelman and colleagues (1995) also show that Latino candidates are evaluated as being more compassionate, but less competent than white male candidates. Unfortunately, the researchers did not consider other possible trait characteristics or issue competencies. Other studies, while not specifically examining issue competencies, find that when a Latino candidate is on the ballot, immigration reform is frequently associated with the candidate even when there are overt attempts to avoid it due to fear of the issue harming the candidacy (Austin and Middleton 2004; McConaughy et al. 2010).

There is a much larger body of research on trait, belief and issue stereotyping of male and female candidates running for different political offices. When voters employ gender stereotypes in evaluating candidates, they are assuming that biological sex is related to differing sets of personality traits, which in turn affects candidates' ideological beliefs, and both of these combine in ways that lead to an assessment that males and females have different issue stances and competencies. Female candidates are typically viewed as more liberal than similarly associated male candidates (McDermott 1997; Koch 2000). Warmth, compassion, honesty, trust, gentleness, and sensitivity have been identified as female associated trait characteristics, while the male-identified trait list includes things such as assertiveness, ambition, leadership, aggression, and strength (Huddy and Terkildsen 1993; Herrnson et al. 2003; Fox and Oxley 2003; Kenski and Falk 2004; Banwart 2010; Winter 2010; Hayes 2011; Meeks 2012).[5] Voters, holding gendered views about trait characteristics, also tend to evaluate female and male candidates as having issue competencies associated with their biological sex, such as female candidates being better at handling poverty, health care, education, child care, and assisting the elderly while male candidates are perceived as more suited to handling foreign affairs, defense, and taxes (Alexander and Anderson 1993; Huddy and Terkildsen 1993; Burrell 1994; Banwart 2010).

Given the well-established findings about the content of gender stereotypes, scholars have explored how these stereotypes are associated with views about which political offices are most appropriate for men and women. Because most of the policy issues that are gendered as female are primarily under the purview of local and state government entities, there is gender congruence when women run for offices such as the school board and city council. In contrast, the issues gendered as male are primarily handled at the national level, which puts female candidates at a disadvantage when running for national and executive office positions (Anderson and Alexander 1993; Kahn 1996; Fox and Oxley 2003; Lawless 2004; Scola 2006). Interestingly, male candidates, who embrace traits and issues gendered as female do not seem to be disadvantaged, but female candidates who attempt to emphasize traditionally male identified traits and issues can be disadvantaged (Rosenwasser and Dean 1989; Kahn 1996; Lawless 2004).

Most of these studies have assessed gender stereotypes toward female candidates in hypothetical experiments in which the partisanship of the candidates is unknown. This has led scholars to ask whether the effects of gender stereotypes persist when partisan cues are also present. Scholarship on this question is mixed. For example, some find that partisan cues can trump gender cues (McDermott 1997; Huddy and Capelos 2002; Matland and King 2002; Hayes 2005, 2011), which can help Republican women in particular combat gender stereotypes, while other research shows that gender stereotypes can trump partisanship (Sanbonmatsu and Dolan 2009). Some studies find that the two interact, particularly in the case of Republican women (Koch 2000). While the findings are mixed, most studies find a reduced impact of gender stereotypes in the presence of party cues.

In sum, while a wide range of studies have documented the trait and belief based stereotypes of candidates based on gender, very few have considered the content of stereotypes toward Latino candidates. Furthermore, no existing studies have looked at how gender and racial/ethnic stereotypes interact to affect evaluations of a Latina candidate. Before we can begin to understand how stereotypes affect the electoral prospects of Latino and Latina candidates and how they may or may not be conditioned by partisan cues, we need to first get a better handle of the content of trait and belief-based stereotypes of these candidates.

TESTABLE HYPOTHESES

In light of the dearth of research on the stereotyping of Latino and Latina candidates, this study should be considered exploratory. We have developed a series of preliminary hypotheses derived from what is known about racial and gender stereotyping, but we recognize that some aspects, particularly those related to interactive effects of racial and gender stereotyping, are difficult to predict without a more established literature. The hypotheses are divided between those associated with trait stereotypes, belief stereotypes, and issue competency stereotypes. We consider Latino and Latina candidates to be distinct categories and compare each candidate type against a male candidate, a white candidate, and a female candidate, as well as against each other.

As noted above, Latino candidates are viewed as more compassionate, but as less competent leaders relative to a white male candidate (Sigelman et al. 1995). Other research also finds that Latinos are viewed as community oriented, which may be linked to higher perceptions of warmth and expressiveness traits (Ramos-Zayas 2001), which typically fall under the basket of female-identified traits. We therefore expect to find that Latino candidates are rated higher than white and male candidates on a wider range of female-identified traits. It is less clear if they will be perceived equally highly compared to a female candidate. There is more limited scholarship that suggests a Latino candidate may be rated lower on male-identified traits, such as strong leadership (Sigelman et al. 1995). However, cultural stereotypes of machismo may point in the other direction (Gutierrez 1993; Quinones-Mayo and Resnick 1996), so we remain agnostic as to differences between a Latino candidate and a male, white, and female candidate on these traits.

It is still unknown how these stereotypes function when the race/ ethnicity and gender of a candidate intersect as in the case of a Latina candidate. Research suggests that minority female candidates face more uphill battles than generic female or minority male candidates (Sigelman et al. 1982; Moncrief et al. 1991; Clayton 2003; Philpot 2007; Bejarano 2013), but these studies have not considered voter perceptions of the traits of minority female candidates. As we discussed above, several scholars find that female candidates are stereotyped as owning traits related to warmth and expressiveness (e.g., Banwart 2010; Burrell 1994; Huddy and Terkild-sen 1993), and there is more limited evidence that the same is true for Latino candidates (Sigelman et al. 1995). Since a Latina candidate has two qualities that reinforce this stereotype, we may find that she is perceived not only higher than male and white candidates on female-identified traits, but also higher than a female candidate or a Latino candidate on those traits. Such stereotypes would fit with existing research that non-white women are seen as politicians who run for office in order to improve the quality of life of their communities (Takash 1993; Hardy-Fanta 1993), and are better equipped to form cross cross-cultural coalitions (Fraga et al. 2007; Casellas 2011). At the same time, since women are perceived as lower on male-identified, or instrumental traits, and there is suggestive evidence that Latinos are as well, a Latina candidate may be doubly disadvantaged on such traits. The lack of visibility of Latinas in politics, until quite recently, only serves to reinforce such stereotypes (García and Marquez 2001). A Latina candidate may therefore be rated lower on male-identified traits compared not only to male and white candidates, but also to female and Latino candidates. In sum, we expect to find:

> *H1a:* Latino candidates will be evaluated more positively on female-identified character traits than male and white candidates.
> *H1b:* Latina candidates will be evaluated more positively on female-identified character traits than white, male, female, and Latino candidates.
> *H2a:* Latino candidates will be evaluated more positively on male-identified character traits than Latina candidates.
> *H2b:* Latina candidates will be evaluated more negatively on male-identified character traits than white, male, female, and Latino candidates.

If we turn to belief-based stereotypes, there is pretty clear evidence with both experimental and survey data that females are perceived as more liberal than are male candidates (McDermott 1997; Koch 2000; Fridkin et al. 2009; Banwart 2010). In the more limited studies of racial stereotypes, scholars find a similar pattern for African Americans, who are stereotyped as liberal (Williams 1990; Sigelman et al. 1995; McDermott 1998; Jones 2013), as well as Latinos (Sigelman et al. 1995; Jones 2013). In line with existing scholarship, we expect to find that a Latino candidate is perceived as more liberal than either a white candidate or a male candidate. However, the Latino candidate may or may not be perceived as more liberal than a female candidate. As with the case of female identified traits, the Latina candidate has two characteristics (gender and ethnicity) that reinforce the liberal stereotype, so we expect to find that she is rated as the most liberal candidate.

> *H3a:* Latino candidates will be evaluated as ideologically more liberal than male and white candidates.
> *H3b:* Latina candidates will be evaluated as ideologically the most liberal of all candidate types.

Finally, we turn to issue stereotyping. We consider a basket of female-identified issues, male-identified issues, and minority-identified issues. With respect to female- and male-identified issues, our expectations overlap with those for character traits. Existing work has not looked at issue competencies of Latino candidates on issues related to racial discrimination and immigration. Scholars have found that African American candidates are perceived as more competent on issues of civil rights (Williams 1990; McDermott 1998), in part because of historical experiences with racism and discrimination. While the historical experiences of Latinos and African Americans are different, Latinos also have a history of racial discrimination (Kaufmann 2003), and may therefore also be perceived as more competent on this issue relative to generic white, male, and female candidates. In contrast, immigration is a policy area that the public tends to associate with Latinos (Austin and Middleton 2004; Abrajano and Singh 2009; Gershon 2012), so we would expect that individuals might perceive a Latino/a candidate as more competent on this issue. Given that race/ethnicity may be most relevant to assessing competency on minority issues, we may not find differences between Latino and Latina candidates.[6]

> *H4a:* Latino candidates will be considered more competent in handling female-identified issues than male and white candidates.
> *H4b:* Latina candidates will be considered more competent in handling female-identified issues than female, male, Latino, and white candidates.
> *H5a:* Latino candidates will be considered more competent in handling male-identified issues than Latina candidates.
> *H5b:* Latina candidates will be considered less competent in handling male-identified issues than female, male, Latino, and white candidates.

H6a: Latino candidates will be considered more competent in handling minority rights issues than the male, female, and white candidates.

H6b: Latina candidates will be considered more competent in handling minority rights issues than the male, female, and white candidates.

DATA AND EXPERIMENTAL DESIGN

In order to explore stereotypes voters hold of Latino and Latina candidates, we fielded our own study using YouGov. The study was in the field from July 20, 2012, to August 8, 2012. YouGov interviewed 1,420 respondents who were then matched down to a sample of 1,300 to produce the final dataset. The respondents were matched on gender, age, race, education, party identification, ideology, and political interest. YouGov then weighted the matched set of survey respondents to known marginals for the general population from the Census Bureau's 2007 American Community Survey.

Respondents were randomly assigned to one of five candidate conditions. As previously noted, the candidate conditions varied on race/ethnicity and on biological sex. Therefore, after answering a battery of demographic questions, respondents were asked to evaluate a "typical" male, white, female, Latino, or Latina candidate on a host of questions related to character traits, ideological placement, and issue competencies. Since so little work has been done on stereotypes of Latino and/or Latina candidates, we included a wide range of trait and issue competency questions. To be clear, respondents only answered these questions for the candidate type they were randomly assigned to. In other words, the only thing that varied was which candidate type they were evaluating, and the only information provided about that candidate was their race/ethnicity and their biological sex, and this information was embedded within the questions they were answering (see next section for a more detailed example).

We use this strategy of assessing stereotypes rather than asking participants to evaluate all five candidates on ideology, traits, and issue competencies for two reasons. First, we did not have the space to ask a wide range of questions about each candidate type. Second, and more importantly, if we asked about each candidate type, then it may have led to social desirability biases by which individuals would give similar evaluations to each candidate type so as not to appear biased. By only asking about one candidate type, such social filters are less likely to influence responses.[7]

In the sections that follow, we consider a stereotype to be present if we find significant differences in responses to the trait, ideological placement, and issue competency questions between experimental conditions. This is the way that past work has looked at gender and/or racial/ethnic stereotypes (e.g., Huddy and Terkildsen 1993; Leeper 1991; King and Matland 2003; Banwart 2010). So, for example, if participants in the male candidate condition report higher evaluations on strong leadership than participants in the Latina candidate condition, that signifies the presence of a stereotype. If there is no significant difference between the two conditions, then it would mean that participants view a male and Latina candidate as equally strong leaders. We compare the male and female candidate conditions first to see how well our sample measures up to prior work. We then assess our hypotheses with respect to Latino and Latina candidates.

Trait-Based Stereotypes

To assess trait-based stereotypes, respondents were presented with the following screen:

Thinking about the typical "(Randomize: male, female, white, Latino, Latina)" candidate running for public office, how well do the descriptions below characterize the average "(male, female, White, Latino, Latina)" candidate?

	Not too Well	Quite Well	Well	Extremely Well
Warm				
Compassionate				
People Skills				
Assertive				
Aggressive				
Ambitious				
Administrative Skills				
Able to Compromise				
Democratic				
Trustworthy				
Strong Leader				

The computer program randomly assigned participants to one of the candidate types. All of the traits above are considered positive traits, and would be beneficial for political office. We did a principal components factor analysis of all of the trait measures and found two factors with eigenvalues over 1. On one factor, all of the trait measures that have been associated with females loaded highly (warm, compassionate, people skills, administrative skills, able to compromise, democratic, and trustworthy), with one instrumental trait, strong leader. The factor ranges from 0.6842 to 0.8781. Given that all of the female-identified traits loaded highly on this dimension, we label it feminine trait factor. On the other factor, three out of the four male-identified traits loaded highly (assertive, aggressive, and ambitious) and we label this the masculine trait factor. This factor ranges from 0.7794 to 0.8586. The rotated factor loadings are presented in table 3.1.

Table 3.1.   Rotated Factor Loadings for the Feminine and Masculine Trait Factors

	Feminine Trait Factor	Masculine Trait Factor
Warm	0.8495	0.1516
Compassionate	0.8470	0.1617
People Skills	0.6940	0.4685
Administrative Skills	0.7154	0.4065
Able to Compromise	0.8256	0.1554
Democratic	0.6842	0.1448
Trustworthy	0.8781	0.1237
Strong Leader	0.8044	0.3241
Assertive	0.3934	0.7794
Aggressive	0.0017	0.8586
Ambitious	0.2292	0.8260

We begin by looking at whether there are any meaningful differences across experimental conditions on the feminine trait factor (figure 3.1).[8] Since the individual traits that make up this factor have been linked to female candidates in the existing literature, we expect to find that individuals in the female candidate condition give higher evaluations on this factor relative to individuals in the male candidate condition. With respect to our primary conditions of interest, we hypothesized that a Latino candidate would be rated higher on the female-identified traits compared to the baseline male and white conditions (H1a), but may or may not be different from a female candidate. Finally, since Latino and female candidates are perceived as higher on these traits than a male or white candidate, we expect to find that individuals in the Latina candidate condition report the highest evaluations on female-identified traits since she has two characteristics (gender and ethnicity) that reinforce that stereotype (H1b).

Respondents were evenly distributed across the experimental conditions according to a host of demographic and political variables, so we proceed by presenting the weighted mean response on the feminine trait factor within each experimental condition in figure 3.1. We test for sig-

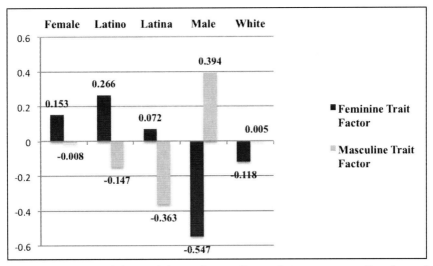

Figure 3.1.   Mean of the Feminine and Masculine Trait Factors across Experimental Conditions. Author made.

nificant differences across conditions using difference in means tests and report the results of those tests in the text. Turning first to the comparisons between individuals in the male and female candidate conditions, as expected, the female candidate is rated higher (mean=0.153) than both the male (mean=−0.547) and white (mean=−0.118) candidate on the feminine trait factor and the differences are statistically significant (p=0.000 in each comparison). These findings therefore nicely replicate those found in other research on gender stereotypes (e.g., Huddy and Terkildsen 1993; Lawless 2004; Banwart 2010). If we turn to the Latino candidate condition, we see that this candidate is rated more highly (mean=0.266) than the male and white candidates and the results are also statistically significant (p=0.000 in each case). Therefore, the Latino candidate is perceived as higher on the feminine trait factor relative to generic male and white candidates, as expected (H1a). One interesting question is how the Latino candidate compares to the female candidate since both are rated highly on these traits. In figure 3.1, we see that while those in the Latino candidate condition rate the candidate more highly than those in the female candidate condition (mean=0.153), the difference between the two conditions is not statistically significant (p=0.167). In sum, the Latino candidate is particularly advantaged on this factor of traits, but only in comparison to the male and white candidates. The work of Sigelman and colleagues (1995) seems to line up with our results here. They find that when comparing a Latino candidate to a white candidate the Latino is perceived as more compassionate, which is similar to these results considering that compassion is a female trait (Sigelman et al. 1995). We however show that this pattern holds for a wider array of warmth and expressive traits.

Turning next to the Latina candidate condition, she is rated higher on the feminine trait factor (mean=0.072) relative to a male candidate and a white candidate and these differences are significant, as expected.[9] However, in comparison to the Latino candidate, she is rated lower on the feminine trait factor and this difference is also statistically significant (p=0.028). In other words, respondents in the Latino candidate condition rated this candidate higher on female-identified traits than did the respondents in the Latina candidate condition, which is contrary to our expectation. Turning to the difference between the female and Latina candidates, the Latina is rated lower but the differences here are not statistically significant (p=0.366). In short, the Latina candidate does not get an even greater boost in perceptions of having female-identified traits that are considered desirable for public office, even though she has two characteristics, gender and ethnicity, that reinforce these positive stereotypes. We therefore find only partial support for H1b, in that the Latina candidate is only seen higher on female-identified traits compared to the white and male candidates. One potential reason for these findings may be the limited exposure that the general population has with a Latina candidate.

We next look at whether there are any meaningful differences across experimental conditions on male-identified traits. Given the existing literature, we expect to find that the female candidate is rated lower on the masculine trait factor relative to the male candidate. To refresh, the only clear expectation we have for the Latino candidate is that he will be perceived higher than the Latina candidate (H2a), and we are less certain where he will fall relative to the other three candidate types. Finally, we expect to find a Latina candidate as being perceived as the lowest on the masculine trait factor since there are two characteristics (gender and ethnicity) that may reinforce stereotypes (H2b).

We present the mean masculine trait factor across experimental conditions in figure 3.1. Turning first to the comparisons between the male and female candidate, the female candidate is rated lower (mean=−0.008), than the male candidate (mean=0.394), and the difference is statistically significant (p =0.000), which is consistent with past scholarship (Alexander and Andersen 1993; Larson 2001; Lawless 2004; Hayes 2011). If we turn to the Latino candidate, he is rated significantly higher (mean=−0.147) than the Latina candidate (mean=−0.363; p=0.016), as expected according to H2a. However, he is rated significantly lower than the male candidate and the white candidate (mean=0.005).[10] As we found with the feminine trait factor, the Latino candidate is statistically indistinguishable from the female candidate (p-value=0.11). In line with expectations (H2b), the Latina candidate is perceived the lowest on the masculine trait factor relative to all of the other conditions and the differences are all statistically significant at p<0.05. In short, the Latina candidate is doubly disadvantaged with respect to male-identified traits, which is a novel finding.

In sum, we find that a Latino candidate is perceived as higher than a white candidate or a male candidate on female-identified traits, but lower on male-identified traits. Masculine qualities are highly valued in leaders, particularly among those serving in executive offices, so being perceived as lower on these measures may make running for these offices more difficult. Overall, the stereotypes toward a Latino candidate are similar to those individuals hold toward a female candidate. The candidate type that is most disadvantaged is the Latina candidate. This candidate type does not get a further boost in perceptions of feminine qualities even though she has a race/ethnicity and gender that should further reinforce these positive stereotypes. At the same time, she is doubly disadvantaged such that she is seen as lower on the masculine factor when compared to all of the other candidate types. These findings suggest that Latinas in particular may face an uphill battle for higher levels of office, especially in a low-information climate where people are more likely to rely on stereotypes to aid in decision making. In the next section, we assess whether perceptions of ideological stances and issue competencies vary across the five types of candidates.

Ideology and Issue Competencies

In this section, we look first at whether there are differences across candidate types with respect to ideological placement. We then examine whether there are differences with respect to competency in handling a range of issues.

To assess ideological placement, respondents were asked to place the candidate type they received in the trait battery on a seven-point ideological scale ranging from extremely liberal (1) to extremely conservative (7). To review, female candidates are generally perceived as more liberal than male candidates. Existing scholarship also suggests that Latinos are perceived as more liberal than male and white candidates (H3a). Because the Latina candidate has two characteristics for which there are liberal stereotypes (gender and ethnicity), we expect this candidate to be perceived as more liberal than all of the candidate types (H3b). The mean ideological placements across experimental conditions are presented in figure 3.2.

The pattern of results is generally supportive of expectations. The female candidate is rated as significantly less conservative (mean=3.570) than the male (mean=4.190; p=0.000) and white candidate (mean=4.437; p=0.000). In fact, the white and male candidates are the only ones to the right of the middle point on the scale. These findings are in line with

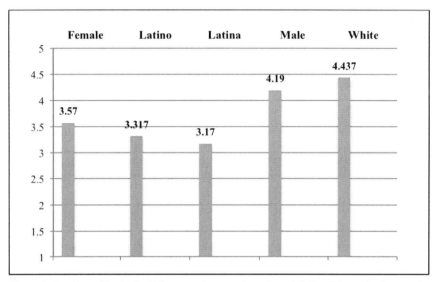

Figure 3.2.   Mean Ideological Placement across Experimental Conditions. Author made.

prior research (Koch 2000; Hayes 2011). The Latino and Latina candidate (mean=3.317 and 3.170, respectively) are significantly less conservative than the male, white candidate and female candidate (p<.05 in all comparisons), as expected. Our results here are similar to those that Jones (2013) finds, indicating that Latino politicians are viewed as more liberal than their white counterparts, though that piece did not look at evaluations of a Latina candidate. Finally, while the mean ideological placement of the Latina is less conservative than the Latino, the difference is not statistically significant (p=0.270). Therefore, the Latina candidate does not suffer an additional bias because of having two qualities that reinforce the liberal stereotype. While this strongly confirms our hypothesis with respect to the Latino candidate (H3a), we cannot fully confirm that the Latina candidate is perceived as the most liberal of all groups (H3b) since she is viewed as roughly having the same ideological placement as a Latino candidate.

Following the ideological question, respondents were asked to evaluate the same candidate type along another dimension. More specifically, respondents were asked: "What is your best guess about a [insert candidate type] candidate's competence in handling the following issues? We asked about female-identified issues, including education, assisting the poor, reproductive health, and health care. We also asked about more male-identified issues, such as foreign affairs, national security, and crime and public safety.[11] We also included two minority rights issues: racial discrimination and immigration. These were presented in a grid similar to the trait evaluation questions. Respondents rated competence on a seven-point scale in which higher values are more competent. We did a principal component factor analysis for each basket of issues and found an eigenvalue of 1 for each one. All of the policy issues that have been associated with females loaded highly (education, assisting the poor, reproductive health care, and health care) onto one factor and we labeled it feminine issues. All of the policy issues associated with males loaded highly (foreign affairs, national security, and crime and public safety) onto another factor and we labeled it masculine issues. Finally, the immigration and civil rights issue competency questions loaded highly on one factor, and we labeled it minority issues. All of the rotated factor loadings are presented in table 3.2.

Table 3.2. Rotated Factor Loadings for the Feminine Issues, Masculine Issues, and Minority Issues Factors

Feminine Issues Factor	Masculine Issues Factor	Minority Issues Factor
Education=0.8838	Foreign Affairs=0.9334	Racial Discrimination=0.946
Assist the Poor=0.8817	National Security=0.9434	Immigration=0.946
Reproductive Health=0.9329	Crime=0.9222	
Health Care=0.9464		

First, we turn to the feminine issues. To refresh, our expectations mirror those that we had for female-identified traits. We show the mean on the feminine issues factor across experimental conditions in figure 3.3. Turning first to the comparisons between the male, white, and female candidate, as expected, the female candidate is rated as significantly more competent (mean=0.400) than both candidate types (male candidate mean=−0.471 and white candidate mean=−0.207) on feminine issues (p=0.000 in each case). These findings therefore nicely replicate those found in other research on gender stereotypes that we noted earlier. If we turn to the Latino candidate, we find that the candidate is rated as significantly more competent (mean=0.093) than the male and white candidates, in accordance with H4a, but is rated as significantly less competent than the female candidate on these issues.[12] If we turn to the Latina candidate, she is rated as significantly more competent (mean=0.009) than both the male and white candidates, as expected (p<0.01). However, she is seen as no different from the Latino candidate, and as significantly less competent than the female candidate for the feminine policy issues (p<0.01). As with feminine traits, the Latina candidate certainly does not benefit from the combination of gender and racial/ethnic stereotypes on female identified issues. Overall then, we are unable to confirm the expectation (H4b) that she would be perceived as more competent than any other candidate type on female-identified issues. All of these findings for the Latino and Latina candidate have not been explored in prior literature.

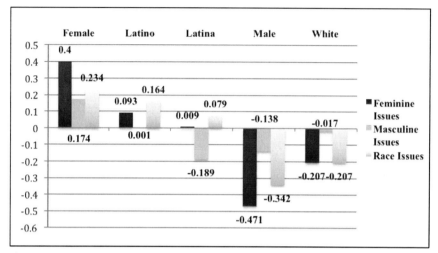

Figure 3.3.   Mean of the Issue Factors across Experimental Conditions. Author made.

We next discuss the masculine policy issues. Our expectations for these issues follow our expectations for male-identified traits, and the mean perceptions for each experimental condition are also in figure 3.3. We can see that the female candidate is considered significantly more competent (mean=0.174) on the masculine policy issues than the male (mean=−0.138; p=0.000) and white candidates (mean=−0.017; p=0.047). These findings are contrary to the existing literature on gender stereotypes, where the male candidate is usually perceived as higher on these issues than the female candidate. If we turn to the Latino candidate, he is rated similarly to the male and white candidate (mean=0.001; p=0.121 and p=0.853, respectively), but significantly lower than the female candidate (p=0.053). Finally, the Latina candidate is ranked significantly lower (mean=−0.189) than all the other candidate types, except for the male candidate. As with male-identified traits, we find that the Latina candidate is often doubly disadvantaged, with this one exception. Overall these results are supportive of our hypotheses (H5a and H5b) that a Latino candidate is perceived as more competent than a Latina candidate on male-identified issues, and that the Latina candidate is generally viewed as the least competent in these issue areas. Finally, it is important to note that existing scholarship has not assessed the content of these stereotypes for Latino and Latina candidates.

Finally, we look at two issues where Latinos and Latinas might be perceived as more competent than the other candidate types: racial discrimination and immigration. We expect Latino and Latina candidates to be perceived as more competent on both issues compared to the male, white, and female candidates (H6a and H6b).[13] Looking at figure 3.3, we see that the Latino and Latina candidates are perceived as significantly more competent (mean=0.164 and 0.079, respectively) than the male (mean=−0.342) and white (mean=−0.207) candidates on the minority issue factor.[14] Furthermore, there are no significant differences between the Latino and Latina candidates, as expected (p-value=0.388). However, the female candidate (mean=0.234) is rated similarly to the Latino candidate and higher than the Latina candidate (p=0.091). Past work has found that female candidates perform better than male candidates on issues of civil rights (Alexander and Andersen 1993; Atkeson and Krebs 2008), so this might help explain the minimal differences between the Latino candidate and the female candidate. Research also shows that women in the general population are more supportive of immigration reform than men (Burns and Gimpel 2000; Knoll, Redlawsk, and Sanborn 2010; Gershon 2012), so we might expect higher competence ratings on the issue compared to male and white candidates, but it is surprising that a female candidate is rated higher than a Latina candidate on these issues. These findings are among our most surprising ones. While generally consistent with the expectation that a racial minority candidate would generate high scores on these issues, we did not expect a female candidate to be perceived as equally competent to the Latino candidate on these issues and significantly higher than the Latina candidate. Hence we only receive partial support for H6a and H6b.

In sum, the Latino and Latina candidate are perceived as more liberal compared to male, white, and female candidates. This finding is consistent with past research on a Latino candidate (Sigelman et al. 1995; Jones 2013) and our work extends these to a Latina candidate. With respect to female-identified issues, a Latino candidate and a Latina candidate are generally perceived as less competent than a female candidate, but as more competent than male or white candidates. On these issues then, a Latina does not get any additional boost from her gender. On male-identified issues, both Latino and Latina candidates are disadvantaged on national level issues, such as foreign affairs and national security, but the disadvantage is greater for the Latina candidate. As with our analysis of traits, Latinas appear to get hurt from the intersection of gender and race on male-identified issues but do not reap the benefits of this intersection for female-identified issues. On issues of racial discrimination and immigration, as expected, the Latino and Latina candidate are perceived as more competent than the male and white candidates, but not any more competent than the female candidate.

DISCUSSION

For many years, scholars and activists described the Latino population in the United States as a "sleeping giant," and pontificated about when the "giant" would awaken and what that would mean for politics in this country. While there is general agreement about Latinos becoming more politically active—just consider the 2016 presidential campaigns mounted by Ted Cruz and Marco Rubio as well as the presence of influential national politicians such as Linda Sanchez (D-CA), and Joaquin Castro (D-TX) (pictured in photo 3.1)—there has been scant research into how the electorate views Latino and Latina candidates. We believe this study provides important insights into public perceptions of the ideological stances, trait characteristics, and issue competencies of Latinos and Latinas running for political office. By manipulating the demographic makeup of the hypothetical candidates that our survey respondents were to evaluate, we were able to make comparisons across race/ethnicity (white or Hispanic) and across biological sex.

Photo 3.1.   Photo courtesy of the Congressional Hispanic Caucus.

While much of what we discovered about trait stereotypes was consistent with our expectations (and previous findings), there were some significant surprises. We found great similarities between the evaluations of Latino and Latina candidates and those of female candidates. Latino candidates were rated higher than male and white candidates on the female-identified trait measure as expected, and actually were rated higher than female candidates on almost half of the these trait characteristics (see appendix). While Latinas were perceived higher on the feminine factor than the male and white candidates as expected, somewhat surprisingly, Latinas actually rate lower than female candidates and lower than Latinos.

This confounded our expectation that Latina candidates would have advantages in terms of the feminine trait characteristics given the intersection of gender and race/ethnicity. When we turned to the masculine factor, Latinos again had a pattern similar to that of females, in that they scored lower than males and whites. Latinas, on the other hand, had the double disadvantage that we hypothesized and scored lower than all other groups on the male-identified trait characteristics.

With respect to ideology, our results showed that both Latino and Latina candidates were perceived as being ideologically liberal relative to male, white, and female candidates. However, Latinas were perceived as no different from Latinos, which was again surprising given that we thought the intersection of gender and race/ethnicity would cause the Latina to be perceived as even more liberal than the Latino candidate.

When we turned to evaluations of issue competencies ascribed to each group, most of the results were congruent with what we discovered in the analysis of trait characteristic perceptions. Latino candidates were positively evaluated on the feminine policy factor when compared with male and white candidates. Latinas, again, do not get a boost by being both female and Hispanic when it comes to female policy issues. Evaluations of her competency are roughly comparable to that of Latinos, in that she scores higher than males and whites, but below that of female candidates. On the male-identified issue areas, we found that Latinos and females are at an advantage in that they are rated significantly higher than the male and white candidates. Latinas, however, are disadvantaged in that they are rated the lowest on this factor. As with traits, Latinas are not doubly advantaged in the more feminine domain, but are doubly disadvantaged in the masculine domain. On the minority issues factor, again there is congruence between Latinos, Latinas, and females, though the latter are perceived as more competent on immigration compared to Latinas.

Although one needs to be cautious about making generalizations about the viability of Latino and Latina candidates from knowledge of the content of stereotypes, since there are many other factors that influence candidate emergence and voting decisions, we believe this research holds out the possibility of both promises and pitfalls for aspiring candidates. Latino candidates appear to have some of the same advantages as generic female candidates, both in terms of scoring high on trait characteristics, such as being warm and compassionate, and in terms of being viewed as competent in female-identified policy areas. What this implies is that Latino candidates are likely to have success when they run for local political office, as well as some state-level offices, but will experience challenges in being viewed as qualified in very important national policy domains, such as foreign policy and defense. Latinas do not appear to gain a further advantage from being female, while at the same time they are doubly disadvantaged in male-identified policy domains. This may mean that they will face a greater hurdle in attaining electoral office, especially in low-information elections, where voters may be more apt to apply stereotypes.

NOTES

1. Acknowledgments: Support for this project was made possible from the Lear Foundation.

2. The voter registration rate among Latinos, which was only 34.9 percent in 1974, just prior to the adoption of the minority language provisions to the Voting Rights Act, increased almost immediately after its adoption, and is now nearly twice that rate (Tucker 2009, 230).

3. Trait, belief, and issue stereotyping are interconnected. Trait stereotyping involves making generalizations about personality characteristics, such as women are more compassionate. Belief stereotyping involves assumptions about the overall political and ideological orientation of individuals belonging to a particular group, such as the assumption that white evangelicals are conservative. Issue orientation is the assumption that individuals belonging to a particular group hold policy stances and competencies related to their membership in the group, such as Latinos favoring immigration reform.

4. When comparing an African American candidate to a generic politician, Schneider and Bos (2011) find that African American politicians are thought to be more empathetic and to hold more integrity. The authors also created a scale of traits they labeled *Black Politician Stereotypes* consisting of eleven traits highly associated with this group. They found that Black politicians are described as ambitious, driven, survived adversity, have something to prove, passionate, charismatic, opinionated, confident, motivated, vocal, and interested in their group only. They also found that an African American politician is rated higher than a generic politician on issues of affirmative action, race relations, welfare programs, equal opportunity, unemployment and job creation, and urban issues.

5. The studies also sometimes label the female-associated traits as "warmth and expressive traits" and the male-associated traits as "instrumental traits."

6. It may be that candidate motivations for running for office vary between Latinos and Latinas (Takash 1993; Hardy-Fanta 1993), but the stereotypes voter apply to each one may not vary on these issues.

7. There may still be some social desirability effects present in the current design, but these are minimized relative to asking about each candidate type on each trait/issue. Even though the study was exempt by the Institutional Review Board at CGU, and the questions we used were based on prior research, we ended up sending a debriefing to participants since some participants were put off by answering questions about different candidate types.

8. For a closer look at the analysis of the individual female-identified trait measures please see the tables in the appendix. They contain the individual trait measures, their mean values, and the respective p-values.

9. The p-value for the difference between the male and the Latina candidate is 0.000. The p-value for the difference between the white and Latina candidate is 0.055.

10. The difference between the Latino candidate and the male candidate is statistically significant with a p-value of 0.000, while the difference between the Latino and white candidate is significant with a p-value of 0.089.

11. We also asked about the economy, for which findings have been mixed in the existing literature. Given the mixed expectations, we present these findings in the appendix.

12. The p-value for the difference in means test between the Latino candidate and each of these candidates is <.0.01.

13. Our expectations diverge from Dolan (2013) who labels immigration policy a male issue.

14. The respective p-values for these differences are as follows: Latino versus male candidate =0.000; Latino versus white candidate =0.000; Latina versus male candidate =0.000 and Latina versus white candidate =0.004.

FOUR

Latina Legislators in Congress

Assessing the Experiences and Influence of the First Generation of Latina Lawmakers

Walter Clark Wilson and Juan Luis Urbano

A record nine Latinas won election to the U.S. House of Representatives in November 2012. Unrepresented in Congress prior to 1989, Latinas slowly but steadily gained presence as U.S. Representatives over the next twenty-five years. By 2014, eleven different Latinas had served a collective sixty-six terms in Congress. Now, with a path blazed by the first generation of Latina representatives in Congress, a second generation appears poised to build upon the political legacies of their predecessors. In this chapter, we explore those legacies by analyzing the legislative behaviors of the first generation of Latina U.S. Representatives. Our goal is to better understand how the intersecting factors of gender and ethnicity have shaped the experiences and influence of Latinas in Congress, and to gain insight into how Latinas might shape the legislative process in future congresses.

We approach our inquiry from a race-gendering perspective that views Latinas in Congress as participants in and parties to institutional processes that shape and constrain their legislative behaviors and experiences (Hawkesworth 2003). Within the race-gendered context of Congress, we also explore how the unique experiential influences of intersecting ethnic and gendered identities prompt the policy agendas of Latina members of Congress (Fraga et al. 2008). From theories that institutional race-gendering and descriptive characteristics shape patterns of legislative activity and substantive representation, we derive and test hypotheses regarding the legislative behaviors, success, and substantive policy focus of Latinas as legislators.

Our approach in this study pursues both descriptive and causal inference. Our primary analyses examine data coded by the *Congressional Bills Project* in order to assess the overall legislative activity of Latina members of Congress and the substantive nature of their contributions.

We supplement insights from the empirical analysis with qualitative data gleaned from the congressional websites of Latina representatives. The findings of our research illustrate that both gender and ethnicity appear to influence the legislative experiences and agendas of Latinas in Congress, sometimes independently and occasionally in combination with one another. These findings shed light on the empirical implications of theoretical arguments that Latina ethnicity and gender yield distinctive legislative representation.

GENDER, ETHNICITY, AND CONGRESSIONAL REPRESENTATION

Questions about the political importance of intersecting gender and ethnic or racial identities are increasingly prevalent in political science literature. The concept of *intersectionality* describes interrelated processes of racialization and gendering that combine to reproduce patterns of privilege and subordination in societal groups (Crenshaw 1989; 1997). While racialization produces commonalities across genders within racial groups, and gendering produces commonalities across races within gender groups, the intersection of race and gender reinforces powerful socially constructed hierarchies that are particularly marginalizing to women of color.

Leading research on women of color in legislatures suggests that their experiences as legislators should be understood in the context of institutional *race-gendering* (Hawkesworth 2003). Women of color in institutions like Congress are subject to processes by which both actors and institutions confine them to subordinated status. Theory suggests women of color are included, but not as equals. They "legislate against the grain" of an establishment that often ignores or defers rather than incorporates their agendas and that renders them invisible (546). Sometimes, invisibility is tactical. Hawkesworth argues that successfully negotiating a legislative process in which power is distributed asymmetrically often means that women of color must identify and work with more powerful patrons, at times "groveling" to achieve the incorporation of their ideas into legislation sponsored by others (538). At other times, more powerful representatives simply take credit for passing legislation championed primarily by women of color, concealing the contributions of these minority female legislators from public recognition (537). Hawkesworth points to instances of marginalization within the Democratic Party in Congress to support her argument that race-gendering, and not merely partisanship or ideology, accounts for the subordination of legislative women of color (540–41).

The barriers to success women of color face in legislatures arguably have consequences for the representation of minority interests. Legislative achievements by women of color may come at the cost of moderated policy positions and the avoidance of race-oriented legislative agendas by minority women lawmakers, assuming they adopt the advice that such moderating concessions are necessary in order to successfully navigate the legislative process (Hamilton 1977; Aberbach and Walker 1973; Wilson 1980). Even when women of color in Congress adopt such strategies, cooperation from white conservatives may not be forthcoming (Hawkesworth 2003, 547).

The notion that race-gendering significantly stifles contributions by women of color in Congress, and in turn the representation of minority interests, implies that women of color contribute uniquely as representatives. These women come to Congress with experiences that differ from those of whites and men, and have "indelible" effects on the political process (García Bedolla et al. 2014). Their personal experiences as members of marginalized groups are expected to shape patterns of responsiveness (Mansbridge 1999; Burden 2007). With respect to Latinas, expectations about legislative behavior flow from experiences related to both gender and ethnicity (Fraga et al. 2008). Latinas in Congress may use their political positions to address issues such as traditional sex roles and culture (Baca Zinn 1980; Cruz 2004). Beyond representing Latinos as a group, studies suggest that Latinas in politics often perceive multiple identity-based constituencies and attempt to represent the interests of diverse groups (Fraga et al. 2001).

We agree with Sierra and Sosa-Riddell that in the political arena "Latina activity is highly complex and comprised of many diverse forms of political practice and intervention" (1994, 307). Latina political motivations appear to transcend individual identities and connect to multiple spheres (Sierra and Sosa-Riddell 1994; Pardo 1990; Takash-Cruz 1993; Montoya et al. 2000; García and Marquez 2001; García et al. 2008). Research suggests that Latina political involvement often stems from community activism and empowerment efforts (Montoya et al. 2000; Hardy-Fanta 1993). Assuming such motivations shape the legislative agendas of Latinas in Congress, we might expect Latina representatives to emphasize priorities related to the empowerment needs of women, Latinos, and Latinas in the communities they represent.

A small but growing body of empirical research supports the notion that Latinas make unique representative contributions, presumably related to the intersecting influence of their ethnic and gendered experiences. At the local level, Rocha and Wrinkle show that support for bilingual education by Texas school boards is positively related to Latina representation (2011). At the state legislative level, Fraga et al. (2006) find evidence that Latinas differ from their Latino counterparts by prioritizing conflict resolution, as well as the special interests of non-Latino minority groups like African Americans, Asian Americans, and immigrants (133). State-level research also suggests Latina legislators address certain constituencies more often depending on their state. In California, Latinas appear to be significantly more vocal than their peers on Latino issues such as immigration; while in Texas, Latinas are more likely to address women's issues such as equal pay (Fraga et al. 2001). Although some quantitative research on Latinas in the Texas legislature has failed to identify evidence that Latinas better represented the interests of women of color (Lavariega Monforti et al. 2009), qualitative research on Latina politicians in Texas suggests they "serve as connectors for their communities . . . on policies that assist families, women, and the Latino community" (García et al. 2008, 133).

Research also provides some limited evidence that the legislative strategies of Latina representatives may be impacted by institutional race-gendering as they attempt to represent their constituencies. For example, Latina representatives may pursue symbolic initiatives in lieu of substantive legislation. Sharon Navarro echoes Jane Mansbridge (2003) in arguing that such initiatives are important to the representation Latinas provide because they foster trust and facilitate communication between Latinas and their constituents, lending legitimacy to governing institutions (Navarro 2008, 37). Latina representatives may also act as "powerbrokers" capable of collaborating and building consensus by drawing together diverse groups, and be more likely to pursue such strategies if more traditional legislative methods prove unproductive (Garica et al. 2008, 11). In sum, growing theoretical consensus and empirical evidence support the notion that Latinas approach their jobs as legislators and representatives in ways shaped by both their gender and their Latina ethnicity.

Based on existing research, we see two subtly different patterns by which Latina representatives might be expected to pursue unique issue agendas in Congress. First, it seems plausible that Latinas might pursue agendas that clearly distinguish them not just from other members of Congress, but also from other Latino and non-Latina female representatives. Such a pattern would appear consistent with the theory of institutional race-gendering which presumes that the intersection of characteristics like ethnicity and gender generates patterns of behavior that are unique from those of both other women and male members of minority groups. Following this logic, we would expect Latina representatives to prioritize issues that are especially salient to Latinas, but less so to Latinos or non-Latina women. The double minority status Latinas face makes them an especially vulnerable population. This vulnerability is evident in numerous issues in which gender and poverty, and perhaps culture, intersect to create interests that weigh disproportionately on Latinas, including issues associated with caring for and educating children, immigration, housing, teen pregnancy, and domestic violence (Purple Purse 2014; Tjaden and Thoennes 2000).

Alternatively, it seems plausible that Latinas draw upon identities *as women* and *as Latino/as* in shaping their issue agendas, but that the extent to which these identities inform agenda setting behaviors depends on the priorities derived from each set of experiences. Such a relationship is reflected in findings elsewhere that black female representatives respond to both women's interests and black interests (Bratton, Haynie and Reingold 2006) and suggests that Latinas might draw upon gender identities in shaping their legislative agendas on issues traditionally associated with gender such as women's rights or childcare, while drawing upon ethnic identities to shape agendas on issues like immigration. In either case, Latina representatives would be acting largely as surrogate representatives on behalf of constituencies they descriptively represent. But in the former theoretical framework, that constituency is a narrower, more specifically Latina constituency.

LATINAS IN THE HOUSE

The history of Latina service in the United States Congress is short. Just eleven Latinas (two Republicans, nine Democrats) have held office in the U.S. House; none has ever served as a U.S. Senator. With just two exceptions, all Latinas elected to Congress continue to serve there as of this writing. Only two Latinas (Ileana Ros-Lehtinen and Nydia Velasquez) have chaired full committees, and Latinas have occupied positions as full committee chairs or ranking members only seven times. Constituencies in southern California have elected seven different Latina representatives, all Democrats. The other two Latina Democrats serve constituencies in New York City and in New Mexico. The only Latina Republicans in Congress represent areas of South Florida and, much more recently, Washington. With one exception, Latinas in Congress have served districts where Latino/as comprised a majority of the population.

The first Latina elected to Congress, Republican Ileana Ros-Lehtinen, took office on August 29, 1989, following a special election. In addition to being the first Latina, she was also the first Cuban-American, and the first Republican woman from Florida elected to Congress. Ros-Lehtinen has established herself as a prominent conservative voice on foreign policy, and served in top committee positions, including as chair of the House

Photo 4.1.   Rep. Illeana Ros Lehtinen (R-FL) chairs a hearing of the House International Relations Committee on "Why Taiwan Matters," June 16, 2011. Screenshot from the House International Relations Committee youtube.com channel, accessed April 29, 2015.

Committee on International Relations during the 112th Congress. She has also served on the House Budget and Government Reform Committees.

The first two Latina Democrats were elected in 1992. Congresswoman Lucille Roybal-Allard, daughter of former congressmen Edward Roybal, serves California's 40th Congressional District. Roybal-Allard is the first Latina to serve on the House Appropriations Committee. In 1999, she became the first Latina to chair the Congressional Hispanic Caucus, an organization founded by her late father. Rep. Nydia M. Velasquez (NY-7) is the first Puerto Rican woman elected to Congress. By her third term she was named ranking member of the House Small Business Committee. In 2007, she became chair of the Small Business Committee and the first Latina to head a full committee in the House. She also chaired the Congressional Hispanic Caucus during the 111th Congress (2009–2010).

Congresswoman Loretta Sanchez (CA-46) was the second Latina elected to the House from California, and the first to win a competitive general election with her plurality victory over the six-term Republican incumbent Bob Dornan in 1996. Sanchez has served on the House Armed Forces Committee, but spent the bulk of her legislative career as a member of the House Homeland Security Committee.

In the next six years, three more Latinas were elected to represent California districts. Rep. Grace Napolitano won the 34th Congressional District seat vacated by Rep. Esteban Torres in 1998 and subsequent to redistricting in 2002 and 2012, won elections in the 38th and 32nd districts. She serves on both the House Natural Resources and House Transportation and Infrastructure committees, and was chair of the

Congressional Hispanic Caucus during the 109th Congress. Rep. Hilda Solis, was elected to represent California's 31st Congressional District in 2000, and after redistricting, won election as the representative of the 32nd Congressional District. Solis served as a member of the House Energy and Commerce and House Natural Resources committees until December 2008 when President-Elect Barack Obama nominated her to be the twenty-fifth Secretary of Labor of the United States. Confirmed over Republican opposition (Fletcher 2009), Solis is the first Latina to serve in a presidential cabinet and the first Latino/a to hold the position of Labor Secretary. Rep. Linda Sanchez, Loretta Sanchez's younger sister, won election to California's newly redrawn 39th Congressional District in 2002. She handily defeated Republican Tim Escobar and now represents California's 38th Congressional District. A former member of the House Judiciary Committee, Linda Sanchez now serves on the House Ways and Means and Ethics Committees. She was elected chair of the Congressional Hispanic Caucus in 2015.

Photo 4.2. Rep. Nydia Velasquez (D-NY) speaks at a rally to reform discriminatory police practices on the steps of New York City Hall, September 24, 2012. Communities United for Police Reform, changethenypd.org, accessed April 29, 2015.

Following Linda Sanchez's election, it would be eight years before another Latina was elected to the House. Jaime Herrera-Beutler, at the age of 31, was elected to represent Washington State's 3rd Congressional District in 2010. Herrera Beutler is the second Latina Republican ever elected, second Latina ever to serve on the House Appropriations Committee, and the only Latina in Congress who does not represent a large Latino/a constituency. Rep. Michelle Lujan Grisham was elected to represent New Mexico's 1st congressional district in 2012 and is the first Latina U.S. Representative from that state. A former state Secretary of the Department of Health under then-governor Bill Richardson, Grisham serves on the House Oversight and Government Reform, Agriculture, and Budget committees. The same year, Rep. Gloria Negrete McLeod won a bitterly fought election in California's 35th congressional district, defeating veteran incumbent and former CHC chair Joe Baca. Negrete McLeod served just one term in the House as a member of the Agriculture and Veteran's Affairs committees before resigning to run instead for the San Bernardino County Board of Supervisors (Cameron 2014). Norma Torres, who had previously served on the Pomona city council, as mayor of Pomona, and in the state assembly and state senate, won the 2014 election to replace McLeod. Born in Guatemala, she immigrated to the United States at age five to escape the violence of her home country (Torres 2014). She now serves on the House Homeland Security and Natural Resources committees.

LATINAS AS LEGISLATORS

Using data coded by the *Congressional Bills Project,* this section explores the legislative activities and successes of Latina representatives from the 101st through 112th Congresses. The *Congressional Bills Project* is a publicly available dataset that includes information about the topical subject matter of and congressional actions taken on every bill sponsored in the U.S. Congress. We augment our empirical analysis with qualitative data from congressional websites.

During the twelve congresses examined here, Latinas sponsored a total of 565 pieces of legislation. Sixty-two of those bills passed the House, and twenty-nine were signed into law. As figure 4.1 illustrates, Latinas' contributions have increased steadily alongside their growing presence in Congress. They were most active as bill sponsors during the Democratic-controlled 110th and 111th congresses when they collectively sponsored 133 and 100 bills, respectively. This pattern of sponsorship is consistent with the notion that majority party status, and therefore greater opportunity for legislative success, generates greater legislative activity. The idea is bolstered by the fact that Latinas achieved their greatest legislative successes during these congresses. During the 110th Congress, twenty-two bills sponsored by Latinas passed the House, and eight became law. During the 111th Congress, ten Latina-sponsored bills passed the House and six became law. During the 112th Congress, the return of a Republican majority coincided with reductions in legislative activity and success by Latinas. Despite increasing their overall presence from six to seven, they sponsored just seventy-five bills collectively, five of which passed in the House, and two of which became law.

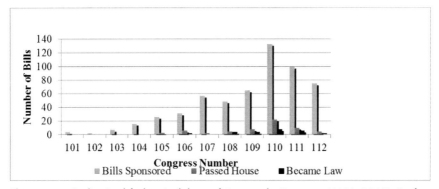

Figure 4.1. Latina Legislative Activity and Success in Congress (1989–2012). Author made.

The theory of race-gendering advanced by Hawkesworth and others suggests that Latinas are marginalized in Congress, and less likely to achieve visibility, credit, or legislative success as a result (2003). Based on this theory, we might expect Latinas to sponsor legislation at lower rates than their Latino, non-Latina female, and non-Latino male counterparts, and also to achieve lower rates of success with regard to the passage of legislation. The argument by Fraga et al. (2006), that Latinas may be more likely to form policy coalitions, appears consistent with Hawkesworth's to the extent that Latinas may achieve less recognition by pursuing such strategies even if they prove successful (2003). With that in mind, it is important to acknowledge that our analysis examines only cases of legislative activity and success that are clearly visible—those related directly to bill sponsorship—and leaves less traceable cases of legislative agenda influence to future research.

It is also important to acknowledge the possibility that Latina ethnicity may be a political asset in certain contexts. Bejarano argues that Latinas' electoral successes are due to their broad appeal to diverse constituencies (2013). They are able to fundraise and campaign as Latinas and as women, and may be seen as less threatening by the white voting population than male minority candidates. Although no direct implications from these arguments are evident in the legislative arena, it seems plausible that Latinas might enjoy enhanced abilities to appeal to and work with a variety of House colleagues, and perhaps enjoy both cooperation on their own legislative initiatives and opportunities to achieve concealed victories by incorporating their ideas into bills advanced by others. But again, we focus only upon those legislative initiatives where Latina representatives played an explicit role as sponsor.

To test the hypotheses that Latina ethnicity is associated with different, and presumably limited legislative activity and success, we model patterns of bill sponsorship, House passage, and laws authored by each representative from the 101st through 112th congresses using negative binomial regression analysis. The technique essentially counts activity in each of these areas while controlling for other factors that might contribute to legislative activity and success.

In addition to analyzing whether status as a *Latina representative* impacted legislative behavior, we examine a number of other factors that may have shaped legislative activity and success. First, we examine whether status as a male *Latino Representative* or *Non-Latina Female* representative significantly impacted sponsorship patterns. Past research shows that Latino representatives sponsor fewer bills than their non-Latino counter parts (Rocca and Sanchez 2008). Some research suggests that only the most qualified women choose to run for Congress and this leads them to outperform their male colleagues in obtaining federal discretionary funds for their district and in bill sponsorship and co-sponsorship (Lawless and Fox 2010; Aniza and Berry 2011).

We control for whether the representative was in the *Majority Party* based on the expectation that majority party status encourages both legislative activity and success. We control for whether the representative was a *Republican* given the possibility that ideology or partisanship might contribute systematically to legislative behavior. We control for whether a representative was a *Chair* or *Ranking Member* of a full committee in the house because these positions enhance influence over legislative agendas (Jones and Baumgartner 2005). We examine several constituency level variables, including *Percent Latino, Percent Black,* and *Median Family Income* in districts in order to examine whether representatives' legislative behaviors relate to these broad constituency contours. We also control for the *Democratic Vote Share* in each House race corresponding to the observation in question, which provides a rough measure of the ideological character of constituencies. In analyses of bill passage and laws, we control for the *number of bills* a representative sponsored because more prolific bill sponsors should, at least from the perspective of probability, see action on a larger number of their bills. Finally, the following analyses control for the impact of time by including a dummy variable for each of the 102nd through 112th congresses. These controls are important for ensuring that patterns observed in the cross-sectional data occurred independent of unique political contexts.

Table 4.1 presents results from our analyses of bill sponsorship, bill passage, and sponsorship of bills that became law. The first model demonstrates that Latina representatives sponsored significantly fewer bills than other Latinos, other women, and non-Latino members of Congress. Interestingly, non-Latina women sponsored significantly more bills compared to Latinas and men. Predicted probabilities calculated from the analysis show that, holding other variables at their means, Latinas sponsored an

Table 4.1. Latina Legislative Activity & Success, 101st–112th Congresses (1989–2012)

	# Sponsored		Passed House		Became Law	
	Coef.	S.E.	Coef.	S.E.	Coef.	S.E.
Latina	–0.330*	0.167	–0.025	0.262	0.162	0.288
Latino	–0.115	0.109	0.112	0.114	0.117	0.155
Female	0.114+	0.060	–0.196*	0.080	–0.242*	0.105
Majority	0.190***	0.028	1.041***	0.049	0.980***	0.064
Republican	–0.073	0.049	0.105	0.066	–0.063	0.089
%Latino	0.006***	0.002	–0.001	0.003	–0.001	0.004
%Black	0.005*	0.002	–0.005+	0.003	0.000	0.004
Income	0.000***	0.000	-0.000+	0.000	0.000+	0.000
Dem. Vote	0.059	0.102	–0.008	0.108	–0.028	0.149
Chair	0.520***	0.061	0.983***	0.064	1.139***	0.077
Ranking	0.256***	0.072	0.388***	0.103	0.350*	0.138
# Sponsored	—	—	0.035***	0.003	0.029***	0.003
102nd	0.045	0.032	–0.005	0.058	–0.019	0.081
103rd	–0.364***	0.057	–0.073	0.084	–0.010	0.114
104th	–0.535***	0.061	0.024	0.097	0.091	0.123
105th	–0.432***	0.061	0.043	0.097	0.028	0.121
106th	–0.255***	0.063	0.311***	0.094	0.494***	0.122
107th	–0.243***	0.063	0.073	0.095	0.251*	0.121
108th	–0.125*	0.054	0.195*	0.085	0.399***	0.108
109th	0.043	0.055	0.035	0.084	0.205+	0.111
110th	0.123*	0.051	0.421***	0.075	0.054	0.106
111th	–0.530***	0.100	0.514***	0.127	0.047	0.189
112th	–0.453***	0.097	–0.004	0.134	–0.417*	0.211
Constant	2.138***	0.092	–1.115***	0.118	–1.604***	0.159
Observations	5129		5129		5129	
Wald Chi-Square	472.78		2146.06		1302.45	
Log pseudo-likelihood	–17702		–7234		–4849	

Note: +p≤.10, ***p≤.05, **p≤.01, *p≤.001, two-tailed significance tests; Robust standard errors adjusted for 1182 clusters by representative.

average of 9.35 bills per congress, while Latino representatives sponsored an average of 11.54, non-Latino men sponsored an average of 12.87, and non-Latina women sponsored an average of 14.47. Given that bill sponsorship is a relatively unconstrained legislative behavior that is presumably shaped in part by an author's perception that legislative success is possible or that the activity is in some way politically useful, it appears that Latinas perceive less advantage to sponsoring bills compared with others. This finding is consistent with the argument that race-gendering marginalizes Latinas in Congress.

Like other female members of Congress, Latinas sponsored fewer bills that passed the House and fewer bills that became law compared to male members of Congress. Although differences were small in substantive terms—for example, Latina and non-Latina women sponsored an average of .93 and .84 bills that passed the House, respectively, while Latino and non-Latino men passed an average of 1.14 and 1.02 bills, respectively— these findings nonetheless underscore the theory that Congress is a gendered institution, and that women enjoy disproportionately less influence over legislative agendas than men.

Not surprisingly, members of the majority party, committee chairs, and ranking members sponsored significantly more bills, passed significantly more bills, and saw significantly more of their bills become law, on average. Also as expected, more prolific bill sponsors passed more bills and saw more of their bills signed into law. All else equal, representatives with larger Latino and black constituencies, as well as wealthier constituencies, were more active as bill sponsors. However, the size of black populations and constituency wealth were both negatively associated with bill passage, and constituency income was also negatively associated with law authorship, all else equal.

While legislative activity and success are important to understanding Latinas' impacts in Congress, perhaps even more interesting are their legislative agendas. We began our analysis of legislative agenda setting by comparing bill sponsorship patterns by Latinas and all non-Latinas on issues where Latinas sponsored at least one bill. Using simple difference of means tests, we found that the proportionate focus of Latinas as sponsors was significantly greater than that of other representatives in twenty-one issue areas. Table 4.3 displays these topics, along with information about the numbers of bills and Latina sponsors associated with each. These agendas appear to have been governed by three primary factors: the interests and opportunities of sponsors (sometimes related to their committee positions), parochial needs within the districts represented by Latinas, and the more generalizable policy agendas of Latina congresswomen guided by their experiences as Latinas.

Table 4.2. Latina-led Legislative Agendas, Difference of Means Tests, 101st–112th Congresses (1989–2012)

Issue	Latina Representatives			Non-Latina Reps.			Sig.	# Latina Sponsors	Lead Latina Sponsor
	# of Bills	Mean	S.E.	# of Bills	Mean	S.E.			
Freedom of Speech and Religion	6	0.011	0.004	208	0.003	0.000	t = −3.24	2	Sanchez, Loretta; Ros-Lehtinen
Infants and Children	16	0.028	0.007	527	0.008	0.000	t = −5.55	4	Roybal-Allard
Alcohol Abuse and Treatment	3	0.005	0.003	42	0.001	0.000	t = −4.37	1	Roybal-Allard
Youth Employment, Child Labor	4	0.007	0.004	82	0.001	0.000	t = −3.96	1	Roybal-Allard
Immigration and Refugee Issues	28	0.050	0.009	1316	0.019	0.001	t = −5.23	5	Ros-Lehtinen
Elementary and Secondary Ed.	15	0.027	0.007	805	0.012	0.000	t = −3.26	5	Sanchez, Linda
Vocational Education	2	0.004	0.003	44	0.001	0.000	t = −2.67	2	Solis; Sanchez, Linda
Other Education Issues	4	0.007	0.004	86	0.001	0.000	t = −3.84	2	Sanchez, Loretta
Indoor Environmental Hazards	2	0.004	0.003	65	0.001	0.000	t = −1.98	1	Roybal-Allard
Family Issues	22	0.039	0.008	599	0.009	0.000	t = −7.61	6	Roybal-Allard
Low and Middle Income Housing	12	0.021	0.006	292	0.004	0.000	t = −6.10	3	Velasquez
Small Business Issues	35	0.062	0.010	680	0.010	0.000	t = −12.22	3	Velasquez
Arms Control	10	0.018	0.006	149	0.002	0.000	t = −7.70	1	Ros-Lehtinen
Western Europe, Common Market	2	0.004	0.003	28	0.000	0.000	t = −3.57	1	Ros-Lehtinen
Asia, Pacific Rim, Australia, Japan	4	0.007	0.004	65	0.001	0.000	t = −4.61	1	Ros-Lehtinen
Middle East	25	0.044	0.009	174	0.003	0.000	t = −18.52	1	Ros-Lehtinen
Human Rights	6	0.011	0.004	144	0.002	0.000	t = −4.35	1	Ros-Lehtinen
International Organizations	6	0.011	0.004	154	0.002	0.000	t = −4.14	1	Ros-Lehtinen
Terrorism	5	0.009	0.004	125	0.002	0.000	t = −3.85	2	Ros-Lehtinen
U.S. Diplomats	5	0.009	0.004	155	0.002	0.000	t = −3.26	1	Ros-Lehtinen
Water Resources Development	18	0.032	0.007	814	0.012	0.000	t = −4.36	5	Napolitano

In nearly half of the issue areas in which Latinas sponsored legislation at a disproportionately higher rate than other representatives, a single bill sponsor drove legislative agendas. In a number of cases, these agendas appear to have been guided by personal issue interests. For example, Rep. Lucille Roybal-Allard sponsored three bills on alcohol abuse and treatment. Roybal-Allard is a former assistant director of the Alcoholism Council of East Los Angeles. She identifies alcohol as the major substance abuse threat to minors, and has successfully passed legislation creating an interagency committee chaired by the Health and Human Services Committee to coordinate federal efforts to combat underage drinking (Koszczuck and Stern 2005, 137).

Rep. Illeana Ros-Lehtinen sponsored ten bills on arms control, two on the European common market, four on Asia/Pacific Rim issues, twenty-five on the Middle East, six on human rights, and five on U.S. diplomacy. Her patterns of sponsorship in these areas arguably reflect both personal interests and clear coincidence with her committee membership and issue expertise. Ros-Lehtinen is a long time member and former chair of the House Committee on International Relations, as well as a former chair of its subcommittee on the Middle East and Central Asia. Her foreign policy agendas, particularly those related to human rights, stem in large part from her upbringing in predominately Cuban and anti-Castro South Florida. Notably, Ros-Lehtinen is the only Latina to have a link dedicated to "Foreign Affairs" on her issues webpage. So Ros-Lehtinen's major policy agendas appear to reflect elements of personal interest, a strategic selection and use of committee positions, and interest in representing the opinions and priorities of her largely Cuban-American constituency.

Rep. Nydia Velasquez, former chair of the House Small Business Committee, also has a legislative resume that appears to have been influenced in part by personal interests related to her committee position. Velasquez sponsored twenty-nine bills on small businesses during the congresses analyzed, and molded a strong leadership role on the topic. The emphasis Velasquez places on small businesses is evident on her website as well. She has links to articles on her small business advocacy, a link to the House Small Business Committee website, and while her "Issues" tab is the most limited of the Latina legislators, it is the only to have a link dedicated to small business issues (also available in Spanish). Although two other Latina representatives have sponsored small business legislation too, Velasquez appears disproportionately responsible for the significant impact of Latinas in this issue area.

Latinas also appear motivated by their constituencies to pursue non-identity based policy agendas. Perhaps the most prominent of these is in the area of water resource development. Five Latina representatives have collectively sponsored eighteen bills on the topic. While such issues are not clearly recognizable as Latino/a issues or women's issues, they are vital in areas of the southwest where population growth is quickly outstripping the availability of water. Perhaps not surprisingly, then, it was a Latina representatives from Southern California who sponsored seventeen of the eighteen bills. On her website, Linda Sanchez proudly details her policy work on funds dedicated to study clean water in the greater Los Angeles area. The newest Latina in congress, Norma Torres, was recently appointed to the Natural Resources Committee and its Water subcommittee.

In addition to bills that appear closely motivated by personal and constituency interests, Latina representatives have taken the lead on a number of issues that comport with the expectation that they advance a "Latina" policy agenda that is associated with their common experiences and perspectives as Latinas. These include legislative agendas addressing the health of infants and children, immigration and refugee issues, elementary and secondary education, low and middle income housing needs, and family issues. In each of these issue areas, at least three Latina representatives have sponsored legislation, and in four of the five, between four and six different Latina representatives sponsored bills.

Latina-sponsored bills addressing child health included H.R.1968, a bill to provide grants to improve positive health behaviors among women and children sponsored by Rep. Solis during the 110th Congress, and H.R. 2691, a bill to prohibit discrimination in exposure to hazardous substances (a serious reproductive health issue in many minority communities), sponsored by Rep. Velasquez during the 104th Congress. Examples of Latina-sponsored immigration legislation include H.R. 2235, a bill to provide enhanced protections for vulnerable unaccompanied alien children and female detainees sponsored by Rep. Roybal-Allard during the 112th Congress, and H.R. 3980, a bill to provide for humane policies and procedures related to the treatment of aliens in immigration enforcement operations sponsored by Rep. Solis during the 110th Congress. Latina-sponsored youth education bills included H.R. 3132, a bill to incorporate bullying and harassment prevention programs into the Safe and Drug Free Schools Act, and H.R. 3439, a bill to fund additional guidance counselors in schools with high dropout rates, both sponsored by Rep. Linda Sanchez during the 110th Congress. Examples of Latina-sponsored housing legislation include H.R. 44, a bill to preserve affordable housing options for low-income families sponsored by Rep. Velasquez during the 110th Congress, and H.R. 5487, a bill to establish the Affordable Homeownership Preservation Fund of the Neighborhood Reinvestment Corporation, sponsored by Rep. Loretta Sanchez during the 110th Congress. Finally, examples of Latina-sponsored family issues bills include H.R. 3185, a bill to promote the safety and security of victims of domestic violence sponsored by Rep. Roybal-Allard during the 109th Congress, H.R. 3921, a bill to educate minority and immigrant communities about domestic violence sponsored by Rep. Solis during the 109th Congress, and H.R. 468, a bill to provide grants for teen pregnancy prevention in minority and immigrant communities sponsored by Rep. Solis during the 110th Congress.

The concentration of interest on child health, youth education, immigration, housing, and family issues by Latina representatives is suggestive of a generalizable pattern of agenda setting, and worthy of more in-depth analysis. The connections between each of these issues and the special needs of minority and/or female constituents—particularly women of color—are evident. The health of infants and children, immigration issues, childhood education, family issues (including domestic violence and teen pregnancy), and access to housing are all acute problems in minority communities. Most are arguably of particular concern to women in those communities given their disproportionate involvement in childrearing, and the disproportionate economic vulnerability of minority women. It seems plausible that intersecting experiences as women and as Latinas may lead Latina members of Congress to prioritize these issues and influence the congressional policy agenda accordingly through their sponsorship behaviors.

To assess whether Latina members of Congress significantly and systematically pursued unique issue agendas in Congress, we analyzed sponsorship patterns in each of the issue areas on which Latinas stood out statistically after difference of means tests, and on which at least three Latinas sponsored legislation. These include child health, youth education, immigration, family issues, housing, small business, and water resource development. Modeling techniques similar to those used in our analysis of legislative activity and success were employed, although these models did not control for committee leadership status because there is no clear theoretical connection between that factor and the focus of a representative's issue agenda.

There are good reasons to think that Latinas, Latinos, and women in Congress might influence the legislative agenda on issues like child health and education, immigration, family issues, or housing, because they may be motivated by experiences that lead them to identify such issues as priorities. If Latinas stand apart from Latinos and non-Latina women, it would suggest that representative ethnicity and gender intersect to influence substantively unique policy agendas. On the other hand, if gender or ethnicity appears to influence agenda setting behavior by Latinas independent of one another, it would suggest that ethnicity and gender act as alternative sources of experience or perspective that influence Latinas' legislative behaviors.

In addition to hypotheses about the influence of representatives' characteristics, there are strong reasons to think that representatives with large Latino and/or black constituencies might sponsor more legislation on issues including education, healthcare, immigration, or housing because problems associated with those issues disproportionately impact minority communities. By contrast, Republican members of Congress should be less likely, all else equal, to sponsor legislation on issues like child health and education, family issues, and housing, given that their most ardent supporters generally demand responsiveness in other issue areas. Although our dependent variable addresses the subject matter rather than the ideological orientation of bills, meaning that conservative and liberal proposals alike may appear within each category of bills, our review of the bills sponsored by Latina representatives showed that they generally proposed policies congruent with more liberal ideological preferences. This gives us confidence that any differences between Latinas and other representatives with respect to topical focus can also be interpreted as impacting the legislative agenda in ways that represent Latina interests in those policies.

Findings from the analysis, which appear in table 4.3, reveal that the agenda setting behaviors of Latinas differed from their Latino and non-Latina female counterparts on two of the seven topics examined: family issues and small business. Latino men sponsored significantly more immigration-related legislation than their non-Latino colleagues, and significantly less legislation associated with small business. Female members of Congress sponsored significantly more child health, youth education, family issue, and housing legislation than their male counterparts. With the exception of child health legislation, an issue on which they sponsored fewer bills, and immigration, an issue on which they sponsored more bills, Republican patterns of agenda setting did not differ significantly from those of Democrats in the issue areas examined. Larger Latino constituencies were positively associated with sponsorship of immigration bills, as well as legislation on water resources. But Latino population size was negatively associated with sponsorship of small business bills. Black population size was positively associated with legislation addressing child health, youth education, and family issues, and was negatively associated with sponsorship of legislation addressing water resources.

Table 4.3. Latina Legislative Agenda Setting, Bill Sponsorship Patterns, 101st–112th Congresses (1989–2012)

	Child Health	Immigration	Youth Ed.	Family Issues	Housing	Small Bus.	Water Res.
Latina	0.500	-0.194	-0.161	1.465*	0.402	2.390**	0.501
	(0.661)	(0.478)	(0.607)	(0.704)	(0.607)	(0.845)	(0.668)
Latino	-0.178	1.056***	0.443	-0.303	0.403	-0.713+	0.429+
	(0.475)	(0.270)	(0.367)	(0.524)	(0.488)	(0.365)	(0.254)
Female	1.147***	0.187	0.282+	0.778***	0.765***	0.226	-0.313
	(0.171)	(0.248)	(0.156)	(0.156)	(0.260)	(0.245)	(0.213)
Majority	0.015	-0.229*	-0.012	-0.073	-0.003	0.074	0.031
	(0.121)	(0.096)	(0.098)	(0.096)	(0.148)	(0.123)	(0.091)
Republican	-0.427*	0.356+	-0.286	-0.052	0.414	-0.010	0.165
	(0.199)	(0.208)	(0.197)	(0.189)	(0.297)	(0.237)	(0.179)
% Latino	0.012	0.016*	0.001	0.003	0.001	-0.032***	0.015**
	(0.010)	(0.007)	(0.006)	(0.007)	(0.010)	(0.006)	(0.005)
% Black	0.020**	-0.007	0.015+	0.028***	0.012	0.001	-0.039**
	(0.007)	(0.008)	(0.008)	(0.007)	(0.010)	(0.007)	(0.013)
Income	0.000	0.000*	0.000+	0.000***	0.000	0.000	-0.000***
	(0.000)	(0.000)	(0.000)	(0.000)	(0.000)	(0.000)	(0.000)
Dem. Vote	0.206	0.419	0.042	0.289	1.824**	0.055	-0.747*
	(0.400)	(0.492)	(0.357)	(0.377)	(0.620)	(0.435)	(0.302)
# Sponsored	0.050***	0.057***	0.042***	0.050***	0.046***	0.050***	0.033***
	(0.006)	(0.006)	(0.005)	(0.004)	(0.005)	(0.008)	(0.005)
Output for dichotomous variables representing congresses 102–112 not shown							
Constant	-3.527***	-3.321***	-3.599***	-4.044***	-4.899***	-3.612***	-1.034**
	(0.376)	(0.423)	(0.381)	(0.341)	(0.568)	(0.498)	(0.345)
Observations	5129	5129	5129	5129	5129	5129	5129
Wald Chi-square	250.77	210.76	221.29	315.05	189.19	136.01	159.26
Pseudo Log-likelihood	-1539	-2917	-2112	-1716	-1016	-1911	-2234

Note: +p≤.10, ***p≤.05, **p≤.01, *p≤.001, two-tailed significance tests; (Robust standard errors in parentheses and adjusted for 1182 clusters by representative).

We believe these findings provide compelling evidence that Latinas impact the congressional agenda in unique and interesting ways. With regard to family issues, Latina representatives stand significantly apart from their Latino and non-Latina female colleagues. Given the subject matter of much of this legislation, which addresses problems that are especially prevalent among Latinas, the finding suggests that Latinas may draw upon their intersecting ethnic and gendered Latina identities as motivations for agenda setting on issues like domestic violence and teen pregnancy.

Perhaps just as interesting are cases in which Latinas appeared to draw upon either gender or ethnic experiences, and to behave similarly either to their Latino or non-Latina female colleagues, but not both groups. Agenda setting by Latinas on issues like child health, youth education, and housing did not differ significantly from agenda setting patterns by other female representatives, suggesting Latinas may have drawn substantially upon their gendered identities when setting those agendas. Meanwhile, Latinas presumably drew substantially upon their ethnic identities when it came to sponsoring immigration legislation, as they differed insignificantly from their Latino counterparts on that issue. We attribute the significant finding that Latinas sponsor more small business bills primarily to Rep. Nydia Velasquez's strong leadership on that issue.

While there is substantial evidence to suggest that Latinas impact the Congressional policy agenda through their bill sponsorship efforts, we found little direct evidence that Latina representatives systematically influence public policy outputs through their sponsorship activities. In and of itself, this may say little about their actual influence because Latinas almost certainly exercise indirect influence over legislative language that evades our limited analysis. For example, Rep. Linda Sanchez's 2007 bill H.R. 1512, which sought to compensate states for incarcerating undocumented aliens who were charged with a felony or multiple misdemeanors, passed the House in May of 2008, only to die in the Senate. But the next year, similar language was incorporated as an amendment sponsored by Rep. Rep Alan Mollohan (D-WV) to H.R. 2847. That bill became part of Public Law 111-147, which made appropriations for the Departments of Commerce, Justice, Science and Related Agencies. Like most policy success stories in Congress, Sanchez's legislative victory in this case was real but nearly invisible to the casual observer. It seems reasonable to assume that Latina representatives' influence over public policy often occurs in this relatively concealed fashion. With this in mind, we must acknowledge that the limited evidence of direct influence observed here only scratches the surface when it comes to evaluating Latina influence over public policy in Congress.

Of the twenty-nine Latina-sponsored bills that were signed into law between 1989 and 2012, more than one-third were associated with redesignating federal properties such as post offices under new names. Symbolic legislation, then, comprises a substantial portion of Latina representatives' most visible public policy legacy in Congress. This pattern is consistent both with arguments that institutional race-gendering limits visible legislative achievement by Latina representatives (Hawkesworth 2003) and with arguments that Latina legislators are likely to embrace symbolic legislation as a way to provide policy responsiveness to their constituencies (Navarro 2008).

The importance of institutional power is also evident in the limited record of Latina legislative accomplishment in the House. For example, of thirteen foreign policy-related bills sponsored by Rep. Ileana Ros-Lehtinen that passed the House, seven passed while she was either Chair or Ranking Member of the House International Relations Committee. Five of the six small business bills sponsored by Rep. Nydia Velasquez that eventually became law were advanced during her four-year tenure as chair of the House Small Business Committee. Clearly and not surprisingly, Latina influence over substantive policy outputs appears tied to institutional power within Congress.

A key task for future research will be to step beyond the analysis of direct legislative agenda setting and policy influence, and to dig deeper in search of Latina representatives' indirect influence, and more concealed victories. If, as theories of institutional race-gendering predict, Latinas must often work behind the scenes in order to influence legislative outputs, then the policy impact of the first generation of Latina legislators may extend beyond the limited record of accomplishment that is most readily observable. We therefore see reasons to both acknowledge evidence that Latina representatives face substantial barriers to influence in Congress, but also to be optimistic that institutional race-gendering can be maneuvered around, if not yet directly overcome. In any case, much remains to be explored before we fully appreciate the policy impacts of Latinas in Congress.

CONCLUSION

This study examines the legislative activity, success, and agendas of the first generation of Latina members of Congress in an effort to test the theory that institutional race-gendering impacts their behaviors, and to better understand how Latinas influence the congressional policy agenda. Although our findings draw upon only a handful of cases, and thus remain limited in terms of their generalizability, we believe they contribute some interesting and important new insights to scholarly understandings of the impact of Latinas in the U.S. House of Representatives.

An initial conclusion to be drawn from our analysis is that it provides no evidence that Latinas enjoy any advantage in terms of legislative activity or success. Rather, our study provides significant evidence that race-gendering negatively shapes patterns of bill sponsorship in Congress and that Latinas face gendered barriers when it comes to passing legislation through Congress and to presidential signature. At least a portion of this effect may be associated with the limited seniority and institutional power exercised by Latinas and other women in Congress relative to men. The general lack of Latina influence at the institutional level may therefore help both to explain the limits of their legislative activity and success and to provide a possible avenue for attaining more proportionate influence in the future.

With regard to policy agenda setting, we find substantial evidence that Latinas draw upon their ethnic and gendered identities, and that the priorities they appear to derive from these identities often differ. On a number of issues like childcare, youth education, and housing, Latinas exemplify legislative agenda setting behaviors characteristic of other female representatives. On immigration, on the other hand, they share heightened patterns of prioritization with their Latino counterparts. Their interest in family issues as a legislative issue appears even more disproportionate than the interests exhibited by other women. This may reflect the especially acute nature of interest in those issues among Latinas and provides perhaps our strongest evidence of a Latina agenda in Congress.

While we uncover some evidence that ethnicity and gender intersect to shape Latina policy agendas, we also find evidence of personal policy agendas—especially in the legislative records of the longest-serving Latina members of Congress. The activity and success of representatives like Ileana Ros-Lehtinen, Lucille Roybal-Allard, and Nydia Velasquez on issues that are not clearly associated with Latino or women's interests suggest that Latina representatives tend to build careers around legislative expertise and personal interest in much the same ways as other members of Congress. Furthermore, and also like other members of Congress, they appear responsive to constituency interests when those interests are fundamental to the vitality of their districts. Their advocacy on water resources offers evidence to support that notion.

Looking ahead, it seems likely that current Latina members will both deepen their influence over agendas in which they have personal interests and expertise, and also contribute to gradually expanding congressional attention on issues associated with their intersectional identities. Increasing seniority and institutional influence may also begin to expand opportunities for and achievement of legislative success by Latinas in Congress. As Latina representation in the House of Representatives enters its second generation, the pathway forward remains far from fully defined. Still, our findings suggest that the first generation of Latinas in Congress have begun to establish themselves as an influential legislative force, both collectively and as individuals.

FIVE

Virtually Shaking Hands and Kissing Babies

Congressional Candidates and Social Media Campaigns

Samantha L. Hernandez

The 2012 presidential election saw an unprecedented increase in the use of social media as a campaign tool. President Obama's campaign team utilized social media to mobilize voters, spread information, and perhaps most importantly, increase visibility. The use of social media sites such as Twitter, Facebook, and Instagram has provided candidates with new platforms to chart their campaign progress. With smaller political offices, social media has enabled candidates' access to publicity that would otherwise be unattainable. While social media has undoubtedly played a role in recent political campaigns, an understanding of that role and its effectiveness remains unclear. Furthermore, although the use of social media by candidates has been discussed in general, it has yet to examine the role of intersectionality. In this chapter, I examine the use of Twitter by Latina congressional candidates. The focus on Latina candidates provides an opportunity to explore an understudied group of candidates. The investigation begins with an in-group comparison to better understand the workings of these candidates within the framework already established in the field of women and politics. Though exploratory in nature, I offer the theoretical argument that Latinas, in an attempt to navigate the intersection of gender and race, use social media as a way to personalize campaigns and connect with constituents.

To begin, I briefly discuss the literature on campaign advertisements and micro-targeting of Latinos, and follow with a discussion of social media and campaigning. A brief exploration of Latino targeting by Democrat and Republican candidates provides an understanding of how targeting has evolved over the years and the trends Latina candidates are either following or changing in terms of campaign patterns.

The theoretical background of this project is within the field of women and politics, with an emphasis on campaigning.

CAMPAIGN OUTREACH HISTORY

Latinos are now the largest minority group within the United States and the increase in population has drawn more interest from politicians over the past few decades. However, Latino voter turnout (Subervi-Velez 2008) is low and the question of how candidates reach out to this voting block remains. Starting in the 1984 election cycle, the Republican National Party (RNC) voiced the need to address Latinos in Spanish to gain their support. The Democratic National Committee (DNC) took a more standard approach of registering Latinos to vote and spent little money on actual advertisements (Subervi-Velez 2008). During later election cycles in the 1990s and early 2000s, both parties funneled money into bilingual Latino-focused ads. This attempt was largely centered in battleground states with high Latino populations in such markets as Los Angeles, New York, San Diego, Philadelphia, Miami, Phoenix, and San Antonio (Subervi-Velez 2008; DeSipio 1996; Abrajano 2010; Connaughton and Jarvis 2004). Although the Democratic Party has historically spent more money in previous elections, in the 2000 and 2004 election cycles the RNC outspent the DNC in an attempt to reach Latinos (Subervi-Velez 2008).

In 1984, the RNC began a comprehensive plan in that included using Spanish ads to gain support from Latinos (Subveri-Velez 2008) and centered around two specific themes. First, they promoted the concept of the "American Dream" to create a connection with Latinos by touching an emotional nerve. The RNC also ran ads focused on Latinos as United States citizens first, not stereotypes of the perceived Latino culture. In an attempt to appeal to all Latinos, the GOP did not address specific Latino issues, nor did they use stereotypes. Instead, they brown-washed[1] the group, using generic emotional appeals. In national campaign plans, the RNC allotted more money for Spanish ads than the DNC throughout the candidacy and subsequent presidency of Bill Clinton (Subveri-Velez 2008). In 1996, the DNC created a budget for Latino outreach during the election cycle. In so doing, the two parties began focusing on states with high Latino populations. The DNC ran ads throughout the campaign season rather than just the last few days. Latinos in seventeen markets were targeted by the DNC in both English and Spanish. The Democrats chose to focus on the work that President Clinton had done to solve Latino issues rather than on the current issues. In short, the Democrats used ads in English and in Spanish to show why Latinos tended to register as Democrats than Republicans. Both parties ran into problems with wording and targeting the group as a whole. Concerns also arose with specific phrases that had different connotations for different Latinos. Since then, both parties have sought out the Latino community and have used different strategies (Subveri-Velez 2008).

The brief history of Latino micro-targeting identifies problems that have emerged with political campaigns. How can candidates connect with a voting block composed of multiple subgroups that span variations of one language as well as different cultural symbols and multiple viewpoints? As demonstrated by Subervi-Velez, the simple solution has often been to address the group in general, or brown-washing. However, we see Latina candidates taking the opportunity to use their own cultural experiences within districts that share a similar culture. This provides a connection that other candidates cannot use.

CAMPAIGN ADS

Campaign advertisements provide a 30- to 60-second connection between potential voters and candidates. The idea of catching voters' attention has led to candidates spending hundreds of thousands of dollars on this type of outreach. These forms of advertisements, I argue, are most similar to social media usage. The similarities between Twitter messages and campaign advertisements largely derive from the shortly crafted messages and allow for a comparison of how small amounts of information are put together and packaged to voters.

Although research has been conducted on senate and gubernatorial campaign advertisements, presidential advertisements have received the most attention due in large part to the number of people they affect and the number of advertisements they can afford to produce.

The effect of political advertisements on presidential campaigns has been substantial. While most of the literature comes from Ansolabehere and Iyengar's (1997) study that focused on ways in which negative ads decrease voting, studies on the broader correlation between campaigns and mobilization have also been conducted. Finkel and Greer's 1998 regression analysis of the National Election Survey 1960–1992 data demonstrates the positive effect of media on voter turnout. Looking specifically at this data from 1992 and 1996, Ansolabehere, Iyengar, and Simon (1999) found a faintly negative correlation between voter turnout and television advertisements.

Analyses of voting rates in state media markets shows that the volume of advertisements bought in the last part of the election cycle have an insignificant effect on voter turnout. In 2008, Krasno and Green (2008) conducted a natural experiment on the effects of televised presidential ads and voter turnout. The authors examined seventy-five media markets by state and analyzed ads for content tone. They found no evidence that negative advertisements decreased turnout.

Studies on the psychological effects of presidential campaign advertisements have also been shown to be of great importance (Huber and Arceneaux 2006). Huber and Arceneaux argued that past studies on the topic do not account for the persuasive power of presidential advertisements on citizens. In particular, they examined the effects by conducting a natural experiment using data from the 2000 presidential campaign that focused on the amount and bias of ads shown in states close to battleground states. To determine voting effects, they matched spot records with election survey data from the National Annenberg Election Survey (NAES). Although there was little evidence that citizens were mobilized by or learned from presidential advertisements, there was strong evidence that the ads were persuasive.

Although political advertisements have been extensively studied, various aspects remained largely undiscovered. Connaughton and Jarvis (2004) utilized identification theory to determine whether Latinos were invited to vote via televised presidential ads. This study used spots to run content analysis for Latino-based symbols and American symbols and controlled for language. It was determined that advertisements purchased by candidates and their political parties to invite Latinos to vote do so by recognizing them as an emerging political force. In addition, Connaughton and Jarvis demonstrated attempts by political ads to create a strong party identification with Latinos via language and symbolism. This study appears to be the first to examine both English and Spanish advertisements.

In perhaps the most detailed investigation of political advertisements and the effects on Latinos, Marissa Abrajano (2010) conducted a national test controlling for variables that could affect mobilization. Conducting a multi-part experiment, the author studied the type of advertisement spots bought by political campaigns on both English and Spanish channels. After coding for language, symbolism, and the ability to mobilize, the author hypothesized that Latinos who have been fully acculturated into American culture are more affected by presidential advertisements than those that have not. In addition to analyzing spots purchased and the times they aired on Spanish and English channels, Abrajano used NAES survey data from 2000 and 2004 to measure mobilization. She found that an advertisement with Latino symbols motivated English-dominant Latinos and that Spanish advertisements, though significant, were not as significant as English advertisements. However, Abrajano noted that both Spanish and English ads remain important because they help maintain previous opinions of candidates.

Research on Twitter and sending messages has largely focused on the pace at which information is disseminated. The work of Jason Gainous and Kevin Wagner (2014) showed that when examining race, White candidates are more likely to tweet than Black or Latino candidates. The authors stated that this is due in large part to effective campaign teams with challengers tweeting more than incumbents. The inherent understanding of these two findings demonstrates a hole that cannot be reconciled. Assuming that oversaturation does not exist based on pure numbers of Whites in political office, the second concern—that challengers tweet more than incumbents—raises a question on campaign management. Though methodologically sound, the overall effects of Latinas' Twitter usage should demonstrate a slight uptick in the number of tweets. While examination of party difference will be looked at in this chapter, I expect to see findings that show Latina Democratic candidates tweet more than Republican Latina candidates. In addition to the measures that Gainous and Wagner (2014) use, I also seek to determine whether a generational difference between Latinas exists and if a candidate's age plays a role in their preferred types of messaging systems.

THEORY

The theoretical framework for this chapter lies within a crucial debate of the women and politics literature. Focusing on gender as the main variable, scholars are now trying to see when gender matters and if gender bias exists. Two schools of thoughts have emerged; the first focuses on double standard theory, and the second on women as leaders. While this debate is ongoing, a question must be taken into consideration. When focusing on politics, how are Latinas perceived, and how do they use this perception? The argument in this chapter focuses on the ways Latinas navigate race and gender stereotypes using social media. This outlet provides an opportunity that is unprecedented in campaign strategy. The use of social media allows for a one-on-one relationship that used to be fulfilled by traditional campaigning such as block walking. I propose that social media provides a way for candidates to show that they can be leaders as well as "everyday" people.

DOUBLE STANDARDS THEORY

Research on female candidates and the media has largely been centered in the United States. The study of female candidates' relationship with the news media began in the early 1990s with an emphasis on gender differences (Kahn and Goldenberg 1991; Kahn 1992, 1994, 1996). The double standards model argues that male candidates receive better treatment from the news media and puts women at a disadvantage when running for office. In her 1996 study, Kim Fridkin Kahn explained how women candidates are treated differently from men in gubernatorial and senatorial races. She found that the media is more likely to focus on the viability of a female candidate and that they receive less coverage than men. Kahn (1996) also found that the level of a race results in a difference in coverage. She showed that in gubernatorial races, the media is more likely to focus on a female candidate's personality traits while in senatorial races, the media focuses on the likelihood of a female candidate's electoral success. Overall, Kahn found that the level of office that the female candidate is running for affects how the media covers the candidate and that women running for governorships benefit from less dramatic media coverage changes than their male counterparts in contrast to women who run for senate positions.

The double standard research indicated that women running for office needed to focus on personality traits that were deemed to be more masculine, such as leadership. However, later research showed that running as a female candidate with masculine traits might also prove to be unsuccessful for women (Lawrence and Rose 2010). Past research has shown that portraying women with such traits has led to negative media coverage. In the United States, the best example has been the 2008 presidential race in which Hillary Clinton's team decided to run her as an "Iron Lady." This decision led to male journalists focusing on her lack of femininity rather than the experience she was trying to tout (Lawrence and Rose 2009; Kornblut 2011). In contrast, the same election showed that if a female candidate is running for office, portraying the candidate as too feminine leads to the sexualization of the candidate with an increased focus on her looks and intelligence rather than leadership ability (Woodall et al. as cited in Murray 2010; Lawrence and Rose 2009; Kornblut 2011). The media treatment of Hillary Clinton and Sarah Palin highlighted the masculine/feminine traits that women are held to. This hyper masculine/feminine paradox places a burden on female candidates. Although one would hope that this treatment of female candidates was U.S. specific, scholars of women and media have demonstrated that this type of coverage occurs in Latin America and Europe as well (Hinojosa as cited in Murray 2010; Murray 2010). The double standard forces female candidates to have to choose how they will be framed by the media, which has been found to affect women's decisions to run (Lawless and Fox 2010).

LEADERS NOT LADIES

More recent studies related to women candidates and the media suggest that stereotypes are no longer as salient as they had been in the past

(Bystrom, Robertson, and Banwart 2001; Hayes and Lawless 2015; Jordan Brooks 2013). These authors determine that other factors affect women running for and being elected to office. Most notably, Hayes and Lawless (2010) argued that past research has not incorporated key aspects such as political knowledge, party identification, and ideology. They maintained that these aspects need to be incorporated and that the examination and use of gender stereotypes from a methodological perspective has problems due to limited scope. To prove their hypotheses, the authors conducted a content analysis of U.S. congressional candidates and found that there was no reason to believe that stereotypes affected voter opinion in the 2010 congressional election cycle. Hayes and Lawless acknowledged that although their study was just one election cycle, the volume of data made the case more impressive and telling than past work.

Deborah Jordan Brooks (2013) argued that past findings of women and politics scholars relating to gender stereotypes and standards are no longer relevant. Brooks (2013) stated that past work on stereotypes and standards faced by female candidates occurred in the late 1970s, 1980s, and early 1990s, thus rendering the findings irrelevant in a political climate more tolerant toward female candidates. To support her claim, Brooks proposed an alternate theory to the double standards theory, the leaders-not-ladies theory. Applying this theoretical framework to various experiments, Brooks ultimately found that gender stereotypes would affect inexperienced female candidates. Moreover, in regards to showing emotion and public opinion, women do not face a double bind compared with men.

The use of stereotypes highlighted by women in politics demonstrates the ways female candidates view themselves portrayed and perceived during campaigns. Latinas, facing stereotypes based both on race and gender, have a magnified experience. The ways they use social media gives them the opportunity to recast themselves and identify as the candidate with the best chance of succeeding. Congressional races capture unique aspects, such as the comparison of Latina candidates to their male and female counterparts, the development of social media usage, and the qualities candidates perceive to be important to constituents. These are all components that can be captured via Twitter. While there is a belief that strategic intersectionality provides an opportunity for Latinas to win office over white women and minority men (Fraga et al. 2008; Bejarano 2013; Scola 2013), the question remains: How are Latinas navigating this space and leveraging it to their advantage? My argument is that Latina candidates, in an attempt to overcome obstacles spanning race and gender, use social media to create their own identities. They use social media for more control of content placed out and to have the ability to immediately respond to media coverage and opponents without excessive spending.

DATA AND METHODS

Tweets were collected from August to November in the 2014 general election. Sixteen Latina congressional candidates were followed. Of the sixteen candidates, eight were incumbents, seven were challengers, and one was running for an open seat. Four Latinas were Republicans and twelve were Democrats. The candidates' age range was considerable—from 31 to 62. Tweets were analyzed for language used, images produced, emotional appeal, and tone. For this analysis, I compared the candidates within three groups: age, party, and incumbency. Although other research has focused on the number of re-tweets, favorites, and followers, the importance of the content in these tweets should be examined as it shows how and when Latinas choose to identify with their heritage and culture.

Of the sixteen women that ran for Congress, ten had Twitter accounts. Table 5.1 shows the breakdown of candidates by party, race type, and race result. Not surprisingly, incumbents were more likely to win than challengers, and the only non-incumbent to win was Norma Torres (D-CA) who was competing for an open seat.

Table 5.1.   2014 Latina Congressional Candidates

Candidate	Party	Race Type	Election Outcome
Ileana Ros-Lehtinen	Republican	Incumbent	Won
Marilinda García	Republican	Challenger	Lost
Jamie Herrera Beutler	Republican	Incumbent	Lost
Loretta Sanchez	Democrat	Incumbent	Won
Linda Sanchez	Democrat	Incumbent	Won
Lucille Roybal Allred	Democrat	Incumbent	Won
Norma Torres	Democrat	Open	Won
Susana Narvaiz	Republican	Challenger	Lost
Amanda Renteria	Democrat	Challenger	Lost
Cheri Bustos	Democrat	Incumbent	Won
Gabriela Saucedo Mercer	Republican	Challenger	Lost
Luz Robles	Democrat	Challenger	Lost
Nydia Velasquez	Democrat	Incumbent	Won
Roxanne Lara	Democrat	Challenger	Lost
Grace Napolitano	Democrat	Incumbent	Won
Suzanne Aguilera Marrero	Democrat	Challenger	Lost

FINDINGS

The exploratory content analysis focused on four main categories: images, language, tone, and emotional appeal. To begin, I will discuss the breakdown of candidates on Twitter. As shown in table 5.1, all five Republican candidates had Twitter accounts. Each account contained at least 100 tweets[2] as well as images put out by the campaign. The importance of the number of tweets lies with the findings of Jason Gainous and Kevin Wagner (2014) and suggests that Latinas use Twitter at a higher rate than other candidates. In addition, of the sixteen Latinas that ran for office, older Latinas were less likely to use social media—for example, Grace Napolitano and Lucille Roybal-Allard. These candidates may have chosen not to use social media for a variety of reasons such as age, tenure in Congress, and race security. The first category, images, produced interesting findings. Latina candidates of both parties chose images that showed them embracing friends, family, or supporters. Photo 5.1 shows Ileana Ros-Lehtinen at a fundraiser embracing donors.

Photo 5.1. Ros-Lehtinen with Constituents Courtesy of "Ros-Lehtinen for Congress."

Although taking pictures with donors is not out of the norm, the way Ros-Lehiten is positioned is unique to Latina candidates (although not unique when looking at in-group comparisons). Latinas tend to show more pictures of themselves with their families. They also appear within close proximity to their constituents. In addition, regardless of age, Latinas running as Democrats have pictures of themselves playing some type of sport or dressed in sports gear. I believe this is an attempt to demonstrate a willingness to be close to their district as well as showing a competitive edge. Following the research of Grabe and Bucy (2007), I examined how these candidates were photographed. As seen in photo 5.1, images are typically shot in mid- to close range. Grabe and Bucy hypothesized that this is done to show emotion. Further, the authors discussed background images. Other images from Latina candidates' campaigns show pictures of other Latinos (both male and female), American flags, family members, and in particular, babies. In addition, Latina Democrats were more likely to be seen with blue-collar workers than with any other working group.

MESSAGE

Tweet content was relatively similar across the board, with variance coming from incumbents who are typically the well-funded candidates. Incumbents, while still sending messages about their personal campaigns, used Twitter as a means of endorsing other candidates. In addition, Norma Torres, a non-incumbent, also endorsed candidates. Candidates that were endorsed ran for office at city, state, and national levels. While there was not much difference within the Twitter campaigns, the largest difference was between young Latina Republican candidates and the other groups. Young Latinas, such as Marilinda García and Jamie Herrera Beutler focused on blending in more than other candidates and were more likely to have images showing the American flag and veterans while downplaying their culture, as demonstrated in photo 5.2.

In addition to minimizing visual cues of their culture, the candidates' Twitter feeds lacked any Spanish or bilingual tweets. This absence indicates an attempt to show full assimilation into American political culture and to run as a national candidate, not a Latina. The results were mixed, with Beutler maintaining her seat and García losing. This blending phenomenon should be further studied to determine its effectiveness and if it is utilized in northern U.S. regions or seen in any other state.

CONCLUSION

Candidates from the fastest-growing voting block are slowly being elected to office, a fact demonstrated by the 2014 congressional elections. With continued population growth and changing campaigning techniques, the atmosphere lends itself to Latinas. This particular group has shown that it will use social media to its advantage. In addition, the barriers of race and gender that Latinas face can be overcome by using social media as a means to frame themselves. Overall, this campaign technique shows promise and requires further study. Since social media research is in its infancy, a comparison between Latinas and other candidates is

Photo 5.2. Image of Marilinda García campaign. Marilinda García. Used with permission.

one avenue to explore. What is the difference in weight between a tweet and a political ad? I would argue that the difference is minimal, as exposure would largely happen for the politically sophisticated who already know the candidate they support. However, the sharing or re-tweeting ability that social networks provides is another avenue that needs to be examined. If a follower of a candidate re-tweets, and the information is disseminated to people that are not politically inclined, how does this affect their likelihood to vote? Studies have begun to look into this question; however, adding the race and gender component taps into a willingness to trust a new venue for information about a non-traditional candidate. Overall, as we are seeing Latinas largely embracing certain political traditions yet changing others, the investigation into Latina political candidates requires further review.

NOTES

1. Brown-washing refers to the grouping of all Latinos and Hispanics into one category and assigning them to a general "Latino" stereotype or profile.

2. Ros-Lehtinen had 397 tweets, Saucedo Mercer 120, Marilinda García 112, and Jaime Herrera Beutler, 100.

Two

STATE ELECTIONS: POLITICAL ASCENSION, CAMPAIGNS, COMMUNICATION, AND GOVERNING

Six

Networked Representation

Latina Legislators on Twitter

José Marichal

The presence of Latina legislators at the state level has increased significantly in recent years. The increase has led to a corresponding interest in examining the ways in which Latina legislators impact democratic representation and governance. In this chapter, I look at how Latina state legislator's use of Twitter is representative of the new forms of representation Latinas bring with them to state capitals. I build off of recent work in the Latina politics literature that highlights the unique "bridging" role that Latina legislators play in the governing process (Bejarano 2013) and my previous work on U.S. members of Congress' use of Facebook to cultivate a *virtual home style* (Marichal 2013). Through an analysis of sixty-one Latina state legislator Twitter accounts, I develop a theory of *networked representation* to explain the novel ways in which Latina legislators use Twitter to build legislative coalitions. Networked representation goes beyond the traditional "descriptive" and "substantive" representation models (Pitkin 1967) to factor in how a member positions herself vis-à-vis her constituents and includes different groups into the democratic process through network building and cultivation on social media. Networked representation has three components: virtual home style, intra-party coalition building, and personalization.

TWITTER IN THE LEGISLATIVE PROCESS

Twitter is one of the fastest growing social media applications in the world. Twitter is a *micro-blogging* platform that allows users to send discrete *status updates* to a network of followers. What makes Twitter distinctive is that it restricts users to 140 characters when posting status updates.

This constraint allows users to see a great many updates from more members of their networks. Information is presented to users in the form of a continuous information cascade. Users can send links, text, images, and short videos making the site particularly effective at disseminating information to a targeted audience. By 2013, one out of four social media users were regular users of Twitter. This is up from eight percent in 2013 (Duggan et al. 2013).

Twitter has gained prominence as a critical tool within social movements. In the past year, Twitter has served as a focal point for a number of social movements. As an example, the outrage over the police shooting of Michael Brown in Ferguson, Missouri, in 2014 was collected and galvanized on Twitter through the use of hashtags like "#dontshoot" and "#blacklivesmatter." The transmission of sentiments attached to these hashtags within and across networks has been dubbed *hashtag activism*. This form of activism focuses on the ability of users to help reframe political events through the use of compelling words and phrases that travel across different Twitter accounts and help frame mobilization activities. Examples like #dontshoot and #rapeculture help create advocate networks by serving as an identity marker and a mechanism for the individual expression of voice. These identity-based communities are "flattened" by Twitter in that they allow for the *mass communication of the self* in ways heretofore not possible (Castells 2011). Anyone can create a hashtag and anyone can retweet a post. Each retweet introduces a user's thoughts to a new web of relationships.

Because of these new network dynamics, social media platforms like Twitter have transformed the nature of representation. The elected official on Twitter is part of a flattened networked of relationships where the member's influence is contingent upon her ability to use the *architecture* of Twitter (tweets, hashtags, and retweets) to gain the attention of other actors in the network. If elected officials want to build support for a cause or policy within the network, they are subject to the same rules of "hashtag activism" as the other members.

Little work has attempted to theorize how social media changes the constituent/representative relationship. Previous studies on the use of social media by elected officials focuses on the tightly circumscribed nature by which the tools are used. Lilleker and Jackson (2010) refer to the use of social media by elected officials as *Web 1.5*, more participatory than the early Web, but far short of the true interactive promise of Web 2.0. Members often used social media sites as glorified newsletters, informing constituents of activities but not seeking avenues for communicating with them. Recent work has found that members of Congress use social media to extend Fenno's (1978) *home style* theory whereby members seek to cultivate an image that engenders trust among constituents (Chi, Yang et al. 2010, Lassen and Brown 2011, Marichal 2013). In previous work, I examined the ways in which members of Congress use Facebook (Marichal 2013). I argued that they adopted on-line a *virtual home style* that closely mirrored Fenno's (1978) classic formulation.

LATINA LEGISLATORS AND DEMOCRATIC INNOVATION

Do Latina legislators use social media in distinctly different ways than has been identified in previous work? A growing body of scholarship looks at the ways in which increasing the number of women in elected office impacts representation. A consistent finding is that women legislators are generally more prone to support and advocate for women's and children's issues (Saint-Germain 1989; Dodson and Carroll 1991; Carroll 2001; Bratton 2002; Swers 2002; Escobar-Lemmon and Taylor-Robinson 2014). Additionally, a number of scholars argue that increasing the number of women of color legislators has descriptive representational benefits by legitimating democratic governance and providing diverse views and perspectives (Campbell and Wolbrecht 2006; Guinier 1989; Johnson, Kabuchu, and Kayonga 2003).

Latina legislators in particular bring a unique set of experiences that can affect their governing focus and style. Chicana feminist scholars note how the marginalized position of Latinas can serve as a form of transformational resistance by introducing novel critical approaches to addressing problems into formal institutions (Solorzano and Bernal 2001). As Mary Pardo's (1990) classic work on economic and environmental injustice in Los Angeles pointed out, Latinas' unique social experiences as marginalized allowed Chicana activists to make pointed critiques about power and inequality in society.

More recent scholarship on the role of Latina legislators challenges the notion of Latina ethnic identity as fixed and immutable. Models of representation that emphasize an ethnic advocacy role for Latina legislators miss the complex, contingent and shifting nature of Latina identity. Embedded in Latina identity is an "in-betweenness" that requires Latinas to emphasize different aspects of identity to navigate an increasingly diverse socio-political context (Anzaldua 1987). As Beltran (2013) skillfully points out, *latinidad,* as applied to protest politics diminishes difference at the expense of perceived commonality muting otherwise salient class and gender based identities. Understanding how Latina legislators govern requires understanding this diversity and multiplexity of experience.

Christina Bejarano (2013) contends that this "in-betweenness" can serve as an asset for Latina candidates. Bejarano found that Latinas could build diverse voter coalitions by leveraging their multiple identities, what she calls a *multiple identity advantage,* to win support. She found that in many instances, gender helped Latina candidates mitigate racial bias among voters that might keep them from supporting minority candidates. By taking opportunity to present themselves as mothers and community advocates, they were able to override negative racial framings. Bejarano's insight of "multiple identity advantage" suggests that the intersectional nature of Latina identity allows these candidates to draw from a broader template that merges race, ethnicity, gender, and other salient identities to build electoral coalitions.

An intersectional identity is not only useful as a mechanism for capturing votes or adding a different dimension to legislative debates, I argue that an intersectional identity as applied to outreach to constituents also has a unique representation dimension, by presenting to constituents a model of representation that advocates for cross-cutting policies. Fraga et al. (2007) found that "Latinas place greater emphasis on representing the interests of multiple minority groups, promoting conflict resolution, and building consensus in both the legislature as a whole and within the Latino caucus" (121). If true, it would seem that social media applications like Twitter would provide Latina legislators with new tools for consensus building, but no work to date has looked at this question.

LATINA LEGISLATORS AND NETWORKED REPRESENTATION

To examine the question of how Latina legislators use Twitter, I examined status updates for all sixty-one Latina state legislators who had active Twitter accounts in March of 2015. I examined each account by collecting data on their followers, who they follow, and examined their posts from March 1, 2015, to March 31, 2015. Using grounded theory and constant comparative analysis (Glaser and Straus 1967), I compared posts to one another and sought patterns in the Tweets. From this analysis, I developed a theory of *networked representation* that highlights the novel ways in which Latina legislators use social media tools as part of their governing style. I grouped the legislator's Twitter behavior online into three distinct elements: *virtual home style,* intra-party network building, and personalization.

Networked representation is the ability to use social media applications to build a web of relationships that both change the nature of the constituent/representative relationship and can build capacity tools that can be used later for effective legislative behavior. This is akin to *regime theory* in urban/local politics (Stone 1989) where power is predicated upon the ability to effectively engage in *social production,* or ability of groups to mobilize the resources of disparate actors to realize a common goal. This social production approach has been used more at the local government level because of the structural limitations of local actors. At the local level, you need the help of the private sector to accomplish capital construction projects; thus there is more of an emphasis on "power to" mobilize resources rather than "power over" in the form of direct legislative mandate. It has always been assumed that state legislators had access to more direct forms of power and were less likely to employ social production as part of their governing approach.

Latina legislators, however, have two reasons for being more disposed to govern in a network style. One is the aforementioned "in-betweenness" of Latina legislators who often find themselves identifying with multiple groups and seeking to build bridges between them to achieve policy aims. Second, many members have only been in their respective bodies for a few years and are thus more dependent upon network relationships to achieve legislative victories. Networked representation is facilitated by tools that allow individuals to speak to and with discrete communities. The emphasis toward building communities of interest is exacerbated by the Internet. Bennett and Segerberg (2013) note that politics has moved from Mancur Olsen's classic conceptualization of a "logic of collective action" built on distributing resources or ethnic/racial solidarity to a "logic of connective" action oriented around identity-based mobilization and the reliance of networks of shared interest. This "personalization of politics" means that collective action requires the formation of cross-cutting, fluid networks around issues of personal concern.

NETWORKED REPRESENTATION:
NETWORK BUILDING IN GENERAL

Table 6.1 lists the names and Twitter handles of the Latina members of state legislatures that have active Twitter accounts. In all, sixty-one out of the eighty-four Latina state legislators in 2014 had accounts on the site (71 percent). Predictably, this rate falls below that of members of Congress. In January of 2013, 100 of U.S. Senators and 90 percent of members of the U.S. House of Representatives had active Twitter accounts (Sharp 2013, online). This is our only point of reference since no comparable data exists how many state legislators have Twitter accounts. Nevertheless, a 71 percent adoption rate suggests that Latina legislators as a whole view Twitter as a useful application in communicating with external publics.

An important dimension of networked representation is how frequently social media like Twitter are employed for the purposes of network building. Most Latina legislator accounts were actively used. California state assemblywoman Lorena Gonzales of San Diego is far and away the most frequent tweeter with 18,500 tweets. This constitutes more than double

Table 6.1. List of Latina State Legislators with Twitter Accounts

Member District	Member name and Twitter Handle	Member Position
NJ 36	Marlene Caride (D)—@AswCaride	Assem.
NM 43	Stephanie García Richard (D) @StephanieNM43	Rep.
NM 41	Debbie A. Rodella (D)—@debbierodella	Rep.
IL 04	Cynthia Soto (D)—@StateRepSoto	Rep.
RI 11	Grace Diaz (D) @repgracediaz	Rep.
NC 40	Marilyn Avila (R)—@MarilynAvila	Rep.
IL 24	Elizabeth Hernandez (D) @RepHernandez	Rep.
MI 90	Daniela García (R)—@RepDGarcía	Rep.
CA 39	Patty Lopez (D)—@PattyLopez_D_39	Assem.
IL 20	Iris Martinez (D)—@ILSenMartinez	Sen.
NJ 32	Angelica Jimenez (D) @angiemj319	Assem.
NJ 35	Nellie Pou (D)—@NelliePou	Sen.
NJ 08	Maria Rodriguez-Gregg (R)—@MariaRGregg	Assem.
AZ 04	Lisa Otondo (D)—@RepOtondo	Rep.
MN 63	Patricia Torres Ray (DFL)—@LaSenadora	Sen.
MI 95	Vanessa Guerra (D)—@VanessaMGuerra	Rep.
NM 25	Christine Trujillo (D)—@elect_christine	Rep.
NM 59	Nora Espinoza (R)—@RepNoraEspinoza	Rep.
MD 18	Ana Sol Gutierrez (D)—@asolg	Del.
CA 20	Connie M. Leyva (D)—@senatorleyva	Assem.
AZ 27	Rebecca Rios (D)—@Rios_Rebecca	Rep.
CO 24	Beth Martinez Humeni (R) @Beth4HD31	Sen.
TX 143	Ana Hernandez (D) @AnaHdzTx	Rep.
NJ 20	Annette Quijano (D)—@AnnetteQuijano	Assem.
CO 34	Lucia Guzman (D)—@SenGuzman	Sen.
CO 27	Libby Szabo (R)—@LibbySzabo	Rep.
MD 21	Joseline Pena-Melnyk (D)—@JPenaMelnyk	Del.
FL 062	Janet Cruz (D)—@RepJanetCruz	Rep.
TX 77	Marisa Marquez (D)—@MarisaMarquez	Rep.
NM 15	Sarah Maetas Barnes (D)—@smaetasbarnes	Rep.
NJ 04	Gabriela Mosquera (D)—@Gabby_Mosquera	Assem.
NM 11	Linda Lopez (D) @Lopez4Gov	Sen.
CO 32	Irene Aguilar (D)—@AguilarFor32	Sen.
TX 21	Judith Zaffirini (D)—@JudithZaffirini	Sen.
NV 27	Teresa Benitez-Thompson (D)—@Assemblywoman27	Assem.
CA 27	Nora Campos (D)—@NCamposAssembly	Assem.
CO 47	Clarice Navarro (R)—@ClariceHD47	Rep.
NM 07	Kelly Fajardo (R)—@KellyFajardoNM	Rep.
OR 47	Jessica Vega Pederson (D) @JVPforOregon	Rep.
FL 119	Jeanette Nunez (R)—@RepJNunez	Rep.
MA Suf2	Sonia Rosa Chang-Diaz (D) @SoniaChangDiaz	Sen.
MD 19	Marice I. Morales (D)@Marice_Morales	Del.
NV 11	Olivia Diaz (D)—@oliviadiaz	Assem.
TX 148	Jessica Farrar (D)—@JFarrarDist148	Rep.

Member District	Member name and Twitter Handle	Member Position
AZ 27	Catherine Miranda (D)—@Miranda4Arizona	Rep.
NM 68	Monica Youngblood (R)—@MonYoungblood	Rep.
TX 50	Celia Israel (D)—@CeliaIsrael	Rep.
IL 83	Linda Chapa-LaVia (D)—@lindachapalavia	Rep.
UT 024	Rebecca Chavez-Houck (D)—@rchouck	Rep.
FL 038	Anitere Flores (R)—@anitereflores	Sen.
TX 145	Carol Alvarado (D)—@RepAlvarado145	Rep.
TX 75	Mary Edna Gonzalez (D) @RepMaryGonzalez	Rep.
UT 026	Angela Romero (D)—@AngelaRomeroH26	Rep.
CA 13	Susan Talamantes Eggman (D)—@SusanEggman	Assem.
CO 05	Crisanta Duran (D)—@Crisantaduran	Sen.
IN 87	Christina Hale (D)—@HaleIndy	Rep.
NY 25	Nily Rozic (D)—@nily	Assem.
TX 06	Sylvia García (D)—@SenatorGarcía	Sen.
CA 80	Lorena Gonzalez (D) @LorenaSGonzalez	Assem.

the next most frequent Tweeter, Sylvia García (TX-6), an assemblywoman representing Houston (7,650 Tweets). However, there were a number of Latina legislators that used the medium as a regular form of communication. Even the median Latina legislator account (Marissa Marquez—TX-77) had 501 total tweets, suggesting a reasonable amount of usage. To get a better sense of the distribution of Latina legislator account use, I created a distribution of each account's Twitter activity. From figure 6.1, we can identify three clusters of users. The first is a small cluster of ten "power

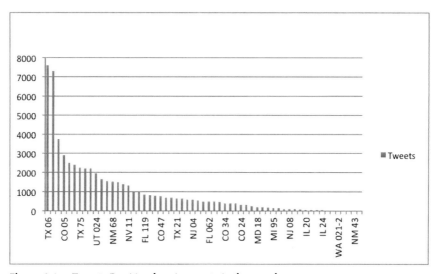

Figure 6.1.   Tweets Per Member Account. Author made.

tweeters" who have over 2,000 tweets from their account. A second cluster of members (21) have between 500 and 2,000 tweets from their account. These members still use the account, but their tweet volume is not several per day. The last cluster (30 members) have less than 500 total tweets, suggesting they either do not Tweet on a regular basis or are still new members and have not accumulated a large body of activity.

Another key characteristic of a Twitter account is the number of followers a user accrues. This network building effort is an important element of networked representation. One index that can shed some more light on the formation of Twitter networks is the follower/following ratio (figure 6.2). The number and quality of followers is one indication of network density. On average, Latina legislator accounts had 1456 followers and followed 517 people. This 3/1 ratio of followers to followed is reflective of an *asymmetrical social graph* between public figures and the general public.

However, a wide range exists among Latina legislator accounts in terms of the follower/following ratio. The follower/following index ranges from an index of roughly 34/1 for Rep. Teresa Benitez-Thompson (NV-27) who represents a district that includes Reno. She has 2411 followers but only follows 68 Twitter accounts. Twenty-seven of the 61 members had follower/following ratios of over three to one. This suggests that for a significant cluster of Latina legislators, Twitter is more a megaphone than a network building tool.

However, more than half of Latina legislators with Twitter accounts (thirty-four out of sixty-one) have a follower/following ratio of less than three to one. A common notion among Twitter observers is that a 1/1 ratio

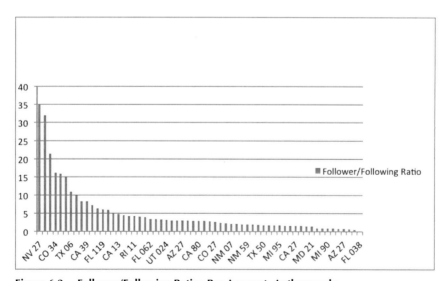

Figure 6.2.   Follower/Following Ratios Per Account. Author made.

between followers and those followed reflects a balance between contributor and listener. However, ratios of below three to one are seldom found among members of the U.S. House and Senate, whose ratios are more often closer to 70/1. This suggests a more balanced relationship between representative and public, at least among the Latina legislators studied, than typically found at the national level. Indeed, seven Latina legislators had ratios under one (e.g., they followed more people than were followed).

This ratio of below three to one is not an arbitrary distinction. One to one ratios would seem sub-optimal for public officials who do have a role to play in communicating the work of the body to their constituents. Conversely, a main function of being a representative is listening and the number of followers is a proxy for how many people the member is willing to hear. While there are a great many caveats to consider, having a reasonably close ratio of follower to following is a good yardstick for how willing the member is to use social media to both talk and listen. The act of following connotes the expectation that one is being heard on social media. At the very least, it provides whoever is running the member's Twitter account with a steady stream of content that a member/staff can choose to listen to if they desire. For instance, a large number of followers from one's district would give the member the ability to "take the pulse" of collective constituency concerns (both within and outside of the district).

DIMENSIONS OF NETWORKED REPRESENTATION: INTRA-PARTY NETWORK BUILDING

A key dimension of networked representation is the use of Twitter to communicate beyond the traditional constituent base described by Fenno (1978) in *Home Style*. In this classic work, Fenno noted that most members of Congress wanted to get re-elected, amass power in Congress, and become effective policy makers. To do this, they crafted an image of a reliable and effective "regular Joe" to their constituents that allowed them to gain constituent trust. Fenno called this a "home style" whereby they convey effectiveness to their constituents through tactics like doing constituent work, claiming credit for legislation or district appropriations, and position taking on issues of concern in the district.

However, traditional home style behaviors take on a new posture when thought of through the lens of social networking. Prior to social media, the development of home style was a "one to many" enterprise. The member would attend a community meeting and expect that the news media would cover the event so constituents could see the member doing "district work." Social media has allowed members to create their own mechanisms for distributing this information. In this way, Twitter is not unlike a newsletter. However, the low-cost mechanisms for presenting information provides members with an ability to engage in the networks of countless numbers of constituencies. I call this in previous work a *virtual home style* (Marichal 2013).

Indeed, many tweets from Latina legislator accounts reflected this "virtual home style." As an example, Rep. Rebecca Chavez-Houck's (D-UT) Twitter feed in March of 2015 resembled many of the member of Congress Facebook pages I studied in 2013. In addition to the standard recognizing constituents, there were a number of retweeted posts that advocated for their party's policy positions. As an example, Rep. Chavez-Houck retweeted this tweet from the Association for Federal, State, County, and Municipal Employees (AFSCME):

> **Rebecca Chavez-Houck** @rchouck Mar 20
> "@AFSCME: New York Times: Data on #Obamacare Shows Largest Drop in Uninsured in 4 Decades http://nyti.ms/19tuZhs #1u"

This is similar to Heclo's (1978) notion of position taking and practically every account studied had some component of it. Similarly, almost all of the member Twitter accounts also engaged in a bit of "home style" work in the form of boosterism. Members would often Tweet about visits to the capital from community organizations. As an example, Representative Linda Chapa LaVia (IL-83) tweeted a "selfie" she took with members of the fire department in her Aurora, IL, district:

> **Linda Chapa LaVia** @lindachapalavia Mar 17
> Members of the Aurora Fire Department at the Capitol here in Springfield. We have the BEST group of guys! . . . http://fb.me/7a3fAv9Pj

Another element of home style I found in the Tweets was "boosterism" or the ability to laud accomplishments in the district. This is an essential element of appearing as a "regular Jane" to members of the district. Twitter and other social media allow this to be done via a tweet. The lowered transaction costs involved with engaging in coordinated action on the Interent (Benkler 2006) allows members to increase the number of plaudits they give to individuals and organizations in their district. As an example, Rep. Monica Youngblood retweeted

> **ABQ Business First** @ABQBizFirst Mar 16
> Two ABQ breweries reach final four of national IPA challenge. http://bit .ly/1BLWugn

Further, almost to a member, Latina legislators spent some time on Twitter engaged in what Hugh Heclo (1978) called *credit claiming*, or signaling effectiveness to a member's constituents. As one of many examples, Celia Israel (TX-50) Tweeted her vote on a bill that would ban driving while texting.

Celia Israel @CeliaIsrael Mar 10
Happy to support statewide ban on texting; voted out of Trans. Committee; Thanks @PatriciaHarless @TXRepE3 @GeneforTexas for your leadership

NETWORKED REPRESENTATION: INTRA-PARTY NETWORK BUILDING

While this Tweet is typical of elected officials, it also signals the distinct ways in which Latina legislators engage on Twitter. One new element Latina legislators bring to the "virtual home style" is the tendency to laud their legislative colleagues. Just like Rep. Celia Israel made sure to thank the supporters of the bill for their leadership, many Latina legislators made sure to celebrate the accomplishments of their fellow legislators. As an example Rep. Monica Youngblood (NM-68) re-tweeted a credit-claiming tweet by her Latina legislator colleague Rep. Kelly Fajardo (NM-7):
Kelly Fajardo retweeted

Monica Youngblood @MonYoungblood Mar 19
.@KellyFajardoNM just got a do pass in SJC on HB 125, protecting our kids! #nmpol #nmleg

This practice of celebrating a colleague's accomplishment via retweet came up repeatedly in the accounts I studied. It falls outside of Fenno's (1978) focus on cultivating a home style. More importantly, it is different from what I observed in my 2013 study of how members of Congress use Facebook (Marichal 2013). In that work, there was very little lauding of other colleagues on congressional Facebook pages. Lauding other legislators is of little consequence to constituents in the development of a home style. One could argue it makes the member appear gracious to her constituents, but she could appear that way by celebrating the accomplishments of members of her district (also a common practice on Twitter). This *intra-party network building* on a public medium like Twitter suggests something distinctly different. It makes public the process of *capacity building* through the cultivation of social capital between members. Re-tweeting the accomplishments of colleagues mirrors the process of *social grooming* between members of a network (Dunbar 1992). Through this social grooming process, members gain trust with one another and are likely to work together by periodically acknowledging others in your network.

As Fraga et al. (2007) noted, Latina legislators were likely to be cross-group coalition builders. This was evident in my study of Latina legislator tweets. In many instances, support would not be simply reserved for other Latina legislators, but for a range of different actors. For example, Rep. Angela Romero's (D-UT) Twitter account was often used to celebrate the accomplishments of fellow members. As an example, this March 3rd tweet congratulated fellow Democratic colleague, Sandra Hollins (UT-23), an African-American member of the Utah House, for representing Utah's 23rd district for having her bill passed out of committee.

Angela Romero @AngelaRomeroH26 Mar 3
Congrats @SHollinsD23! #HCR004 passed cmte. w/ a favorable rec. Now on the Senate Consent Calendar. #utleg #utpol

This effort to engage in social grooming with fellow legislators falls in line with theories of political party development as an important element of a member's job. Butler and Neff Powell (2012) in particular emphasize the growing importance of cultivating a "party brand" at the national level. This idea of promoting the member's party by touting its accomplishments did regularly take place on Twitter. But in the instances highlighted, members were engaged in public support of other individual members rather than the party itself. It is this careful cultivation of within-party networks through tweeting and retweeting each other is a key element of *networked representation*.

Ethnic solidarity formation was also an essential part of intra-party network building on Twitter. On several occasions, members would use Twitter to signal solidarity with fellow Latina colleagues. For example, Assemblywoman Olivia Diaz (NV-11) re-tweeted a "selfie" of the members of the Nevada Latina delegation taken by one of her colleagues (see photo 6.1).

Olivia Diaz retweeted

Benitez-Thompson @Assemblywoman27 Mar 17
Crazy comments from legislative colleagues on race won't get us down! Our spirits, families & hearts fight on #**nvleg**

In this instance, the member was using the medium to communicate support and solidarity with legislative colleagues in ways that go beyond simple party building. These intra-party networks often extended beyond state delegations and towards Latin legislators in other states. In this conversation thread between Rep. Mary Gonzales (TX-75) and Rep. Nily Rozic (NY-25) we find two Latina legislators from different states sending wishes of support to each other during a long legislative session.

Photo 6.1. Used with permission of Assemblywoman Teresa Benitez-Thompson

Nily Rozic 李羅莎 retweeted
Mary Gonzalez @RepMaryGonzalez Mar 31
Amiga! Sending you love from TX! "**@nily**: **@RepMaryGonzalez** we're on hour 17 in New York, sending you good vibes!"

This networked approach stands in stark contrast to my study of the U.S. Congress where members rarely cited one another and stuck to traditional forms of home style that emphasized the member's relationship with constituents. It highlights the importance Latina legislators place on building networks horizontally across legislative colleagues, both within and across ethnic boundaries.

NETWORKED REPRESENTATION: PERSONALIZATION

A key element of networked representation is the "letting in" of network members (e.g., Twitter followers) into the day-to-day work of the body. Members used the medium to give constituents a "first-person" view of the legislative body by "live tweeting" or documenting daily events. As an example, Rep. Nily Rozic (NY-25) Tweeted a photo of the end of a New York's legislative session with the tagline:

@CarlHeastie wraps up the #nybudget—his first as Speaker! #thepeopleswork

Even in this instance, the "live-tweet" was congratulating the Speaker on concluding his first legislative session. This tweet has the dual purpose of letting constituents into the work of the body while also engaging in *social grooming* by acknowledging a colleague's accomplishment.

One dimension of this "letting in" process was "live tweeting" floor votes. Rep. Rosanna Gabaldon (AZ-2) repeatedly retweeted floor vote announcements to a voter ID proposal in the Arizona state house. In this instance, she "live tweeted" the vote of Rep. Bruce Wheeler, the house whip for the Arizona Democrats.

Rosanna Gabaldon retweeted

> **AZ House Democrats** @AZHouseDems Apr 3
> .@BruceWheelerAZ votes no on #SB1339 calling R attempts to make it more difficult to vote "obnoxious."

This "live tweeting" is a familiar trope to anyone who uses social media. However, it is a new element of constituent/representative relationships in that it gives constituents the ability to get a real-time (albeit curated) look at what members are doing while they are doing it. This is a fundamental feature of a public institution, but it is one that members of Congress seldom did when I looked at the Facebook pages of twenty-five members of Congress in 2013 (Marichal 2013).

Twitter allows its members to regularly engage in what Arendt (1958) referred to as "small things . . . between chest and bed, table and chair, dog and cat, and flowerpot" (Arendt 1958, 57). Members would share posts about family vacations, recognize staff birthdays, or post pictures of their meals. For instance, Rep. Kelly Fajardo (NM-7) tweeted the result of a charity basketball game between the two branches of the New Mexico legislature.

> Kelly Fajardo @KellyFajardoNM Mar 4
> House vs Senate basketball game this evening. The senate won, but most importantly over 25k was raised for cancer . . . http://ift.tt/1zMt8JD

While Arendt regards these as problematic, discussions of "small things" between member and network helps build relationships among constituents, particularly when it pertains to the inner working of the legislature.

Twitter also allowed for constituents to share ideas with members. The flattened nature of Twitter networks allows citizens and groups to access members of their networks that can have an impact on issues of concern. Guo and Saxton (2014) calls the practice of tweeting influential people in the hopes of gaining their attention *celebrity poking*. While state legislators are not celebrities, they are influentials that have the ability to effect change. In a large number of cases, members retweeted posts from citizens that lent support to an issue of the member's concern, thereby bringing them into the debate over policy issues.

As an example, Monica Youngblood (NM-68) re-tweeted a claim from one of her followers regarding the disproportionate lobbying between the taxi industry and Lyft.

Monica Youngblood retweeted

Joel @Joel505H Mar 16
For every $1 @**Uber** | @**lyft** have spent on legislative lobbying, the taxi industry has paid $3,500. #**nmleg** #**nmpol**

At the time, Youngblood was the author of a bill opposed by taxi companies that would regulate Lyft and Uber. The ability to retweet information that is favorable to a member is novel in how it places the member within the broader network of constituents. While Monica Youngblood has less than 900 followers, each of them has their own network and as such content she tweets can be disseminated to like-minded constituencies. A particularly powerful data-point, hashtag, story, or image does have the potential to "go viral" and affect the public conversation, particularly at the local level.

While this doesn't constitute "listening" in an ideal deliberative sense, it does suggest an expansion of voices into the process in ways consistent with networked representation. Latina legislators can serve as effective brokers in ensuring that marginal voices can become part of the public debate. Twitter provides citizens with the ability to "talk to" members and help in their effort to affect policy change; however, members have to be willing to put themselves in a position to hear them. To the extent they do, it constitutes a novel form of network representation between member and constituent.

CONCLUSION

In this work, I argue that social media changes the nature of the relationship between constituent and member. Latina legislators are on the forefront of this transformation. By engaging with different publics on Twitter, many Latina legislators use Twitter to build coalitions with different groups. Networked representation consists of three dimensions: virtual home style, intra-party network building, and personalization. In this chapter, I examine the Twitter accounts for the sixty-one Latina legislators that use the application. Through a descriptive and qualitative look at their accounts, I develop a theory of *networked representation*. Networked representation consists of three dimensions: intra-party network building, dialogic communication, and segmented home style.

This chapter begins an inquiry into how Latina legislators use Twitter. Much more work needs to be done to understand the nature of legislator networks. A "big data" project that includes network analysis of Latina legislators' Twitter accounts would give us more fine-grained detail as to the different ways in which members go about building these "virtual constituencies." By examining networks of followers/following, retweet and "favorit-ing" patterns, and studies of hashtag adoption, we can gain a better sense of how this group of legislators uses emerging technology to reimagine the representational role.

Latina legislators as a whole were not as active in building strong advocacy networks as one might suspect from the literature. Members were not as strategic in their efforts to reach out to advocacy groups. Advocacy groups are critical actors within networks by providing policy information, access to a like-minded community, and the possibility of mobilizing a group to action (Lovejoy and Saxton 2012).

This is something of a missed opportunity since advocacy groups are playing an increased role in how users translate personal identity into collective action (Fenton and Barassi 2011). The coalition building process seemed to focus more on other members or building links to the national party. Twitter provides an opportunity to link to advocacy groups and causes through hashtags in a process Erica Cizsek (2013) calls *advocacy amplification*. However members weren't particularly skilled at Tweeting in ways that linked up to prevalent memes and hashtags. There were some exceptions, State Senator Anitere Flores (FL-37) retweeted a meme that remixed classic Cuba tourism posters to include depictions of human rights violations associated with the hashtag #Dictatorshiptourism. More research is needed to examine the links between effective uses of Twitter by elected officials and policy effectiveness. This chapter serves as a first step in that process.

SEVEN

Advantages and Disadvantages for Latina Officeholders

The Case of New Mexico

Julia Marin Hellwege and Christine Marie Sierra

In 2010 New Mexico elected the country's first Latina governor, Susana Martinez. This was an important moment for several reasons. Martinez's election marked a significant advancement for women in reaching executive leadership positions—to date only thirty-seven women have held a gubernatorial position in any U.S. state (CAWP 2015). In addition, it marked only the third time in history that two women competed for governor as Martinez ran against Democratic nominee and former NM Lieutenant Governor Diane Denish. Martinez's election, as a Latina Republican, also posed an interesting question for Latino partisanship in a time when immigration was (and still is) a highly divisive issue. Finally, her election presents an interesting contrast and point of comparison to Michelle Lujan Grisham, the first female Democrat and the first Latina to win this congressional office (CD1) since its creation in 1969. Lujan Grisham won her seat, which covers the largest urban area in the state, in the 2012 election.

The literature on minority women elected officials, in general, has suggested that minority women face double disadvantages as minorities and as women, but also that minority women, and Latinas in particular, have the potential for strategic behavior in building winning coalitions among both Latinos and women (Scola 2013; Bejarano 2013; Fraga et al. 2008; Githens and Prestage 1977; Fraga and Navarro 2007). The elections and time in office of these two Latinas provide an opportunity to assess, through qualitative analysis, whether, and more importantly, how and when, Latinas are advantaged or disadvantaged as candidates and officeholders in electoral politics. We suggest that there are several contextual variables which must be taken into account to understand not only *if* there are advantages and disadvantages for Latina politicians but also under what conditions they will emerge. In particular we seek to understand

how the established theories of double disadvantage and strategic intersectionality can explain Latina women's behavior by considering the context in which each applies. In order to hone in on the causal mechanisms of
the complex relationship between identity, partisanship, and institutions,
we propose case studies of two New Mexico Latina elected officials, Governor Susana Martinez and U.S. Congresswoman Michelle Lujan Grisham.
Not only have these two Latinas reached significant leadership positions
individually, but jointly they pose interesting contrasts in terms of their
electoral strategies and governing behaviors.

ADVANTAGES AND DISADVANTAGES OF INTERSECTIONALITY

Research on Latina politics has its roots in the literature on intersectionality. Though early scholarship on Chicana and Latina women did not employ the academic term "intersectionality," scholars called for the simul-
taneous study of how race and gender influenced Latinas' political status
in American politics (Sierra and Sosa-Riddell 1994). Understanding how
the dual identities of race and gender work as a joint concept, rather than
individually, has been one of the greater challenges of understanding political behavior (Sierra 2009). Work on the political behavior of minority
women suggests caution in applying behavioral theories of white women
to minority women (Crenshaw 1989; Hancock 2007). Crenshaw states that
minority women are "situated within at least two subordinated groups
that frequently pursue conflicting political agendas" (Crenshaw 1989).
The theory of intersectionality suggests that identities are intimately
linked; in particular, empirical evidence has shown that there are significant differences in regards to both gender and race/ethnicity; thus, it is
important to take both into consideration when analyzing the behavior
of public officials (Smooth 2009, 2006; Sierra 2009; Manuel 2006; García
Bedolla 2007; Hancock 2007). This literature was mostly making theoretical predictions about the nature of the minority woman, but also making
early observations of the few minority women who had made it to higher
levels of elected office (Githens and Prestage 1977). Scholars of Latina
politics have found that many of the fundamental theoretical implications
of intersectionality, which applied to black women's politics, have also
applied to Latinas. In particular, the argument that minority women faced
structural discrimination due to their race and gender—a double disadvantage—emerged in studies of Latina women as well (Melville 1980).

   However, when considering Latina politics, much more so than black
women's politics, scholars must be mindful of the impact of party identification in mediating some political relationships, particularly as it relates
to electoral strategies and policy preferences (Uhlaner and García 2005).

While the Latino-Latina partisan gender gap is certainly not as wide as for their white counterparts, there is more variation in partisan identification among Latinos than there is among blacks (Uhlaner and García 2005). As with whites, though, this gender gap does minimize when it comes to elected officials in comparison to the electorate; that is, there are significantly more Democratic Latina women in electoral politics than there are Republicans. All Latinas, and women and minorities in general, regardless of party, are of course still vastly underrepresented in American politics. In all, the early literature on intersectionality broadly suggests that minority women in comparison to white males are disadvantaged in terms of electoral politics.

Contemporary research, particularly of Latina elected officials, has found seemingly contradictory evidence that minority women may have particular advantages over men and white women. The theoretical suggestion of this "strategic intersectionality" has been corroborated with empirical evidence that minority women are elected at higher rates than white women (Scola 2014; Bejarano 2013; Smooth 2009). This concept, coined by Fraga et al., suggests that Latinas' dual identities may appeal to both Latinos and to women as separate constituencies (Fraga et al. 2008; see also Bejarano 2013). Latina state legislators, they argue, are able to build coalitions and generate a more fluid policy agenda, making them appeal to a broader audience (Fraga et al. 2008). Importantly, the theory of strategic intersectionality does not suggest that Latinas have an advantage over white men, in the way that the double disadvantage theory suggests that minority women are exponentially more disadvantaged in comparison to white men. Instead the strategic intersectionality theory compares minority women's advantages over white women and minority men in reaching higher office. That said, double disadvantage theory still suggests an additive effect of being a woman *and* a minority, thus implying that white women and minority men should be less disadvantaged than minority women, but not have the status quo advantage of being a white man.

In her comparison of election rates of white and non-white women state legislators, Scola proposes that there are geographical as well as institutional factors at play which affect minority women's higher chances of winning public office, though she admits that the results are better at indicating reasons why white women do *not* get elected rather than why minority women do (Scola 2014; see also Bejarano 2013). Bejarano also argues that voters "soften" the impact of race of minority women, in comparison to minority men. In other words, when it comes to minority women candidates, race is less salient than it is for minority male candidates (Bejarano 2013). Essentially, barring party conditions, when it comes to supporting underrepresented candidates (anyone who is not a white man), white women are more likely to support minority women over minority men, because of a descriptive representation connection to women broadly. Additionally, for the same reasons, minority men are more likely to support a minority woman over a white woman, thus yielding a broad winning coalition. Theories of descriptive representation suggest that representatives of the same gender, race, or ethnicity (or other identity) may be preferred by constituents who share these identities (Pitkin 1967; Mansbridge 1999). That is to say that a Latino voter may prefer a Latino candidate because the voter is using ethnic identity as a utility heuristic to make assumptions about that candidate's preferences and priorities (Dawson 1994).

While both women and minorities are underrepresented as elected officials in comparison to white men, strategic intersectionality suggests that minority women have an advantage over white women and minority men in the electoral context as they are better suited to build winning coalitions through multiple descriptive constituencies, are less likely to be "racialized" than their male counterparts, and are better able to present a fluid policy agenda which appeals to a broader audience.

Does this mean that the days of double disadvantage are over? Does this mean that minority women are only marginalized in comparison to white men, but have broad advantages over white women and minority men when it comes to all aspects of political life? Surely not. The literature on the barriers for women and for minority elected officials still suggests that there are additive disadvantages for minority women in the institutional context. In other words, while strategic intersectionality presents a comparative advantage to winning electoral races vis-à-vis white women and minority men, the long-lasting institutional setting created by white men, for white men, still persists.

The literature shows that minority women are disadvantaged as elected officials because they are marginalized by the institutional context, which was created largely by white men. American political institutions have been designed to favor hierarchical, individual, and competitive actors. These institutions generally presume that the actors will not only be able to, but will prefer, to act in their own self-interest and with preferences that are only related to the job at hand, rather than additional external circumstances (such as family obligations). Georgia Duerst-Lahti argues that our institutions are gendered and designed to favor male behaviors because they were created by men (Duerst-Lahti 2002, 2009). She states that male-dominated institutions are not designed for women's cooperative style; acting as a single unitary political actor tends to be a masculine trait, and thus men would be more likely to perform well in such an office and consequently be preferred to fill such a position. Duerst-Lahti argues that although the legislative branch and executive branches are designed differently, each involves the same mechanism of gender-based institutions (Duerst-Lahti 2002, 2010). Her argument about single unitary actors applies well to both Congress and the presidency (and by extension the governor's office) even if it is perhaps more readily visible in the executive branch. Though they are also part of a collective whole, legislators act as individual actors insofar as they are the sole representatives for their districts. On the other hand, the head of an executive branch of government is in a position to act unilaterally with less horizontal collaboration.

Regardless of branch of office, the literature suggests that women's leadership style is more horizontal, more cooperative, and that women are more likely to take family obligations into account when considering a run for public office (Thomas 1994; Carroll and Sanbonmatsu 2013). Thus, the traditional expectation was that if women wanted to become politicians, they would have to behave as men. This line of thinking implies that the reason there are not more women in politics is because of an individual decision on the part of women not to participate in politics, which does not align with most women's preferences and experiences. Instead, we argue that these are symptoms of the institutional context, which creates barriers for women because the institutions were not designed with women's obligations, experiences, and preferences in mind (Duerst-Lahti 2002, 2010; Thomas 1994). These gender differences hold across racial and ethnic groups, and in terms of the Latino community, Fraga et al. (2008) make the case for Latinas acting as collaborators in comparison to Latino men, who may act as "lone wolves who usually do not consult with anyone" (134). Latinas, then, may be institutionally disadvantaged in comparison to Latino men, whose leadership styles are better aligned with the institutional design for single unitary actors.

Just as our institutions are gendered, they are also "racialized" (Preuhs 2006). Democratic institutions are generally designed to favor the majority; as such, it is logical that the minority populations are at a disadvantage in politics. Arguably, this is rightly so, to ensure that no group has undue impact on the policy process. Instead, it can normatively be stated that our representative democracy should be influenced by minority groups in proportion to their demographic presence. However, this is complicated by our institutions which are designed to favor a moderate majority. One such institutional feature which affects both descriptive and substantive representation for minorities is majority-minority districts. Collectively, generating favorable minority policies is difficult through descriptive representation. Majority-minority districts may increase the number of descriptive representatives by design because the majority of voters in the district are likely to favor a minority candidate. Pooling minority voters in a single district increases the likelihood of a descriptive representative in one district. But it also means that surrounding districts are less likely to have any minority representation. In addition, because those districts are likely to have very low descriptive representation, they're likely to favor candidates who are not only ambivalent to minority policies, but likely opposed to them (Cameron, Epstein and O'Halloran 1996). This means that Latinos trying to make policy changes in favor of Latino preferences are likely to, by design, be relegated to a minority opinion.

Taken together, institutional domains are both gendered and racialized producing disadvantages for both women and for minority representatives. Given that these institutional effects are not necessarily overlapping (majority-minority districts do not apply to gender, and women's leadership styles are consistent across racial/ethnic lines), this creates an additive effect, a double disadvantage, for minority women. In addition, when we consider the case of Latina women, there is an overlapping effect of the role of family for an elected official (García et al. 2008). The literature, but perhaps even more so first-hand accounts from politicians, have suggested that public life is relatively incompatible with family life. Many women who run for elected office either do not have children, or run for office once the children are grown (Carroll and Sanbonmatsu 2013). This is because in their governing role, elected officials are expected to work long hours, both in the office, but often attending social engagements. Not only are the work hours long, but also late, likely past the bedtime of most small children. The life of a public official also frequently involves traveling away from family, and simply put, being relatively unavailable. This struggle is well documented and analyzed in the case of women (Carroll and Sanbonmatsu 2013; Thomas 1994); however, given the central role of family in Hispanic culture (Baca Zinn 1975), arguably this challenge also affects Latino legislators broadly.

CONTEXT MATTERS: THEORETICAL APPLICATION

The arguments behind the double disadvantage theory, that minority women are situated within two subordinate groups, are precisely what allows minority women to form multiple electoral coalitions ultimately leading to electoral success. By putting these theories into context through the use of a case study, we will be able to hone in on the factors which contribute to the advantages and disadvantages of intersectionality. We examine two contexts in which Latina officeholders must act: the electoral context (as candidates for office) and the institutional context (as governing officeholders).[1] We pay special attention to the partisanship of Latina descriptive representatives and how Latina elected officials seek to mobilize and respond to a more divided partisan Latino electorate.

We argue that strategic intersectionality and double disadvantage are not at odds, but are reflections of two different contexts: the electoral context as candidates and the institutional context in governing. In addition, we recognize that extending implications of intersectionality from black women to Latinas necessitates a discussion of partisan politics. We argue that strategic intersectionality explains Latina behavior well, but also that it is conditioned upon political party. Third, we argue that Latinas do experience double disadvantages in the institutional context, because governing institutions were created by white men who largely designed public office around their behaviors and preferences.

In attempting to synthesize the literature on the effects of intersectionality on electoral behavior, the question of the co-existence of the double disadvantage and strategic intersectionality theories becomes immediately apparent. How can it be true that Latinas—or minority women generally—can suffer from both advantages and disadvantages due to the same intersection of identities in the same context (as politicians)? As indicated in the review of the literature on the behavioral implications of intersectionality, this answer may lie in how these theories have been applied to varying elite behaviors of minority women as politicians. Elected officials engage in two different types of electoral behaviors, they wear two "hats" to use a common analogy: as candidates and as elected officials for public office. This allows us to consider whether these theories are applicable to each of these contexts.

As the scholarly study of electoral politics broadens and expands, and as our legislatures and executive offices become more diverse (albeit slowly), more nuances of the identities of those office holders begin to take shape. This book, examining Latinas in American politics, is a testament to our scholarly accomplishments in combating essentialism in electoral analysis. However, many studies of women in politics and minority women in politics still suffer from a lack of examination of partisan differences. This partisan lens is important for two reasons: it may color the approach or direction a politician may take even if priorities are similar (Osborn 2012) and second, it may affect our idea of critical mass if members of the same identity group are not in agreement because of partisan divisions (Kanthak and Krause 2012). Given attempted monopolization of Latino and women's issues (with a special focus on immigration and reproductive rights) by the Democratic Party, Democratic Latina candidates, such as Michelle Lujan Grisham, are more likely to be advantaged in the electoral context than Republican ones. Republican Latinas, like Susana Martinez, will find it necessary to make strong appeals to women and Latinos in efforts to convince them that they share fundamental values.

Although women and minorities are making strides in crystallizing interests and symbolically standing as role models for younger generations to run for office, both groups are disadvantaged in comparison to white men in being effective leaders in our institutions. American institutions were created by white men who designed the political process in their image, based on their needs, preferences, and leadership style. The institutional domain, however, is not necessarily designed for women and minority needs, preferences, and leadership styles. The effects of this misalignment with institutional design are additive—this means that minority women face double barriers to their effectiveness in office. Latina officeholders are disadvantaged both because of their gender and also because of their ethnicity. In addition, as Latina women, they are especially prone to find public life challenging because of the premium they are likely to place on family involvement.

NEW MEXICO, SUSANA MARTINEZ, AND MICHELLE LUJAN GRISHAM

New Mexico is a geographically large state (ranked fifth) but a sparsely populated state with just over 2 million inhabitants. There are two important reasons for including New Mexico as a case study in a book on Latinas in American politics: New Mexico has the largest percentage of Latinos of any U.S. state, and New Mexico's shared Spanish, Mexican and American history has created a relatively unique *Nuevomexicano* culture which stands apart from Latino cultures in other areas. The New Mexican case is arguably one of exceptionalism, because of its history, which includes landowning Hispanic elites with considerable political power (Sierra and García 2010). Hispanics as a group have not seen the same degree of marginalization and exclusion from political power as seen in other states. That is, of course, not to argue that Hispanics in the state do not face discrimination or inequality, but rather that the Hispanic experience in New Mexico is considerably more varied than in other parts of the country (Sierra and García 2010). New Mexican Hispanics, then, are not as homogenous in their political behavior as Hispanics in other states—this is important because as Latinos establish themselves in the United States over generations and as the population grows vis-à-vis whites in particular, the national Latino story may become more similar to the New Mexican experience over time. In many ways, New Mexico can be seen as a model state for Latinos in U.S. politics as a case for what the future may hold as the percentage of Latinos, vis-à-vis other groups, increases. New Mexico is a state where Hispanics are neither a token minority population nor recent immigrants, which, according to the Center for American Progress, may be what the United States will look like by 2050 (Cardenas et al. 2011).

Susana Martinez was elected governor of New Mexico in 2010. In a race that would determine the state's first woman governor, Martinez succeeded and became not only the state's first elected woman governor, but the nation's first Hispanic female governor. Martinez was born in the United States in the Rio Grande Valley to Hispanic parents who trace their lineage to Mexico (Office of the [NM] Governor). In a highly touted speech to the 2012 Republican Convention, Martinez recounted her story while evoking her heritage. She started off the speech by stating: "growing up I never imagined a little girl from a border town could one day become a governor, but this is America; *¡en America, todo es posible!*" (Republican National Committee 2012).

Photo 7.1.   Susana Martinez, first elected Latina governor. Public domain.

Unlike Susana Martinez, Michelle Lujan Grisham represents a long-standing prominent New Mexico Hispanic family. Lujan Grisham is a twelfth-generation New Mexican born in affluent Los Alamos, NM, and raised in Santa Fe (Office of Congresswoman Lujan Grisham). Several of the Lujan family members have served in New Mexico public office, including her grandfather, Eugene Lujan, who was "the first Hispanic Chief Justice of the New Mexico Supreme Court" (Office of Congresswoman Lujan Grisham); her uncle, Manuel Lujan, Jr., served in the U.S. House of Representatives and as Secretary of the Interior under George H. W. Bush; and her cousin, Ben Ray Lujan, serves alongside her in Congress representing New Mexico's 2nd district in the northern half of the state (Ralph

Nader Congress Project). Michelle Lujan Grisham represents the New Mexico exceptionalism in terms of Hispanic political inclusion in comparison to Hispanics and Latinos in other parts of the country. The contrast between Lujan Grisham and Martinez also exemplifies the heterogeneity of Hispanics in New Mexico ranging from those who trace their family lineage to landowning Spanish elites and other long-established Hispanic communities to those who have come in later immigrant generations.

ELECTORAL CONTEXT: RUNNING FOR OFFICE

We have argued that theories of Latina elite behavior, including strategic intersectionality and double disadvantage, are not at odds but are reflections of two different contexts: the electoral context as candidates and the institutional context in governing. The electoral context is typified by two distinct settings: the demographics of the state, particularly as it applies to Hispanic vote share, and the level of office establishes the size of the district. In addition we also argue that a Latina candidate's success in running for office, that is her opportunity for strategic intersectionality, will be conditioned upon partisan politics. We suggest that party identification is a primary motivator for a voter's choice of elected officials, and that advantages can only be reaped in comparison to other candidates of the same party. We show that because the Democratic Party has been successful in monopolizing Latino and women's issues, Republican Susana Martinez has and will find it more challenging to rally Latino and women voters in comparison to Democrat Michelle Lujan Grisham.

DEMOGRAPHIC CONTEXT

Perhaps the primary factor in situating the question about generalizability is the demographic context. Nationwide, the Latino population is about 17 percent; however, the density of this population varies greatly by region (Ennis et al. 2011). The Latino population by state ranges from less than two percent in states like West Virginia, Maine, and Vermont to 47 percent in New Mexico (Ennis et al. 2011). The variability in the density of the Latino population means that we should expect varying percentages of Latina elected officials by states, where states with higher percentages of Latinos (such as New Mexico, Texas, and California) should produce more Latina elected officials, but also that Latina elected officials exist in varying demographic contexts. In some states, such as New Mexico, being a Latina elected official is fairly commonplace; it does not generally serve as a distinguishing characteristic that voters can use as a heuristic to voting as many theories of descriptive representation suggest it should (Sanchez and Masuoka 2010).

The theory of descriptive representation for underrepresented groups does not necessarily take into account the scenario where nearly half of the state's legislature is Hispanic, such as in the case of New Mexico (NHCSL 2015). When multiple candidates and elected officials are all of "minority" status, this may change the context of descriptive representation broadly speaking. Descriptive representation, then, is not only a story of identity politics, but a story of tokenism and minority politics. Descriptive representation becomes the most salient and necessary in a context where minority representation is sparse, or at least historically low. Descriptive representation is said to have many benefits, such as increasing legitimacy of the institution as a whole, introducing uncrystallized issues, and giving a voice to historically underrepresented groups (Mansbridge 1999). However, these presume that the group in question is a "minority." Certainly, sheer numbers do not necessarily speak to the degree of political agency a group has; for example, women make up at least half of the population, but do not hold the same political capital as men. That said, Hispanics in New Mexico have held a closer proportion of elected positions to their proportions in the population than in any other state. Thus, Latinas in New Mexico may be more disadvantaged (or advantaged) by their gender than by their ethnicity.

The concept of descriptive representation also plays on the issue of essentialism, that is to say the "attribution of certain characteristics to everyone subsumed within a particular category" (Phillips 2010). In other words, descriptive representation assumes that a Latino candidate can effectively speak for all Latinos. In a context where the minority group is small, one or a few token descriptive representatives may speak on behalf of all, or at least most, members of that community. This is because that minority group may share broad preferences which have not yet been taken into consideration (uncrystallized interests), or may legitimize the institution by including this historically underrepresented group. However, as the group grows larger, more nuances in their preferences may start to take hold (Dawson 1994; Ignatiev 1995). Tokenism then breeds essentialism, both of which are assumptions for the utility of descriptive representation.

In terms of Latino representation, the fundamental aspects of descriptive representation do not always hold water in New Mexico as Latinos make up nearly half of the population. That said, in terms of our analysis here, we must of course consider the other half of the equation which is that women, broadly speaking, and Latinas specifically, are still underrepresented in our state, currently ranking nineteenth among U.S. state legislatures, with women holding about 26 percent of the seats (CAWP 2015).

New Mexico has a long history of Latinas running for public office, including statewide executive office. Nearly all NM secretaries of state since 1923 have been women, most of them Hispanic. The first woman secretary of state in New Mexico was Hispanic; Soledad "Lala" Chacón served from 1923–1926, even acting as governor for two weeks in 1924 (Baker 2010). It is clear that the New Mexican case, particularly in terms of its demographic history, has produced a favorable environment for Latinas in which to succeed. In New Mexico, Hispanics comprise about 33 to 38 percent of the electorate, significantly more than in any other state (Sanchez, Medeiros, and Ybarra 2010). Sanchez, Medeiros, and Ybarra, writing for Latino Decisions in anticipation of the 2010 elections, discussed important estimated gains in Democratic votes for Martinez: "Martinez is polling relatively well with Hispanic voters who have voted for Democratic candidates in larger numbers in recent years . . . between 30 and 44 percent of the Hispanic vote. This is a greater share of the Latino vote than any other Republican candidates in recent memory in New Mexico." The authors correctly estimated that sufficient crossover by Democratic Hispanics voting for Martinez as a co-ethnic would produce the "plus factor" securing her win (Sanchez, Ybarra, and Medeiros 2010; Manzano and Sanchez 2010).

LEVEL OF OFFICE

There are many institutional dynamics at play which may affect the election of women into different levels of office. In our case study, we are looking at two very high profile offices—governor and U.S. Congress. As such, we should expect Latinas, and women generally, to be especially disadvantaged at these higher glass ceilings. Historically women have done better at lower levels of office (Center for American Women and Politics), and currently women fare much better in state legislatures (24 percent) than in the U.S. Congress (18.5 percent). Similarly in the executive branch there have been thirty-seven women governors though no woman has ever been president, nor even been either of the major party's nominees for president. This could of course be a simple matter of sheer size (7383 state legislators compared to 535 members of Congress); however, research shows that the ambition ladder, especially for women, starts at lower levels of office (Hardy-Fanta 1993, 1997; Carroll and Sanbonmatsu 2013; García et al. 2008; Hardy-Fanta et al, Summer 2016). In particular, we know that minority women, who have a history as community leaders, tend to hold lower levels of office because of a feeling that they are making a difference in their community (García et al. 2008; Hardy-Fanta 1993, 1997). Thus, finding out whether Latinas are disadvantaged when it comes to running for higher office, or if fewer Latinas have ambition for high-profile offices, is a difficult question to answer, especially on a larger scale. The recent theories of strategic intersectionality have been studied in particular at the state legislative level; this is likely because these studies have mostly relied on quantitative analysis, for which this level of office has proven most useful because of the larger population available for study. There simply have not been sufficient numbers of Latinas in Congress or in statewide offices to apply similar quantitative techniques; we hope this qualitative case study will shed some light on these higher offices.

THE PARTY EFFECT

During the 2012 Republican Convention, Martinez recounted a now-famous story about her party identity. She states that until the mid-1990s, she and her husband were Democrats, and so had her parents been before her, confirming what we know about political socialization in the family and party identity (Republican National Committee). Also, confirming what we know about most Mexican American families and party identification with the Democratic Party, save for long-standing Spanish families in northern New Mexico (Uhlaner and García 2005). In her story, she describes how she and her husband, Chuck, were invited by some Republican friends to lunch. She says "we talked about issues, they never used the words Republican or Democrat, conservative or liberal . . . and when we left that lunch we got in the car, and I looked over at Chuck and I said, 'I'll be damned, we're Republicans'" (Republican National Committee 2012). This is interesting rhetoric that may resonate with new generations of Latinos who may not have the same ties to the Democratic Party.

In 2011 the immigration status of her grandparents came into question by the local newspaper, the *Santa Fe New Mexican*, which reported that "the 1930 U.S. Census Bureau record lists Martinez' paternal grandparents' citizenship status as . . . neither naturalized nor having first papers [implying illegal entry]" (Clausing 2011). According to Martinez's spokesperson, Scott Darnell, Martinez had "no reason to question that 1930 Census record" (Clausing 2011). Because of Martinez's stance on repealing a New Mexico law granting driver's licenses to undocumented immigrants, protesters challenged Martinez, questioning her connection and commitment to the Latino community. Later in 2011, however, Martinez retracted her previous statements about her family history and revealed additional immigration documents, following a costly investigation, which showed that her grandparents did indeed follow the immigration laws of the time, though they were not naturalized citizens as of the 1930 Census (Massey and Contreras 2011). Arguably, Martinez strategically responded with attempts to increase her favorability to the Latino community but also maintain her position as a conservative with a firm stance on the driver's license issue. In her response to her stance on the issue, she stated, "It's not like I started talking about driver's licenses and then all of a sudden realized, 'Oh my gosh, I came from Mexico and that's a conflict.' I've known where my heritage is from all along" (quoted in Massey and Contreras 2011).

The tension on the issue of driver's license stems from the intersection of ethnic identity and partisan politics. The New Mexico law which allows for undocumented immigrants to receive driver's licenses was created under Democratic leadership and hailed by former governor Bill Richardson (Sanchez 2012, 2014). The expansion of rights to immigrants has unquestionably become monopolized by the Democratic Party. The bifurcation of issues due to the two-party system has produced a party environment where each of the political parties monopolizes one side or another of a political issue generally speaking (Belanger and Meguid 2008; Hayes 2005). On the issue of immigration, Democrats have generally come on the side of favoring expansion of rights to immigrants while Republicans have sided in the opposite direction, favoring restrictionist policies (Sanchez 2014). This leaves Republican Latinos in a sort of limbo and open to be scrutinized and ostracized by either the Latino community or their party, or both in regards to the issue.

During the 2014 campaign season, Democratic gubernatorial candidate Gary King attempted to capitalize on this assumed detachment by saying that the governor "does not have a Latino heart" (Monteleone 2014). In his response to criticism drawn from the remarks, King stated, "I think it points out in an important way that Governor Martinez does not share the same value system as most New Mexico Hispanic families do, such as increasing the minimum wage and supporting our professional educators in the teaching of our children" (quoted in Monteleone 2014). It is evident from this response that, at the very least, Martinez' major opponent was first essentializing New Mexico Hispanics as holding Democratic values, and, secondly, strategically attempting to capitalize on the assumed disconnect between Hispanic values and Republican party stances. This may have been quite shortsighted though, as nearly 40 percent of Hispanics voted for Martinez in 2010, and in 2014 she secured her re-election with an overall 57 percent of the vote (Monteleone 2014; NM Secretary of State).[2]

In her discussion on gender and party stances, Tracy Osborn discusses the very similar case of Republican women and the issue of so-called "women's issues." Similar to immigration issues, the Democratic Party has become the self-proclaimed party of women's issues, including reproductive rights and wage equality. She argues that party identification is not necessarily about priority of an issue as it is about approach to dealing with an issue. She states that Republican and Democratic women state legislators both prioritize issues of special concern to women such as health, education, and wage equality, but that Republican women tackle these with different solutions than their Democratic counterparts (Osborn 2012).

This tension again became evident during the 2012 presidential campaign, though this time it was Martinez who was criticizing Republican candidate Mitt Romney for an insensitive "self-deportation" plan. When asked in an interview about her stance on the Romney plan, Martinez stated, "'Self-deport?' What the heck does that mean?" She followed up with a reflection on how she saw the Hispanic community's incorporation in the 2012 election stating, "I have no doubt Hispanics have been alienated during this campaign" (Sonmez 2012). This case illustrates the complex relationship between party, ethnicity, and even gender. Women are more likely than men to consider the complexity and multiple facets of an issue, and consider the connection between government policy and citizens (CAWP 1991; Thomas 1994). In the same interview, Martinez goes on to say, "Republicans want to be tough and say, 'Illegals, you're gone.' But the answer is a lot more complex than that" (Sonmez 2012). Even when comparing her proposal for comprehensive immigration reform in comparison to Latino Republican Marco Rubio, who in 2012 advocated for a scaled-back DREAM Act, Martinez suggested that focusing solely on the DREAM Act is insufficient for comprehensive change (Sonmez 2012). Even if Rubio's plan was more sympathetic to the Latino community than Mitt Romney's, Martinez still saw the issue as more complex than either of these male candidates suggested. On the case of immigration, in particular, Susana Martinez is cross pressured because of the intersectional nature of her identity interacting with the intersection of policy issues and corresponding party stances.

INSTITUTIONAL CONTEXT: GOVERNING

It is evident that Latinas have performed very well in gaining not only more elected positions, but reaching higher than ever. We have shown in our case study of Susana Martinez and Michelle Lujan Grisham that Latinas have comparative advantages over white women and over minority men when it comes to building winning coalitions. We have also shown that these advantages are especially marked when the candidate is a Democrat because of the Democratic Party's strategic monopolization of women's and Latino issues. However, while Latinas, and minority women in general, have electoral advantages over other underrepresented groups, they are still comparatively disadvantaged in the institutional context. Because of their dual identities as both women and minorities, in a gendered and racialized context, we argue that Latinas are still double disadvantaged when governing. In particular we argue that political institutions tend to favor men's leadership styles which emphasize a single unitary actor over a more cooperative style; that as minorities they are relegated to a minority policy position, making effective change difficult; and that as Latinas who emphasize family obligation, they are less likely to have the kind of flexibility in office that many white men enjoy.

Descriptive representation is important for multiple reasons: it may introduce new priorities and preferences; it is likely to create a sense of legitimacy of the institution; and it may serve an important symbolic function for other (particularly younger) members of underrepresented groups. As Marie Wilson of the White House Project states in the film Miss Representation: "You can't be what you can't see." When young Latina girls see Latina trailblazers pursuing more and higher offices, these young girls can see themselves in those positions in the future and are less likely to self-select out of such possibilities (Siebel Newsom 2011). In 2012, Susana Martinez gave one of the most compelling speeches at the Republican nominating convention, recalling her childhood in El Paso, Texas, and her immigrant parents' up-from-their-bootstraps story. As the nation's first female and Hispanic governor, Martinez described girls coming up to her in the grocery store and the mall. "They look and they point and when they get the courage to come up, they ask, 'Are you Susana?' and they run up and they give me a hug," she said. Clearly recognizing her role as a trailblazing Latina, and as a symbolic role model, legitimizing the role of Latinas in U.S. politics, she stated, "It is in moments like these when I'm reminded that we pave a path, and for me, it is about paving a path for those little girls to follow." She continued by stating: "They need to know, no more barriers" (Republican National Committee). Here she markedly emphasized the institutional underrepresentation of Latinas, like herself, and the recognition that there have been disadvantages for Latinas in reaching political office. In addition, her statement implies that her election and her position as a Latina governor, blazes the trail for future generations to hold political office. In a similar statement upon receiving an endorsement from the PODER PAC, which supports Democratic Latina candidates, Michelle Lujan Grisham stated, "I truly value this endorsement. Endorsements from Latina/o groups like PODER motivate me to continue to be a role model for other Latinas in New Mexico interested in public service" (PODER PAC). Latina candidates are evidently acutely aware of their significance in office for legitimizing the institutions in which they serve, and their symbolic function as role models.

Latinas like Susana Martinez and Michelle Lujan Grisham recognize the difficulties minority women face as elected officials. Even if minority women, including Latinas, win office at higher rates than other underrepresented groups (white women and minority men), the challenges they face in office in comparison to the majority white male counterparts are compounded by their dual minority identity. The institutions to which they are elected are arguably gendered and racialized, putting Latinas at a disadvantage as functions of both their gender and their ethnicity. This is because, as mentioned in the theory section, our political institutions were created by white men who created these institutions in their own image, considering their own leadership style, legislative priorities and preferences, and considered their own personal obligations and experiences.[3] This lack of diverse input into the institutional design means that those with experiences vastly different from the (traditional) average white man will find public service challenging. There are many ways in which we can examine how institutions are gendered and racialized. To explore some of the challenges Latinas in particular face, we specifically consider the institutional features of the New Mexico governor's office, of congressional office, and the challenge of family obligations for Latinas.

Most literature on descriptive representation focuses on the legislative branch of government. This is for two good reasons: first, it is the legislative branch which is created for the purpose of representation, and secondly, the legislative branch is more abundant in terms of individual observations. The executive branch is significantly smaller in size. In terms of state-wide executive office, only thirty-seven women have held the highest office of governor. Of the thirty-seven women governors, New Mexico governor Susana Martinez is the first elected Latina.

The New Mexico executive branch uses the "fragmented" model of leadership (García et al. 2008). The branch is set up with a multitude of independently elected officers as well as several agencies under the purview of an executive board or commission. Multiple offices making up the executive branch, each with control of its own budget, creates a significantly weaker governor than can be found in systems with a more unitary executive branch, such as in New Jersey (García et al. 2008). However, the New Mexico governor is relatively powerful when it comes to the power of appointment, with the authority to appoint about 400 agency heads and other state employees, even if the true executive power for many of these agencies rests with a board or commission. García et al. argue that "achieving a governor's goals through the medium of a board represents one of the most taxing challenges of the office" (García et al. 2008, 103).

Notwithstanding differences between a strong versus weak governor model, both presume a unitary actor at the apex of executive power. This hierarchical leadership model tends to favor male traits over women's more collaborative style. In contrast, legislative office may appear more cooperative and horizontally organized than executive office. Even so, the legislative branch generally, and Congress in particular, still favors majority rule and a hierarchical organization of leadership.[4]

Majority rule is a democratic ideal upon which the U.S. system is based. At its core, majority rule suggests that the preferences of the many should trump the preferences of the few. While this may be preferred over minority positions trumping the views of the many (as might be the case in an undemocratic society), it quickly becomes evident that minority positions are less likely to be crystallized fully into substantive policy changes. In addition, those who defend minority positions are by design less likely to be effective in seeing their proposals come to fruition. Furthermore, because of majority-minority districts, designed to increase descriptive representation, it is likely that for each descriptive representative, surrounding districts will elect white representatives who do not share the same concern for minority issues, further marginalizing minority opinions (Cameron, Epstein, and O'Halloran 1996).

This concept is readily evident in the issue of immigration. As Latina representatives, both Susana Martinez and Michelle Lujan Grisham are likely to consider immigration policy a salient issue, and are more likely than their *partisan* counterparts to have empathetic policy views in favor of immigrants. As we saw earlier in the discussion of the partisan effect, despite the Republican Party's strong restrictionist policy preferences on the issue of immigration, Susana Martinez adamantly spoke out against immigration policies which did not take the immigrant experience and challenges into account. Michelle Lujan Grisham, though certainly privileged by her party's position on the issue, has contributed to the saliency of the issue of immigration. Even if Democrats are expected to favor a pro-immigration platform, which is touted by the party generally, white representatives are less likely to push for the saliency of the immigration issue. Taking different stances on immigration policy, both Lujan Grisham and Martinez are acting as descriptive representatives in highlighting the saliency and complexity of the issue. As Mansbridge (1999) maintains, a key role for descriptive representatives is introducing issues before policy makers for debate, discussion, and action.

In terms of the institutional arrangements, both the executive and the legislative branches favor a hierarchical arrangement of leadership (even if the NM fragmented style is somewhat less hierarchical than others). Even within Congress, which is seemingly a more collaborative decision-making body, there is an organizational structure, which is largely based on seniority. A system based on seniority tends to favor the status quo and disadvantage "newcomers" to the institution. Important leadership positions, such as committee leadership, more prestigious committee assignments, and even speaking privileges are likely to be distributed on the basis of seniority. These leaders can wield great power, especially in terms of agenda setting. Women are currently, and have historically been, underrepresented in leadership positions in Congress, and minority women even more so (CAWP 2015). This means that even if women, and Latinas in particular, are able to have "a seat at the table," they are disadvantaged in their opportunities to be effective because they are not setting the agenda to push salient issues even if they have the opportunity to present them (Childs and Krook 2009).

FAMILY AS A SPECIAL CONCERN

One of the most common concerns for women, and especially Latinas, when considering public office is the toll public life takes on the family and family obligations. Political office was designed around white men's experiences, which often were comparatively independent. While white male politicians throughout history have had families, they have not had the same types of family *obligations*. Women tend to account for family obligations when considering public office much more so than men, and thus are less likely to run if they have small children (Carroll and Sanbonmatsu 2013). Women elected officials are also more likely to be stigmatized and shamed for their decisions to hold public office because of an expectation of family obligations (Siebel Newsom 2011). Latino culture brings an additional layer of family obligations, especially to Latinas who are truly considered matriarchs in a culture that emphasizes care for the family and multi-generational family networks (Baca Zinn 1975).

The centrality of family and the closeness of familial ties in Hispanic culture is evident for our Latina leaders in New Mexico. Both Susana Martinez and Michelle Lujan Grisham have been "constrained" by the care for family. The effects of motherhood are evident in that neither woman ran for higher office (beyond local office) until their children[5] were at least in their teenage years. However, both women have also cared for additional family members, obligations which are likely to have affected their effectiveness and opportunities for institutional ambition.

In a 2013 interview with *People Magazine*, Susana Martinez simply stated, "It's all about my family" (quoted in Clark 2013). As the caretaker for her disabled older sister who has cerebral palsy, Martinez's commitment to family is evident. Martinez's decision to care for her sister was obvious to her, stating that, "I knew that after my mother died, [my sister] Lettie would come back to me, and she would still be 5" (quoted in Clark 2013). Martinez's extensive family commitments have affected her political ambitions, in particular for considering federal-level positions. Holding a federal-level position means working in Washington D.C., something which is a clear constraint on the family. Already in 2012, Martinez was rumored as a possible running mate for presidential candidate Mitt Romney. When asked about her ambitions should a similar opportunity arise in 2016, "Martinez says she'll be flattered, but 'Lettie will always be my priority'" (Clark 2013).

Caretaking has similarly been a priority for Michelle Lujan Grisham both professionally and personally for a long time. Prior to becoming a member of Congress, Michelle Lujan Grisham served as New Mexico's first Secretary of Aging and Long Term Services when the department was elevated by Governor Bill Richardson to a cabinet position, and later headed the New Mexico Department of Health. As a member of Congress, in 2015 Lujan Grisham launched a new bipartisan caucus, the Assisting Caregivers Today Caucus (ACT) in an effort to "bring more attention to the plight of those caring for aging family members" (Coleman 2015). Lujan Grisham has personally faced the challenges of caretaking in caring for her sister until her early death, and now caring for her ailing mother. In Lujan Grisham's first few months in office her mother fell ill, as Stacey Goers reported, "as her mother's primary caregiver, Lujan Grisham had to balance hospital stays and medications and coordination among family and friends, while tackling budget votes, new legislation and caucus work" (Goers 2013). In considering the plight of these two Latinas, it appears that their roles as caretakers have created particular challenges (though not necessarily insurmountable) to their effectiveness as public officials.

CONCLUSION

As the number of Latina elected officials grows, and the scholarly literature follows closely behind, our understanding of Latina elected officials' behavior adapts and in particular becomes more complicated. Early studies considering how an elected official's intersectional identity might be affected by longstanding institutional constraints suggested that the additive barriers created by the dual identity of being both a woman and a minority would create a double disadvantage for any woman seeking and holding elected office. However, as Latina trailblazers have opened the paths of leadership to a growing number of Latina elected officials, analysis has expanded to consider how institutional mechanisms impact styles, preferences, and priorities associated with Latina identity. Coupled with quantitative findings that minority women win at higher rates than white women and the theoretical assessment that minority women are better able to create winning electoral coalitions, a much more dynamic view of Latina leadership has emerged.

In our study we have shown that the seemingly contradictory theoretical implications of strategic intersectionality and double disadvantage are compatible when considering the different contexts in which Latina elected officials are active. We argued that an examination of the electoral context, the (mediating) partisan effect, and the institutional context are crucial to a fuller understanding of the complexity of Latina elected officials' behavior. We also argued that this complex relationship is better seen qualitatively and presented a case study of two prominent Latina elected officials, Susana Martinez and Michelle Lujan Grisham, to test our theoretical assumptions.

In attempting to understand what the advantages and disadvantages are for Latina elected officials, we found that strategic intersectionality explains the comparative advantages Latinas have over other minority groups (white women and minority men) because they are better able to produce a winning coalition, through their connections of descriptive representation with both white women and minority men. We found that both Susana Martinez and Michelle Lujan Grisham were indeed able to rally these important groups in winning their respective races. Importantly, however, we also found that party appeared to be an important mediating factor in the electoral context. We found that because of the Democratic Party's issue ownership of women's issues and pro-immigration stances, the Democratic candidate we examined, Michelle Lujan Grisham, was comparatively more advantaged than Martinez, who would often have to defend her positions both to the community and to her own party.

We also showed that while minority women are comparatively advantaged over other minority groups in the electoral context, they are comparatively disadvantaged in the institutional context, and double disadvantaged in comparison to white men. We found that because of the institutional design, which is at once gendered and racialized, our Latina elected officials will be doubly disadvantaged because of their intersectional identity. We found that these institutions are created to favor single unitary actors with a hierarchical leadership style, whereas women's leadership style is more cooperative. In addition to the additive effects of broad gender and race/ethnicity factors, we also found that Latina familial ties and a strong commitment to extensive caregiving create additional challenges for Latina elected officials.

This study provides one glimpse into the advantages and disadvantages of Latina officeholders. Future studies should consider two directions of study. First, as this study attempted to dig deeper to examine the extent of generalizing established theories of Latina elected officials' behavior, future research should return to examine the extent to which our findings hold beyond our case studies within the state of New Mexico. Secondly, we also recommend deeper qualitative analysis (and perhaps eventual quantitative analysis) to examine if these same factors apply in other states, to other levels of office, and to the judicial branch.

NOTES

1. We acknowledge that theoretically there is the additional pre-candidacy context wherein Latinas decide whether or not to run for office. This question deals much with the structural barriers to office, which are implicated by the double disadvantages that Latinas face as minorities and as women in society. While this may be an extension of our work, we limit the discussion to behaviors of candidates and elected officials who have already passed the initial barrier of running for office.

2. Exit poll data was not available for 2014. However, according to the NM Secretary of State's office, Martinez won all but five counties: Mora, Rio Arriba, San Miguel, Santa Fe, and Taos, all traditional Democratic strongholds. (http://electionresults.sos.state.nm.us/resultsCTY.aspx?type=SW&rid=1803&osn=202&map=CTY).

3. Intentionality to exclude and/or marginalize women and minorities from institutions of power and decision-making can be found in American history and politics. Our purpose is to call attention to the impact of "exclusivity," regardless if intentional or not.

4. While this chapter addresses high-level elected office, we suggest that other decision making bodies which are more horizontal and cooperative, such as smaller local councils, boards, and commissions, may be more appealing to women's preferred leadership style.

5. Michelle Lujan Grisham has two daughters, and Susana Martinez has one stepson.

EIGHT

"Liberal Leticia" and the Race for Texas Lieutenant Governor

Sharon A. Navarro

There is little question that political campaigns make appeals to voters' emotions. Campaign managers must craft television advertisements that not only convey a message, but also simultaneously resonate with voters on an emotional level (Brader 2006). Increasingly, political scientists have recognized that both substantive message content and emotional content are critical in understanding the effects of campaign advertising on voters. More recently, scholars have shown a renewed interest in examining the effects of distinct emotions such as anger, fear, hope, compassion, and sadness on political participation (Bodenhausen, Kramer and Susser 1994; Brader and Corrigan 2005; Valentino et al. 2011; Weber 2007). Other experts focus on the tone, that is, whether a political advertisement is positive, negative, or comparative (Weber 2007). By focusing on the effects of such specific emotional appeals on individual voters, these approaches assume that campaigns attempt to purposefully manipulate voter emotions.

Research finds that individuals experiencing anxiety are likely to increase the assessment of risk when contemplating action (Huddy, Feldman, and Cassese 2007). Thus, individuals who feel anxious about a candidate may see greater risk in relying on easy partisan cues, which leads them to thoughtfully process information about the candidates in the race. According to Marcus et al. (2000), individuals will rely on routine or, in a political situation, partisanship, to make a voting decision (Marcus et al. 2006). Research indicates that the types of emotions invoked by campaigns are likely to depend on the characteristics of the candidate, circumstances of the race, and the desired social or policy outcome (Brader 2005). Schnur (2007) argues that candidates strategically select emotional appeals based on two objectives: enhancing or maintaining their position in the race and targeting the audiences needed to accomplish the first objective.

This study provides descriptive evidence of candidates' use of emotional appeals through a content analysis of political advertising spots by two Texas lieutenant gubernatorial candidates in the 2014 midterm election in which one candidate was a Latina woman. Emotional appeals were used to trigger party cues associated with certain policies. As Texas is a very red state, the average Republican candidate starts off with a 10–12 point advantage against a Democratic rival. The challenge for any Democratic candidate is to close the gap. After the April 2014 Republican primary run-off in which State Senator Dan Patrick defeated longtime incumbent Lieutenant Governor David Dewhurst, a University of Texas/ *Texas Tribune* Poll showed Patrick leading State Senator Leticia Van de Putte by 15 points. Forty-one percent of surveyed voters favored Patrick, while 26 percent supported Van de Putte and 23 percent were undecided.[1] A rule of thumb in any political race is whichever political candidate can successfully define the other candidate first will likely dictate the race. Democratic State Senator Leticia Van de Putte had her work cut out for her. In addition, she was unaware that Patrick's campaign would be run and won using an online strategy.

DATA AND METHODS

To examine the timing and type of candidates' emotional appeals, I examined six campaign television advertisements that aired from September 4, 2014, to November 4, 2014. The ads appeared on thirty-seven television stations and twelve cable networks.[2] Two graduate students coded the advertisements using the questions listed in the Appendix, which were provided by the Wisconsin Advertising Project 2012 and adapted by Samantha L. Hernandez (2017). The Intercoder reliability was calculated using Cohen's test statistic, which has a scale that ranges from 0 to 1, with 1 indicating perfect reliability and 0 indicating almost no agreement (Stemler 2001).

Two graduate research assistants were asked to examine and code each question as a 1 if the ad contained an item from the questionnaire and 0 otherwise. In addition, an ad could contain more than one item from the questionnaire and could be coded as 1 for question 2, parts a through d. As these questions are not mutually exclusive, the assistants understood that an ad could contain multiple types of policy content. If they were unsure or unclear whether an ad contained the item, they were asked to code it as missing data. The result was .90 reliability.

Twenty graduate students then looked at all six campaign advertisements and answered the questionnaire.

Given previous research in political advertising, I categorized the ads by type. Accordingly, I adopted the categories of issue/advocacy, attack, and contrast, as opposed to categorizing as simply positive and negative (see Jamieson, Waldman, and Sherr 2000). I was also interested in the degree to which candidates addressed aspects of their own or their opponent's character as well as substantive political issues. In addition, I examined whether the candidate or his or her opponent appeared in the ads and if so, whether the candidate or opponent was moving or speaking. This is important because men and women emphasize different messages in their campaigns (Kahn 1993).

In conjunction with these typical categories used in content studies of political advertising, I also checked for words or cues directly related to race—that is, the presence or absence of an explicit or implicit racial appeal by the sponsoring candidate (Abrajano 2010; DeFrancesco Soto, and Morella 2008). Of the six campaign advertisements,[3] the statistical significance of three are examined and discussed in this essay.

Given this, I offer two hypotheses:

> *H1:* Leading candidates should be more likely than trailing candidates to use emotions associated with the necessary anger, enthusiasm, compassion, and pride to maintain existing public support.
>
> *H2:* Trailing candidates should be more likely than leading candidates to use emotions associated with fear to encourage political learning and upset existing public support.

THEORY

Politicians have a number of tools for communicating and winning over voters, including campaign appearances, direct mail, websites, televisions debates and speeches, and door-to-door canvassing, among others. Agranoff (1972) writes about a "new style" of campaigning in which televised political advertisements have become the primary means by which candidates communicate with voters. This means of communication is clearly reflected in the way candidates allocate campaign funds. Texas Lieutenant Gubernatorial candidate Dan Patrick's campaign spent about $830,000 on online consulting and advertising, according to campaign filings. That accounts for about 7.5 percent of the roughly $11 million the campaign spent on advertising—much more than the national average of digital political advertising, which is 3.5 percent (Rosenthal and Rauf

2014). This fact is particularly notable given that the amount was for a statewide race, not a national race.

That candidates spend such vast sums on television commercials acknowledges the power of advertising to influence voters. The advent of televised political advertising in the presidential election of 1948 initially raised concerns about this influence among scholars, the media, and the general public. This fear led to popular claims that political ads were deceitful, overly personalistic, and lacked substantive material (West 2001, 44, 46). Scholars and the general public believed that, in advertisements, "the candidate's personality, image, and symbolic appeals [take] precedence over specific issue positions" (Aiken et al. 1973, 10). Alleviating some of these concerns, Berelson and colleagues (1954) concluded that short-term effects, such as campaigns, had a minimal influence on voter decision-making. Berelson and his colleagues argued that political campaigns did not provide new information to voters but instead triggered voters' previous beliefs and opinions. These findings led many scholars to support the "minimal effects hypothesis," which posits that campaigns have little or no impact on a voter's decision-making process.

Decades of research following Berelson's seminal work—along with technological advancements in measuring advertising exposure—have left little doubt that television ads influence voters' opinions and attitudes in elections (Brader 2006; Geer 2006; West 2001; Mendelberg 2001; Just et al. 1996; Herrnson and Patterson 2001; Kahn and Kenny 1999). As one might expect, more frequent advertising positively affects a candidate's vote share (Clinton and Lapinski 2004; Freedman and Goldstein 1999; Nagler and Leighley 1992; and Shaw 1999). Nagler and Leighley (1992) found that an increase in campaign advertising spending positively correlated with a candidate's share of the vote.

A televised political ad contains several distinct elements, all of which can affect the way voters assess candidates. One element is the tone, which refers to the way the message is crafted and is generally categorized as positive, negative, or comparative (Jamieson 1992; Shea and Burton 2006). The tone of political advertising has received considerable attention from political scientists (Bader 2006; Geer 2006; Clinton and Lapinski 2004; Freedman and Goldstein 1999; Lau and Sigelam 2000; Kahn and Kenney 1999; Ansolabehere et al. and Iyengar 1995). For example, Geer (2006) reported that attack ads tend to be more informative and substantive in content than positive ads.

In addition to the overall tone of an advertisement, how the message is presented—what political scientist call "framing"—can influence individuals' opinions and attitudes toward a particular issue (Nir and Druckman 2008; Winter 2008; Druckman 2004; Entman 1993). A frame can be thought of as the message's point of view (Popkin 1994; Tversky and Kahneman 1981). Framing is important because point of view determines the type of information and considerations the message brings to voters' mind. As such, the standards by which an individual evaluates a campaign message may change depending on the frame. One way that an issue can be framed is from a "group-centric" perspective. This approach is advantageous when an issue such as crime, immigration, or welfare, specifically deals with or is identified with a particular group. Nelson and Kinder (1996) have found that frames focusing on groups associated with an issue (for example, African Americans or affirmative action) lead individuals to think about their attitudes toward a particular group rather than about the actual policy being addressed. Candidates may therefore be motivated to frame certain issues in a group-centric manner, rather than positively or negatively, to appeal to particular voters. A candidate might frame a commercial about immigration reform in a way that evokes Latin voters' positive feelings about economic opportunity in the United States or, alternatively, in a way that amplifies Anglo voters' negative feelings about Latin immigrants. Thus, Anglo Americans' opinions on issues have been shaped to some degree by racial bias.

Advertisements attempt to prime voters to respond in particular ways. Priming is a concept drawn from the psychology literature on decision-making (Kahneman et al. 1979). It refers to the idea that individuals will use the information that is most readily available and accessible when making decisions. Thus, a person's decision-making process is influenced to some extent by circumstances, that is, the topics and themes of political ads viewed in the days leading up to an election are likely to affect how a person votes. Although priming does not overtly alter individuals' opinion and beliefs, it has the potential to influence issues that voters consider to be most important (Iyengar and Kinder 1987). Priming has also been found to be effective at activating voters' racial biases. When political advertisements contain subtle racial cues or negative stereotypes about racial and ethnic minorities, an individual's racial attitudes can also become more negative (Mendelberg 2001; Valentino et al. 2002).

Agenda setting, which refers to the order in which political messages are discussed in an advertisement, is also important in relating to voters. If, for example, a candidate consistently emphasizes education as his most important issue, voters might perceive education as the issue most salient in their decision about which candidate to vote for. In this area, Iyengar and Kinder (1987) found that "those problems that receive prompt attention on the news become the problems the viewing public regards as the most important" (16).

THE RACE FOR LIEUTENANT GOVERNOR

Although Dan Patrick won the Republican primary race for lieutenant governor in May 2014, he did not hold any news conferences or give any interviews until November 4, 2014. A survey of political reporters at major newspapers found that no one was able to interview him for six months (Kofler 2014). One news outlet tracked the political movements of Van de Putte and Patrick from October 1 through October 27 and found that Van de Putte attended/participated in seventy-nine public breakfasts, rallies, get-out-the vote events and media interviews. The same news outlet identified twelve events for Patrick, which included mostly unpublicized meetings with Republicans or students and one appearance on a Houston TV program where he answered questions. Patrick was running a low-profile campaign. In the past, as a radio talk show host, he was known or being controversial. As a candidate, he did not want to say anything contentious. Because Texas is a red state, the public does not punish GOP frontrunners like Patrick who choose not to be visible (Kofler 2014).

Patrick coupled his media savvy with the power of Facebook, Twitter, and other social media unlike any candidate in the election to create his own online megaphone—one he wielded to coalesce a Tea Party base and subvert the traditional media in the process. Patrick's strategy stood in contrast to that of his Democratic opponent, Leticia Van de Putte, who had maintained a comparatively low online profile and, like most candidates, had focused her resources almost entirely on television advertising. Van de Putte spokesman Manny García said that Patrick's strategy included less genuine engagement and fewer media interviews. "You have more accountability when you're talking to a reporter, and it's a shame that Dan Patrick had decided that he didn't believe in his values enough to talk about them," García said. Vincent Harris, an American Conservative political digital strategist and CEO of Harris Media, said that the strategy allowed Patrick to communicate with voters more directly and quickly (Rosenthal and Rauf 2014, A3). As the campaign progressed, Patrick's digital strategy moved from social media to television. According to *The Total Audience Report* (Turrill and Enoch 2015), television reaches 87 percent of Americans 18 and older (4). The same messaging he created virtually easily transferred to television. This allowed him to stay disciplined in his messaging and defined the political agenda for the remaining months.

Early on, Harris focused mainly on building Patrick's Facebook page to reach like-minded conservatives and simplified his message to three issues—border security, property taxes, and Texas schools (Harris 2014). He reinforced these issues on television. The issues of illegal immigration, property taxes, and Texas schools were identified on social media and became three 30-second campaign ads that appealed emotionally to voters. Social media also became the Patrick campaign's preferred avenue for responding to attacks.

BORDER SECURITY

Patrick made immigration and border security major components of his platform. He said, "it's important to separate the 'innocent children' from the 'gang members from Mexico and Central America who are coming under the cover of this' increase in unaccompanied minors," and he emphasized that the state could not bear the expense of caring for all immigrants (Ura 2014). On his Facebook page, Patrick went on to defend his stance for border security, writing, "We do care about the poor and disenfranchised. However, we cannot afford to take care of the entire world and every person who wants to come to American legal or illegally. . . . We have a real and present threat from ISIS and al-Qaida" (Rauf 2014, B10).

Van de Putte indicated that the state should secure the border by providing local law enforcement with ample resources to ensure "that troops can focus on catching criminals, not kids," (Ura 2014) while calling for immigration reform at the federal level to get to the root of illegal immigration. At the same time she also talked about the humanitarian crisis in Texas and the importance of properly aiding the tens of thousands of unaccompanied minors coming to the state because of violence in their home countries (Ura 2014).

Patrick responded by saying, "This is not being anti-immigrant; it's not anti-Hispanic. This is about law and order" (Ura 2014). Van de Putte responded to his comments, calling his language "inappropriate" (Ura 2014) and reminding voters that Republicans were using immigration and "the politics of fear and toxic rhetoric just to get votes" (Rauf 2014, B10). In television ads, Patrick portrayed Van de Putte as overly soft on border security. In one 30-second ad, he created the specter of ISIS terrorists invading the U.S. border as illegal immigrants and reported that Van de Putte voted for money directed to Latin America rather than to border security.

He stated that Van De Putte authored a bill that "gave" in-state tuition to "illegal" dreamers, and "refused to send armed troops to secure the border," and voting to "send millions to Latin America" instead. In June of 2014, the University of Texas/*Texas Tribune* published a poll that identified the top three concerns among state constituents. Thirty percent of Texans believed that immigration/border security was the

Photos 8.1 and 8.2.   "Washington Has Failed Us," Dan Patrick television campaign ad.
Courtesy of DanPatrick.Org.

number one issue, followed by 12 percent who identified the economy/
unemployment/jobs, with education in third place at 5 percent.[4] Three
months later, a Texas Lyceum Poll reported similar findings,[5] reporting
that Texans see immigration and border security as the most important
issue facing the state (a combined total of 31 percent), putting education
in third place, while the economy and jobs were seen as the most important issue facing the country (a combined total of 20 percent) (Justus
2014). Patrick's campaign strategist clearly had the pulse of Texans.

PROPERTY TAXES

In another Patrick 30-second campaign ad, viewers witnessed the use of party cues in a low information election. The ad begins with a male voice narrating, "Leticia Van de Putte is consistently rated as one of the most liberal politicians in Texas. Here are the facts: Liberal Leticia opposed property tax cuts. She supported a statewide property tax and even supported a tax on employee wages and an income tax on Texas workers." Patrick then appears. Speaking to the camera, he introduces himself as "a conservative, who sponsored one of the biggest taxes cuts of any state during the recession helping Texas lead the nation in job creation. As lieutenant governor, I will cut property taxes and keep the Texas economy number one in America."

In this ad, Patrick plays on party cues by labeling Van de Putte as a *tax-happy liberal* while emphasizing that he is the strong conservative. This strategy is consistent with the literature on campaign ads and party cues. According to Robinson (2010), parties/candidates are able to communicate to voters not only through policy stands, but also through "messages about the people and places that are important to the party; the affinity parties feel they have with voters; the extent to which voters needs have informed party priorities; myths and histories shared with party and voters; leadership offerings; and the threat parties sense from their competition" (452). In essence, Robinson's argument points to the fact that political advertising is extremely important for parties and candidates in developing and discussing campaign issues and constructing or reconstructing their images to win voters' support and defeat the competition. These types of ads enable a winning candidate to construct a negative group-centric image of their challenger.

Van de Putte's response to Patrick's accusations fell on deaf ears. She pointed out that the state could levy a property tax, so any decreases in property taxes would place restrictions on local governments who set tax rates to fund schools, public safety, and more. "Would firefighters lose their jobs? Would police lose their jobs?" she asked the audience in the one debate she and Patrick had. "It's the cities and counties that would be affected. To burden Texas businesses and families with a sales tax increase—well, that's not pro-business" (McSwane 2014, A1). Despite her efforts, she could not overcome the image Patrick had constructed over her of a tax-spending liberal who supports illegal immigration. Patrick may have appeared more knowledgable on the issues of tax and spending and immigration, but when it came to the issue of education, Van de Putte showed compassion. This played into the stereotype of women having more compassion for social issues than men.

IMPROVING PUBLIC EDUCATION

Van de Putte's first television ad aired September 5, 2014, and ran in several major markets. In the 30-second commercial, she attacks Patrick, reminding viewers that as a state senator in 2011, he voted to cut school funding in Texas by $5 billion while she had opposed the reduction. In the ad, Van de Putte reports, "the funding cuts to schools, supported by most Republicans in the Legislature, resulted in the loss of 11,000 teaching jobs. Last year, Patrick voted against restoring much of that money, while most Republicans and all Democrats in the Senate supported the increased funding. For a second time, Dan Patrick voted against our kids." Patrick defended his vote, stating that he'd had no choice but to cut spending on education (Stutz 2014). When asked if he was willing to invest more in public education if elected lieutenant governor, he replied, "yes, but I want it to be spent wisely" (Rauf 2014, B10).

Despite Van de Putte's position and image as a compassionate advocate of public education funding, not many people knew Patrick voted to cut $5 billion from education. Texas is not a state known for addressing any issues related to education and it has never been a not a top concern for voters, as opposed to immigration. Patrick had crafted himself as a fiscally conservative candidate and succeeded at portraying Van de Putte as a tax-and-spend liberal who would allow the re-conquest or invasion of illegals and threaten citizens' way of life. It was an image that she could not overcome. Patrick was disciplined in delivering his message: he talked up the same policy issues that were initially developed on his Facebook page and subsequently addressed in the Republican primary. These were dominant issues for the state's most conservative voters.

FINDINGS

At the beginning of this chapter, I offered two hypotheses:

> *H1:* Leading candidates should be more likely than trailing candidates to use emotions associated with anger, enthusiasm, compassion, and pride to maintain existing public support.
> *H2:* Trailing candidates should be more likely than leading candidates to use emotions associated with fear to encourage political learning and upset existing public support.

From the outset, Patrick clearly defined the issues for lieutenant governor's race through his campaign advertisements. It was nearly impossible for Van de Putte to get out in front of these issues, as Patrick was only accessible through social media and traditional media such as television. His entire campaign was run through social media and traditional media. There was no direct candidate engagement. Van de Putte could not compel him to engage in a public discourse because he was in the lead, according to the polls. All Patrick had to do was stay on course and not make any errors.

Of the six television campaign advertisements that were watched, twenty graduate students were asked questions about issue recognition, racial appeal (i.e., did a Latina appear in the ad, was she talking, etc.), tone (i.e., was the ad was positive, negative, and/or comparative), and emotion (i.e., compassion, pride, anger, fear, hope, anxiety, and enthusiasm). There was no statistical significant difference between the Van de Putte and Patrick political advertisements when students were asked to observe the perception of fear, particularly after the ISIS television frame. However, on the issue of education, Van de Putte was more likely to use a compassionate appeal than Patrick (.001 significance). This runs counter to both hypotheses: Van de Putte did not succeed at invoking fear to prompt voter appeal. Patrick was more likely to use enthusiasm and pride than Van de Putte (both at the .001) on issues of border security and taxes (see table 8.1), which is consistent with the first hypothesis offered.

CONCLUSION

Social media, newspaper interviews, and all other media help to make televised political advertising more effective than other tools at the candidates' disposal. Moreover, the content of political advertising is valuable in educating voters. Political advertising can serve to reduce voters' misperceptions and uncertainties (Lupia and McCubbins 1998; Conover and Feldman 1989). Some of the most readily available voter cues are provided by messages in the ever-growing number of televised political ads. Howell and McLean (2001) reported that the performance of minority public officials, not race, is a stronger predictor of how they are evaluated by non-minority voters.

Although the findings here are inconclusive because of the small sample size, this study is similar to McIlwain and Caliendo's (2009). It suggests, as does McIlwain and Caliendo's study, that current research is proceeding in the right direction; that is, findings are consistent with what might be expected given our conceptualization of emotional appeals and how these appeals are used. Similar to the literature on women in politics and policy, Van de Putte had a strong association with compassion when

Table 8.1. Advertising Emotional Appeals by Candidate

	Compassion		Pride		Enthusiasm	
	Van de Putte	Patrick	Van de Putte	Patrick	Van de Putte	Patrick
Mean	1.15***	.16	.09	1.55***	.10	1.68***
SD	.37	.37	.37	.51	.31	.48
SEM	.08	.09	.08	.11	.07	.11
T value	7.55		4.98		13.56	
DF	18		38		18	

*** Significant at the .001 level

it came to the issue of education (Bratton, Haynie, and Reingold 1999). This finding was inconsistent with the second hypothesis offered. As the trailing candidate in the race, she did not elicit fear in the education ad discussed in this article, but rather compassion. Patrick, as the leading candidate, succeeded at targeting the emotions of enthusiasm and pride. Van de Putte was never able to close the voting gap. On election night in 2014, Patrick defeated Van de Putte 58 percent to 38 percent.

NOTES

1. The margin of error for the sample with an n = 1200 is +/-2.83. See the UT/ *Texas Tribune* Survey on June 2014 http://texaspolitics.laits.utexas.edu/11_1_1.html.

2. The 37 television stations were culled from http://en.wikipedia.org/wiki/ List_of_television_stations_in_Texas, which is a good source for identifying the most popular television stations across the state. I crossed referenced these stations with the Federal Communications Commission database https://stations .fcc.gov/ to ensure that candidates did buy airtime, the cost of the airtime, and the frequency of the advertisements. I also culled the most popular cable stations from http://www.cablemediasales.com/PoliticalFile/.

3. Campaign TV Ads by Dan Patrick are Liberal Leticia, Washington Has Failed Us. Campaign TV Ads by Leticia Van de Putte are Dangerous Dan, Trust, Respect, Twice.

4. University of Texas/*Texas Tribune*. (June 2014). *Texas Statewide Survey.* Field dates were from May 30–June 8, 2014; 1200 adults were surveyed with a margin of error +/– 2.83 percent

5. Field dates were from September 11–25, 2014; 1000 adults were surveyed with a margin of error +/–3.1 percent.

NINE

"A Force to Be Reckoned With"

Rethinking Latina Leadership and Power

Lizeth Gonzalez and Tony Affigne

The nation's Latino population of more than 55 million remains descriptively underrepresented in government, and within that population it is women—*Latinas*—who are the most underrepresented. At 17 percent of the national population, Hispanics (both men and women) hold just 5.9 percent of seats in Congress, 3.8 percent of state executive offices, and 4.1 percent of state legislative seats. Hispanic women are even less likely to serve in public office. In local governments, for example, there are 5,750 Hispanic officials but only 34.6 percent (1,990) are women.[1] Across all levels of government in the United States, Hispanic men hold about twice as many positions as Hispanic women. This gender imbalance is striking, since the Hispanic population includes nearly as many women as men (49.3 percent), and a recent study by Bejarano (2013) found that compared to Hispanic men, Hispanic women appear to be more successful candidates in racially mixed, multi-ethnic constituencies.[2]

To better understand these gendered dynamics, in this chapter we consider how social, personal, and political obstacles might be hampering Latina empowerment and contributing to the 2-to-1-gender imbalance in Hispanic office holding. At the same time, we recognize that despite obstacles, more than 2,000 Latinas *have* been elected to public office across the United States. An even greater number wield power as senior appointees in federal agencies, state administrative departments, as well as state or municipal agencies, boards, and commissions. What do these successful Latinas have in common? What are the characteristics and backgrounds of Latinas who have been elected or appointed to public office? What can their experiences tell us about career trajectories, aspirations, and self-conceptions, as leaders who face the distinct challenges of being both female and Hispanic?

Our research subjects were women of diverse Hispanic backgrounds who are current or former elected and appointed officials, for state and municipal governments, in the State of Rhode Island. Our research approach was qualitative, using extended confidential interviews with these Latina political elites. In semi-structured 30–80 minute interviews we inquired about political and personal experiences—positive and negative—leading up to and during the women's terms of service. We invited them to describe whether and how their lives were shaped by immigration, civic engagement, and racial and ethnic identity, and to assess impacts of gender and/or racial and ethnic discrimination. Finally, we explored the role of mentors and sponsors, and whether and how the subjects viewed themselves as role models for other women and men, and in relation to the broader Latino community.

THE SOCIAL AND ECONOMIC ENVIRONMENT
FOR LATINAS IN RHODE ISLAND

Compared to the national Latino population Rhode Island's Latinos are in some ways typical and in other ways, distinctive. For example, Rhode Island's Latino population growth rate between 2000 and 2010 was 43.9 percent, very similar to the national rate of 43.0 percent. At 13.2 percent, Rhode Island's Latino population share in 2012 was slightly, but not dramatically, less than the national 16.9 percent. On the other hand, Rhode Island Latinos' national-origin profile is distinctive, with comparatively few Mexicans, but large Puerto Rican, Dominican, and Guatemalan populations in rough parity to one another. Finally, unlike the nation as a whole, the state's cohort of Hispanic elected officials is majority female. Nine of sixteen Hispanic elected are women, serving as municipal councilors, state legislators, and one statewide general officer.

Rhode Island's Latino men, women, and children would appear to be substantively as well as descriptively underrepresented. They are disproportionately poor, undereducated, and underemployed, with a median household income barely half that for non-Hispanic whites, and Latinos have the lowest per capita income of all the state's racial groups—less than $14,000 (see figure 9.1. *Per Capita Income in Rhode Island by Race, Hispanic Ethnicity*). When social data are disaggregated by gender, moreover, it's evident that Latina women experience extreme economic inequality. As a group, for example, they have the state's highest rates of poverty and lowest rates of graduate education. Single Latina householders without children, those with children, and Latinas overall, face higher rates of poverty than Latino men in comparable situations. In fact, nearly two-thirds of Rhode Island's Hispanic single female householders with children live below the poverty level (see figure 9.2. *Comparative Poverty Rates among Rhode Island Hispanics, by Gender*). Their poverty rate of 65.4 percent compares very poorly to corresponding rates for other single female householders with children who are white (25.4 percent in poverty), or Black (36.7 percent).[3] Finally, Latinas are more likely than other workers to be unemployed, or employed in low-wage health care, personal care, and service occupations.[4]

The Hispanic female unemployment rate in 2013 was the highest in the state. Their 20.6 percent jobless rate compared to 15.8 percent for Hispanic men, and 8.1 percent for white women. Black unemployment, by comparison, was 14.4 percent for women, and 13.6 percent for men. For Latinas who were employed, concentration in low-wage sectors and wage discrimination even in higher-status jobs, placed them at the bottom of the state's income rankings: Latinas' mean full-time earnings in 2013 were just $33,562, compared to $74,338 for white men.[5]

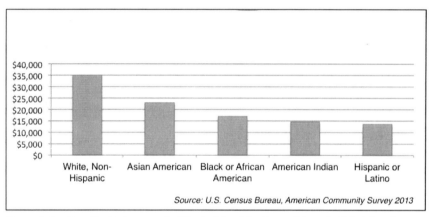

Figure 9.1. **Per Capita Income in Rhode Island by Race, Hispanic Ethnicity. Source: U.S. Census Beureau, American Community Survey 2013.**

In other words, whether they care for children or not; are employed or unemployed; live in families or live independently; and in nearly every age cohort, Hispanic females are disproportionately located at the bottom rungs of the Rhode Island economic ladder, relative to women and men in every other racial group—and compared to men in the Latino community itself. To be sure, economic inequality is far from the only problem confronting Latina women in Rhode Island. Serious concerns include poor access to education, domestic violence, and sparse social capital, among others. For their part, Latino men likewise face daunting social and economic challenges including high unemployment and underemployment, school and workplace discrimination, racial profiling and police violence,

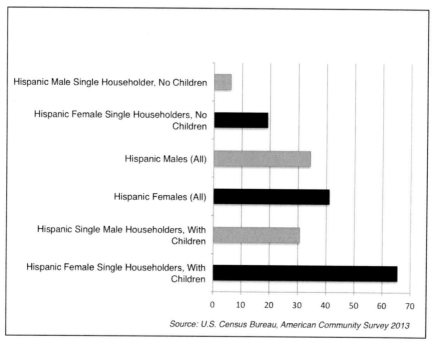

Figure 9.2. **Comparative Poverty Rates among Rhode Island Hispanics, by Gender.**
Source: U.S. Census Beureau, American Community Survey 2013.

and maltreatment in the courts and prison system, to name a few. But severe economic inequality remains the fundamental reality for Rhode Island's Latino communities, and the fact that women face the *most* difficult economic conditions raises important questions about potential impacts of Latina participation in governance.

In addition to Rhode Island's nine Latina elected officials (including the Secretary of State), another two dozen or so politically active Latinas have been appointed to state and municipal offices, including one cabinet position—director of the state Department of Human Services—and the state boards of education, and parole, as well as housing, canvassing, parks, planning, and licensing boards in the cities of Providence, Pawtucket, and Central Falls. These women's experiences achieving and exercising power may be instructive for Latina aspirants and office-holders elsewhere, in states where Latinas have not yet achieved comparable success. They may also help explain how political contexts in small states like Rhode Island are different from—in both positive and negative ways—opportunities and obstacles for Latinas in larger states, including those with better-established Latina leadership.

UNDERSTANDING LATINAS IN LEADERSHIP—A BRIEF REVIEW

As long ago as 1986, political scientists measured gender differences in participation among Mexican Americans, and found that stereotypical views of Latinas—too poor, too oppressed, and too passive to be fully engaged in politics—were false. In fact, registration and voting rates for Latinas in one West Texas county more than doubled between 1974 and 1984—until female participation was higher than for Mexican American males. How to explain these findings? The authors hypothesized that the Latinas' relative youthfulness, an increase in educational levels, and "their role as agents of social change," particularly as mothers of young children, might explain why Latinas were confounding expectations and engaging more fully in political life. The authors noted their findings were striking *because* both scholarly traditions and social expectations defined a less participatory role for Hispanic women. Gender-conscious social analysis, it seemed, was likely to undermine both conventional science and popular misconception (MacManus, Bullock, and Grothe 1986, 610).

In 1993, anthropologist Paule Cruz Takash surveyed Mexican American women who were elected to state and local offices in California, to document the experiences and attitudes of Latina women who had successfully broken through barriers of race, class, gender, and culture. In what she called "the first profile ever of Latina officeholders in the United States," Takash found that Latina officials faced questions about their competence, were challenged by fundraising requirements, and felt persistent pressure to overcome stereotypes to prove themselves both as women and as Hispanics, in a political culture dominated by white people, and by men. Many of the women also reported that limited financial resources, working class backgrounds and constituencies, and comparatively low educational achievement were likely to discourage other Hispanic women from seeking elective office. Takash found that her subjects were troubled by cultural and societal expectations and experienced feelings of guilt about neglected parental and familial duties. In addition, a majority reported that obstacles Latinas may face winning office included their Hispanic ethnicity (60 percent agreed), economic class (56 percent), and gender (60.5 percent)—yet a majority of respondents themselves reported *not* facing such barriers. Still, large pluralities of 46 percent and 41 percent, respectively, felt that ethnic and gender barriers had to be overcome during their campaigns. Significantly, Takash found that these Latinas' rise to official power often came after long careers as community advocates. Takash concluded that grassroots and electoral activism constituted a continuum, not a dichotomy; both were used to promote social change (Takash 1993).

A similar theme—the linkage between Latina public service, and experiences in community-based activism—can be found in Hardy-Fanta, whose study of Latina activists and officials in Boston, reported in *Latina Politics, Latino Politics* (1993), found that

> For Latina women, much more than men, the boundary between [public and private] spheres of life is blurred, indistinct. With their emphasis on grassroots politics, survival politics, the politics of everyday life and through their emphasis on the development of political consciousness, Latina women see connections between the problems they face personally and community issues stemming from government policies (189).

Hardy-Fanta locates her Latina subjects in *communities*, where political styles, aspirations, and leadership preferences are shaped by institutional contexts and opportunities. We read this as evidence that Latina political styles are *not* essentialist, determined by innate characteristics of Latinas *qua* women. Rather, Latina women adopt particular styles and aspire to particular roles because the structure of their communities, families, and culture—and the broader patriarchal society—offer opportunities for women to communicate and engage in collective action in some areas of political life, while constraining access to other political venues. We also imagine, with some confidence, that gendered opportunity structures for Latinas will vary across both location and time. Hardy-Fanta concluded that whatever their roots, distinctive Latina political styles and practices will provide crucial strategies of political empowerment for the broader Latino community. And significantly, she reminds us that despite serious obstacles, Latinas have moved beyond community engagement to become frequent, and successful, candidates for elective office as well (Hardy-Fanta 2002, 196–197).

For those Latinas who do move into electoral politics, important challenges remain, however. In *Políticas,* published in 2008 by García et al., a team of Latina researchers conducted interview-based case studies of fifteen Latina officials in Texas, each of whom was the first Latina elected to the state or local office she held. Like Takash, García et al. found that Latina political ambition and effectiveness were powerfully shaped by both family and cultural factors. Many were raised in politically involved families, and nearly all had experienced cultural marginalization and discrimination, internalizing these as motivations for community engagement and the basis for a sense of linked fate. Importantly, though, these trailblazers did not report being groomed for public service or feeling much initial political ambition, nor did most report being recruited by political parties or established leaders, either Latino or non-Latino. To the contrary, most said they had been asked by community representatives, colleagues, or friends to consider running for office, and most had been previously involved in grassroots community organizations. Significantly, most also cited the importance of supportive spouses and extended families in making the decision to run for office or to accept appointment. On the other hand, obstacles to service included financial burdens on families, and the challenge of campaign fundraising in communities with comparatively low incomes. In addition, family and cultural expectations based on traditional gender roles sometimes made public service more difficult. "Most of the Latinas in this study," the authors found, "had to confront stereotypes when others argued that they should not consider running and would not be taken seriously. They also faced accusations that they would not be able to juggle public service and caring for their spouse and family." Still, the successful Latina officials profiled in *Políticas* were those who overcame such barriers, drew support from families and communities, and were able to succeed. (García et al. 2008, 132)

And succeed they do, in rising numbers. In *The Latina Advantage* (2013), Christina Bejarano actually concluded that Latinas enjoy greater success in electoral politics than Latino men, partly because they benefit from what she calls a multiple identity *ad*vantage (rather than a "double disadvantage"), drawing support from other women, Latina and non-Latina, as well as from racial/ethnic minority voters, both male and female. Minority women candidates, she noted, have surpassed expectations and have enjoyed dramatically increased electoral success in the past decade, with election rates that now exceed those for white women as compared to their white male counterparts. At the same time, she notes a special challenge they face: "The public may assume that Latina elected officials will favor either their Latino or their female constituents over others, and Latinas must prove their authenticity as representatives." (Bejarano 2013, 136)

Latinas in office may represent diverse constituencies, but many have benefited from association with, and support from, Latino ethnic organizations, both local and national, which support the political interests and aspirations of Latina women. García and Marquez (2001) identified a number of such groups, especially in California, Texas, Florida, and New Mexico. In a study asking why Chicanas and Latinas become politically involved, and how they assess risk and develop self-confidence, García and Marquez hypothesized that Latina women may be motivated by either exogenous or endogenous interests—commitment to particular candidates, policies, and parties; or a sense of community responsibility, personal ambition, and peer expectations. They interviewed fifty-one participants drawn from a national Latina candidate development conference in 1990, and Latina delegates to the 1992 Democratic National Convention. They found a distinctive blending (or bridging) of what they call traditional political motivations (vis-à-vis candidates and policies), and a commitment to their own local communities, and the Chicano/Latino community at large. "In effect," they wrote, "Latinas are entering traditional mainstream politics and bringing with them their experiences from grassroots politics and from their cultural networks and resources. Moreover, participants voiced a concern to 'see others like themselves involved in politics.'" From years of experience, the Latina political actors in the García and Marquez study were also intimately familiar with the risks of political involvement, and among these, named as the most serious (1) financial burdens, (2) invasion of family and personal life, and (3) the risk of compromising (Latino) group values. Yet against these risks, participants expressed a great deal of confidence, that they could secure necessary resources while also serving as a resource and role model for others. In short, the Latina elites represented in García and Marquez were motivated by a synthesis of traditional power and policy goals, and community-oriented aspirations; recognized significant risks in a life of political involvement; but felt abundant confidence that their goals could be achieved and the risks managed successfully (García and Marquez 2001, 117–19).

OUR STUDY PARTICIPANTS AND THEIR POLITICAL ROLES

Based on key findings and research questions from these earlier studies, we designed a questionnaire to tap Rhode Island Latina officials' experiences and attitudes. Our twelve participants were of widely disparate ages and years of experience in public office, but collectively they reflect Rhode Island's rich political history, as experienced by the Latino population, between 1992 and the present. Some of the women in this study are responsible for legislation in the General Assembly, affecting the entire state; others share management of old industrial communities, as city council members; while others have directed state agencies or served on public commissions for state education policy, public housing, and urban parks.

Anastasia Williams, *State Representative—Providence*
Shelby Maldonado, *State Representative—Central Falls*
Stephanie Gonzalez, *City Councilor—Central Falls*
Sandra Cano, *City Councilor—Pawtucket*
Melba Depeña Affigne, *Director, R.I. Department of Human Services*
Patricia Martinez, *(past) Director, R.I. Department of Children, Youth, and Families*
Anna Cano Morales, *(past) R.I. Board of Education*
Marta Martinez, *Member, R.I. Board of Education*

Lammis Vargas, *Director of Unclaimed Property, Office of the R.I. State Treasurer*
Stella Carerra, *Housing Authority Commissioner—Pawtucket*
Jackie Parra, *Housing Authority Commissioner—Central Falls*
Marilyn Cepeda Sanchez, *Parks Commissioner—Providence*

The proportion of elected to appointed officials in the study was close to that for all Latina officials in the state—a third of the women who participated did so as elected officials, closely mirroring the one third of Rhode Island's Latina officials who are in elective office, and two-thirds who hold administrative or commission appointments. One of our subjects was the first person of Hispanic descent, male or female, ever elected to Rhode Island public office. Among other participants can be found the first Guatemalan woman elected to the General Assembly, the first Dominican woman or man (perhaps in the country), to serve in a gubernatorial cabinet as director of a large department, and the youngest Hispanic woman (age 28) ever to serve in the General Assembly.

Our participant pool is less reflective, however, of Rhode Island Latinos' national origins. Seven of our subjects are Colombian American, two are Dominican American, one is Mexican American, one is Panamanian, and one is Guatemalan.

RESEARCH DESIGN, INTERVIEWS, AND CODING CRITERIA

We included questions addressing our specific research goals, and whenever possible, incorporated comparable questions from the Latino National Survey and the interview instrument used by García et al. for *Políticas.* (Our full questionnaire can be found in Appendix A.) Invitation letters were sent to all twenty-six Latinas known to currently or previously serve as elected or appointed officials, in Rhode Island's state and municipal governments. Among these invitees were our newly elected secretary of state (who was unable to participate), state representatives, municipal council and school committee members, appointees to senior administrative positions, and members of state and municipal boards and commissions. In the end, twelve subjects participated in the study.[6] Interviews were scheduled at a time and place of interviewees' choosing, and were conducted in English, Spanish, or both, as the subjects preferred. About 20 percent of the interviews were predominantly in Spanish, with occasional reversion to English; the remainder were predominantly in English, with occasional reversion to Spanish. All subjects were asked the same twenty-four questions, in the same order; each was allowed to speak as extensively, or briefly, as she desired, with only occasional interventions by the interviewer. Minimal guidance was offered to ensure that each question was in fact answered, but in most ways the interviews were subject-driven.

All subjects participated willingly and expressed interest in our research goals. They understood that their reflections and experiences would ultimately appear in a book chapter, to be read by scholars and practitioners—including other Latina leaders like themselves—and that the ultimate purpose of the project was educational. They were informed that responses would be coded anonymously, so that individual subjects could not be identified during the analysis or in publication. Subjects were also invited to demur on questionnaire items for which they perceived any personal or political risk. All interviews were recorded, with subjects' permission, to facilitate an accurate transcription of responses.

When the recorded interviews were transcribed, we encountered the major strength and the major weakness of our interview design. Our twenty-four question items were posed systematically, with the same tone and in the same order, but subjects were invited to offer open-ended responses, and to elaborate even on items which might have been answered with simple binary (yes/no) or categorical statements. This interview design gave our subjects consistent guidance, so the set of individual responses could be compared, and collective emphases observed. This was its great strength. On the other hand, our design choices meant that subjects were free to respond, in English and/or Spanish, in a wide variety of individualized ways. This made it impossible to employ straightforward content comparisons, for example, since different subjects used different words and phrasing to describe essentially the same concept, sometimes employing distinctive idioms, or lapsing between English, and Spanish, unpredictably.

Our solution was to code each subject's twenty-four responses along two dimensions—concept *frequency* and concept *intensity*. For example, a subject might have referred to her own or her family's immigration experience frequently, in response to multiple question items; or might have described that experience fewer times, yet with greater apparent intensity of feeling, or with explicit reference to its great significance in her life. In either case, the emphasis we assigned to that theme would be greater, than for a subject in whose answers immigration appeared less frequently *or* with lesser emphasis.

We divided our twenty-four questions into three thematic groups. Questions were posed to the subjects in order, beginning with personal backgrounds (*Personal Background, Identity, and Civic Engagement*), then exploring current empowerment (*Current Position and Experiences*), and finally, inviting self-assessment (*Reflections on Leadership Roles in Social and*

Political Context). Loosely speaking, these categories correspond to each subject's political past, present, and future.

For our post-interview analysis we consolidated the twenty-four responses by combining related items, yielding thirteen distinct themes. The thirteen themes were:

> *Personal Background, Identity, and Civic Engagement*
>> Subject's prior participation in civic activities
>> Presence and impact of role models and mentors
>> Impact of immigration experiences
>
> *Current Position and Experiences*
>> Impact of identity as *Latina woman* on election or appointment
>> Impact of identity as *a woman* on election or appointment
>> Differing expectations for Latina and non-Latina officials?
>> Subject's reception or perception by peers in office: as a *Latina*
>> Subject's reception or perception by peers in office: as *a woman*
>> Tensions between career and personal life
>
> *Reflections on Leadership Roles in Social and Political Context*
>> Subject as role models for others?
>> Subject's sense of commonality with other Latinos
>> Accessibility of political environment for Latinas
>> Unresolved obstacles to Latina leadership?

To get a clear sense of the various themes' importance in our subjects' understanding of their own trajectories and political roles, we needed to sort them according to estimates of emphasis. To do this, we used our rubric ascribing weight to either frequency or intensity, to assign a score of 1, 2, or 3 (low, medium, or high emphasis) to each subject's response for each item. For each item, scores were assigned after three complete reviews of all twelve recorded interviews. After each iteration of the listening-scoring process, we made occasional adjustments to individual scores, until they reflect as consistently and objectively as we could estimate them, the emphasis our subjects expressed when they talked about various aspects of their backgrounds, identities, and experiences.

Our summary of key findings can be seen in table 9.1. We have rank-ordered themes from high emphasis, to medium, to low.[7] Keeping in mind the usual *caveats* about our small sample, the imprecision of oral language, and the potential for coding bias, consider that these findings represent a close look inside the experiences of Latinas who have enjoyed success in the quest for political power, and who have learned, and continue to learn, the practice and limitations of Latina influence in the current political environment. We believe these are significant findings, many of which replicate findings from earlier work, but some of which

Table 9.1. Summary of Key Findings

Themes	Responses
	High Emphasis
PRIOR PARTICIPATION IN CIVIC ACTIVITIES	• Subjects reported a wide range of formal and informal civic activities throughout young adulthood. • Participants described involvement in school, church, and social/cultural organizations. • A majority of subjects who reported high levels of civic activism were involved in the context of a group; rhetoric surrounding civic activism was rarely individual. • Many participants were reportedly introduced to civic lifestyles through their families.
PRESENCE OF LEADERSHIP ROLE MODELS & MENTORS	• A large majority of participants reported the presence of role models, predominantly family and peers. • Family members consciously and unconsciously served as examples of community engagement and acted as a source of encouragement and support. Mothers were the most commonly cited family members, ascribed the greatest impact. • Peers were the second largest group named as role models for encouraging leadership, and teaching subjects how to navigate the political system through networks and processes,
SUBJECTS AS ROLE MODEL FOR OTHERS	• A majority of the subjects self-identify as role models to other Latinos and youth. • Subjects who did not identify as role models acknowledged that others thought they were role models for the community. • All of the women acknowledged their roles as a "resource" to others in the community who lack professional networks and access to other resources.
SENSE OF COMMONALITY WITH OTHER LATINOS	• All of the Latina subjects reported a sense of overarching commonality with Latinos in Rhode Island and across the country. • All of them cited the origination narrative of Latinos as immigrants to a new country, as a source of commonality. • Some subjects reflected on their own (relatively elite) social and economic positions, as distinct from the majority of Latinos.
	Medium Emphasis
IMPACT OF IDENTITY AS "*LATINA WOMAN*" ON ELECTION OR APPOINTMENT	• Subjects' identity as Latina was considered a *positive* factor, helping them succeed in the appointment / election process. • Most subjects perceived others' expectations (during the selection / election process) that as "Latinas," i.e. Hispanic females, they would better relate to the community, and offer new perspectives.
IMPACT OF IDENTITY AS "*WOMAN*" ON ELECTION OR APPOINTMENT	• Subjects viewed their female identity as a *positive* factor in the success of their election / appointment process. • However, while subjects felt their (gender) identity helped them gain office, they believed their qualifications, relative to other candidates, were a more important factor.

Themes	Responses
TENSIONS BETWEEN CAREER AND PERSONAL LIFE	• Subjects acknowledged an ongoing difficulty, striking a balance between their personal and their professional / political lives. • Many reported this balance was achieved through support of family and partners. • Few of the subjects reported feeling guilt over sacrifices they made in regards to their family.
DIFFERING EXPECTATIONS FOR LATINA AND NON-LATINA WOMEN	• Once in office, subjects reported that expectations / standards for them were higher and more acutely felt, than for other (non-Latina) women in comparable positions. • Compared to white female counterparts, these Latina subjects felt their competency was always in question. Participants felt they had to constantly prove themselves. • Expectations from Latino communities were often unrealistic, with a demand for fast policy results, and jobs for supporters.
RECEPTION OR PERCEPTION BY PEERS: AS A "LATINA"	• The subjects reported that their identity as a Latina resulted in an increased level of scrutiny by peers in office. • Increased scrutiny forced subjects to constantly prove their abilities and intelligence, in spite of advanced degrees and proven track records.
Low Emphasis	
IMMIGRATION EXPERIENCE	• Typically, subjects did not emphasize their immigration experiences, generally mentioning them in passing, in the form of personal anecdotes. • Even when mentioned, immigration experiences did not play a very prominent role in subjects' personal stories.
RECEPTION OR PERCEPTION BY PEERS: AS A "WOMAN"	• Most subjects felt their identity as a woman did not have a negative effect on their reception and perception in office, distinct from their identity as a *Latina* woman. In addition, some noted a generally greater acceptance of women in politics.
MORE ACCESSIBLE POLITICAL ENVIRONMENT FOR LATINAS	• Subjects gave some credence to the idea that the political environment had changed for Latinas, but not dramatically. • To the extent political contexts have improved for Latinas, subjects believed the shift was due to the emergence of Latinas as political actors; in other words, the causality went like this: Latina emergence => improved environment, not the other way around.
UNRESOLVED OBSTACLES TO LATINA LEADERSHIP	• At the state and national levels, subjects perceive the most important unresolved obstacles to Latina political leadership to be disparities in formal education, income, and access to resources. • Subjects considered the difficulty of campaign fundraising to be a key obstacle for Latinas in achieving greater political leadership.

are surprising and seem to offer new answers to longstanding questions about which Latinas achieve political power, how they do so, and what obstacles may remain. In the discussion which follows we explore these implications and provide representative excerpts from the interviews, to illustrate our findings in our subjects' own words.

THE RECRUITMENT TRAJECTORY

The first step on a prospective Latina leader's path to empowerment is her decision to become involved in politics in the first place, leading at some later date to a successful electoral campaign, or nomination to an appointed position. Yet this decision typically comes at the end of a long process of socialization and engagement. This *recruitment trajectory* varies by individual, and we gave each subject an opportunity to identify those aspects of her experience, which made her later leadership possible.

THE ROOTS OF LEADERSHIP IN PRIOR CIVIC ACTIVITY

The single theme most emphasized by our subjects was the importance of prior involvement in some form of community organization, neighborhood or ethnic association, or other civic forum, where they learned leadership skills, networked with like-minded people, and became more familiar with community interests. For many subjects, early experiences in youth were most important.

In fact, all twelve of our subjects reported prior involvement in civic activities during youth and early adulthood. The activities varied, including both political involvement in campaigns and volunteering in nonpartisan community-based organizations. A number of subjects reported multiple forms of civic activity, but most frequently mentioned membership and involvement with neighborhood organizations and schools. Church activism was also noted by a smaller subset of interviewees, but even this was described as a springboard for larger community aspirations.

Significantly, ten of the twelve subjects defined civic engagement in the context of *groups*. In other words, our participants seldom described activism on an individual level, but identified their prior civic engagement as embedded in a larger network. One subject explained her preference for group-based engagement:

> I either become part of the organization or have formed different organizations along the way. I believe in the power of teamwork and often times individuals do stand out as the leader on one particular issue, but you will

always find that there is somebody behind them, so everything I did was through groups. (*State Appointee*)

Those subjects who reported prior civic engagement *not* in the context of groups, defined their activities in social entrepreneurial terms. For example, one subject described her activism promoting social and cultural awareness:

I introduced people to my culture. I was tired of people asking about my culture so I turned it around and tried to educate and raise awareness about diversity and what it means. It was simple and subtle; I would bring Spanish songs in church when I went to mass. (*State appointee*)

Though this activism was on a more individual level, her desire to teach others led this subject to another sort of group experience; she would informally hold dinners in her college dorm and share her culture with peers who were unfamiliar with it.

Our subjects' levels of civic activism were also gauged by asking whether or not they had written or contacted a government official to voice a concern. As it turned out, subjects were evenly distributed in their responses. Half the participants reported that they had contacted a government official to voice concerns, while the other half reported never doing so. For two of our subjects, this contact with government took the form of public testimony before legislative bodies. One described her activities this way:

Testifying on particular legislation or in support of a bill, was part of my academic training. I remember we learned how to write legislation and testimony for the state house. Yes. Writing letters, picking up the phone, advocating, but always through a group, like Planned Parenthood, with some kind of agenda. (*Municipal appointee*)

Another subject reported a similar experience testifying on behalf of *Progreso Latino*, the state's oldest Latino advocacy and community service agency. Testifying was one of the forms of gaining direct access and contact with political officials. Working through organizations with political agendas gave our subjects experience advocating for public policies, while helping them understand nuances of the political process.

Finally, about one-fourth of our subjects indicated that after gaining experience working within existing groups, they then went on to found their own new organizations. These include *Fundacion Esperanza*, the Latina Leadership Institute, and *Quisqueya en Accion*. These initiatives served several related purposes; one was to bring Latinas—as women—together. During one interview, a subject declared that she "saw the need for women to be more connected," exactly the motivation of the women who founded the Latina Leadership Institute. At the same time, women who founded organizations serving the broader Latino community did so because they recognized the need for Latinos, both men and women, to be more united for social and political progress. And, several subjects noted that individual and group success was simply more achievable through the efforts of groups. One participant stated,

> You don't have to be a college graduate, or speak English. But this organiza-
> tion gives you access to resources, to let you know where you can find help
> and advocate for what you believe in. We have rights and many Latinos
> don't know. *(State appointee)*

Still, we need to understand *why* our subjects took on community responsibilities, when so many of their peers did not. Most frequently, it was the influence of family norms and practices, as well as cultural expectations, which our subjects cited as the sources of their commitment to community engagement. Fully one-fourth emphasized the crucial role of family expectations and traditions in fostering civic engagement. With these personal and family histories, they described civic participation as "natural" and "a way of life." One subject recalled that she had been very involved in school and neighborhood activities as a child in her native country, and when she found a peer group in the United States who shared her interests, she became more involved here as well:

> I thought that I would continue that kind of participation in school [in the
> U.S.], but I had a very difficult time adjusting. I didn't fit into the culture. I
> found a niche and other people that had similar experiences as very recent
> immigrants. We felt marginalized but that brought us together and we par-
> ticipated in things. *(State appointee)*

Mobilizing to found new organizations, testifying for public policies, or volunteering in communities at home or abroad, these women represent a broad spectrum of civic engagement, typical amongst Latina leaders nationwide. Their civic engagement before rising to positions of public power is consistent with findings from earlier studies, which traced a clear trajectory from community activist to public official.

THE IMPORTANCE OF ROLE MODELS AND MENTORS

Because there are still comparatively few Hispanic public officials, and among these only a small number are women, Latinas who aspire to political office may have few role models and few experienced mentors. Logically, this could present a serious problem for prospective Latina leaders.

Aspirants to political careers, like any other demanding, high-status profession, must first imagine themselves in such a role. Similarly, those who can identify and learn from experienced and well-connected mentors may be more successful than those who enjoy no such sponsorship and support.

Thus when we planned our study, we hypothesized that if role models played a part in our subjects' political ascent, those role models would be Hispanic, and they would be people well versed in political process. Indeed we did find that as expected, our subjects attributed much of their success to examples set by role models, and the support and encouragement of mentors. But the most common exemplars and mentors turned out *not* to be exclusively Latino, nor were they typically politically prominent individuals. Instead, our subjects reported that average people around them, that is, family members and peers in the community, offered the most encouragement on the road to leadership. And outside the family, non-Hispanics were just as likely to be named as role models and mentors, as were Hispanics.

> My first mentor is my mom and my second is my sister. Her vision allowed us to develop leadership skills. Whether it was organizing car washes, banquets, or walks against legislation. I also learned from my friends [*subject names a male Latino state legislator, and a male Latino city councilor*] . . . but my greatest mentors are my mom and sister. (*Municipal appointee*)

Upon reflection, this is not surprising. After all, it seems likely that the first successful representatives of marginalized groups may be compelled to achieve political leadership via unconventional routes, since existing pathways to power may not be easily accessible to groups who have previously *had* few representatives in office. Thus the question of role models and mentors, a theme to which our subjects assigned nearly as great an emphasis as they did for prior civic engagement, yielded somewhat unexpected results. A number of our subjects reported that *organizations* served in the capacity of "mentors," by providing group resources, advice, and encouragement from organizational veterans, and an opportunity to experience both the perils and promise of leadership, even if only at the organizational or neighborhood level. A small number also cited historical figures (e.g., Rigoberta Menchu). By far the most important influences, however, were ascribed to families and community peers.

Three-quarters of our subjects reported that key family members played decisive roles in shaping them as leaders and inculcating the values of community service. About half named non-family peers who provided examples of leadership, and who continued to provide guidance and advice as mentors, even after the subjects had begun to achieve influence in their own right.

Mothers, fathers, and siblings were named as the most important individuals who influenced our subjects' involvement and helped them decide to participate and become leaders in the community. These findings are similar to those reported by Jones-Correa, who found that family members often acted as the first mentors to Latinas, introducing them to a political and civic-minded lifestyle (Jones-Correa 1998, 342). Some of our participants described deliberate efforts by their families to involve them in leadership roles, even if these were initially only informal activities. Encouragement to help organize events for a community group, for example, was cited as one such deliberate family practice. Other interviewees described a more serendipitous process, in which parents inculcated values of service and collaborative work, often by example, that would make leadership roles attractive as subjects came into adulthood. On one occasion a subject described her parents' influence by saying,

> I can't really pinpoint where it started, because I didn't really have anyone saying this is the way to do it, or you should become a leader. But the more I think about it, the more I think about my family. My father was very active in politics and my mom was very vocal at home . . . though they certainly didn't *intend* to raise a woman who was going to be participating in politics! *(State Appointee)*

In this case her role models may not have realized they were teaching her the ways of community activism through example. Her outspoken mother was clearly a step or two away from a traditional image of the Latina woman, said to stand on the sidelines of family and community discourse. Likewise, our subject's father engaged her in conversations about politics, teaching her by example that her opinion was of interest and important. In the existing literature on Latina leadership, the role of the family is often understated relative to the influence of community leaders, but in our interviews the ordering was reversed, indicating that informal role models, especially parents and other elders, may have a greater impact for many Latina leaders than community leaders or peers. In particular, mothers were frequently cited as sources of relentless support, and as examples of perseverance.

This is not to say that our subjects did not find role models in the community. On the contrary, a number of participants who cited family also mentioned peers who helped them navigate the political scene. In these responses, subjects suggested that peers had influenced the nature of the subjects' leadership today through encouragement, but also by example, or in a much more directive way. One respondent described her role model,

Juanita Sanchez [*a Dominican community leader in the 1970s and 1980s, who has since passed away*]. She was the one who literally pushed me and dragged me. . . . She knew the ins and outs about Rhode Island and said, "This is what you need to do." *(State Appointee)*

In this case, the subject experienced Rhode Island leadership and politics through the eyes of another Latina. As with this example, the support and network of associations that Latinas provide one another became evident in the interviews. In fact, many of our subjects named *one another* as role models!

Significantly, in another divergence from the existing literature, a number of our participants ascribed key mentoring roles to non-Hispanic men. One such white man, who is now a senior state official, was singled out for recognition by a subject who described him as the kind of person who worked to empower others. For another subject, key support and encouragement came from a senior Democratic party official, from a powerful Irish-American political family. Another subject described how her (white male) role model actually recruited her to run for office:

The one that encouraged me to take on this political role was [*a powerful male Italo-American political operative*]. There were other minority officials but they never came forward with the opportunity to run. Being a non-minority was instrumental in being a mentor to me. *(State Representative)*

Finally, about a third of our subjects also ascribed to an organization, not just individuals, a key role exposing the subject to politics and teaching her how to navigate the political environment, access resources, and grow her personal network. Those subjects reported that such organizations, including *Quisqueya en Accion*, the Latina Leadership Institute, *Progreso Latino*, and the Rhode Island Foundation, were responsible for a degree of their success. In some cases, moreover, as with the Latina Leadership Institute, the mission of identifying, training, and mentoring Latinas to become leaders was an explicit goal of the organization.

In sum, the impact of role models and mentoring is more complex than expected, and occasionally counter-intuitive. All twelve of our subjects related important experiences with at least one role model who acted as a guide, informally or formally, to learn the political process. None of the subjects claimed sole responsibility for her own rise to power. All described this trajectory as being powerfully influenced by others, including family members, especially mothers, who inculcated values of service and leadership; sponsors and mentors both Latino and non-Latino, women and men, who provided resources, advice, political connections, and opportunities to practice leadership; and peers in the community including influential Latinas, whose political engagement was at the neighborhood or "Latino community" level.

Though a majority of the group emphatically identified families as the main source of political socialization and encouragement, they also made frequent reference to peers and influential women in the community. In short, our findings suggest that while families may shape characters and values, and habits of civic engagement, in adulthood Latina leaders are those women who have been able to identify and engage with community peers and organizations, as well as women and men who are already in positions of knowledge and influence, and who are willing to share resources and support Latinas' emergence as leaders in their own right. Our subjects, after all, are those women who have *successfully* navigated the political process, to be elected or appointed to positions of public power; in all likelihood, the existence of role models and mentors, for these women and not for others, is a key factor explaining why some aspirants succeed in achieving political influence—while others do not.

PERSONAL AND PROFESSIONAL TENSIONS

A common theme in existing literature on Latinas in leadership is the idea that patriarchal Hispanic cultures, traditional family structures, and judgmental community standards conspire to create special challenges for politically engaged Latinas. These challenges can manifest as extreme tension between familial and professional responsibilities. Takash (1993) and García et al. (2008) discovered feelings of guilt among Latina officials over neglected familial duties, and on the part of others, resistance to their leadership roles based on stereotypes about the incompatibility of public service and family commitments. To test the validity of these claims, we included a questionnaire item inquiring about the balance our subjects had achieved between "personal relationships with family and loved ones, and professional lives." As with our inquiry about role models and mentors, our findings here were mixed and somewhat different from expectations based on prior research. The conventional narrative did emerge, to be sure:

> I have not quite been able to strike that balance. Though I have been lucky to have a support system. As a mother and a wife I often feel resentful because I know I have to be at events. *(State Appointee)*

As public leaders, participants in this study lead extremely busy lives with competing demands on their time from their political careers and their personal obligations. Compartmentalizing personal and professional life in order to give full attention to one or the other, as needed, is difficult for most people and often impossible. Women in particular, especially women with children, can feel these conflicting demands acutely, as a result of their desire to fulfill satisfying and successful maternal roles in the family setting, but also to command public opinion through their roles in public office (Takash 1993). Unlike most other professions public officials, whether elected or appointed, live in a world which frequently extends far beyond the desk and the office; to garner and maintain support in their communities or with their superiors, public officials find attendance at special events, fundraisers, and political meetings, for example, critical to maintaining their positions. Being visible and accessible is important to constituents, who favor accountability and transparency. With such an array of external responsibilities, leaders often find themselves compromising some aspect of their lives. For the subjects we interviewed this proved to be, as expected, a challenge—but one which they say they are meeting through careful time management and support from families and friends.

In fact, without prompting, a large majority of subjects used the words "balance" and "organization" to describe how they prioritize demands on their time. Striking this balance, they all admitted, required a conscious effort. One official described an ongoing struggle, noting that sometimes it is the political commitments, which must be sacrificed:

> Balance is something that I have to practice every day. I am reminded by my aging mother and my children that I need to enjoy my family and me. If I say no to an event I'm disappointing someone. (*Municipal Appointee*)

This is significantly different from the conventional understanding, in which Latina officials are said to feel guilt when failing to meet their family obligations; in this case, to the contrary, our subject feels that family commitments have trumped political expectations, and feels guilty on that account. Her discomfort arises from the context of the situation, in which young professionals had invited her to meet, to provide advice and career guidance. When she could not be there for them, she felt she had failed an important aspect of her role as a public servant.

In general, we found that guilt appeared infrequently in our subjects' responses, rarely figuring into discussions of how they balanced demands of politics and family. Most of our subjects are mothers, and as expected maternal responsibilities were complicated by responsibilities to the public. Only two of the women mentioned guilt at all, but even they opted to view their absences from the home in a positive light; one recalled that,

My children were the victims [*with a laugh*]. But I have a great husband who has always supported me. My children grew up with a service-oriented environment that values equality. At that level, it was difficult because I have to go to this event, and make dinner, but my husband helped. My children can see what I did and how I grew. (*Municipal Appointee*)

While this interviewee feels the tension in her roles acutely, she also believes, and takes comfort in that conviction, that her work is instrumental to teaching her children and other youth a greater lesson about life and public service.

This subject also raised another important consideration in how Latina officials can work toward balance between their public and private lives; she acknowledged the importance of her husband's support. A number of other interviewees recalled similar situations, noting as one did that her husband's support meant he would be there for their children on those occasion when she could not be there physically. Another subject reported that bsoth her mother and her husband provided crucial support in helping raise their children. She recognizes that in some ways, it is her husband who defies conventions:

We kinda joke sometimes that I have a really great wife because he is a great husband, wife, and mother. (*Municipal Appointee*)

Not all of our subjects were married, nor did all have children. Even for these unmarried women, however, romantic relationships were equally stressed by demanding political careers. And when they imagine how their lives might look should they someday start families, they anticipate dilemmas they don't currently face. One speculated on future prospects saying,

Right now I don't have kids or a family, and right now I don't think I could handle both [*family and career*]. I would have to let one or the other go. (*Elected Official*)

For all of our subjects, whether married or not, one common approach has been to include spouses, partners, or children in political events whenever possible. Another way tensions between political leadership and family life are managed is by maintaining a circle of friends, comprised of other women in the same situation. One subject noted that her most important network of friends is comprised of other women who are just as busy and just as involved in leadership, as herself. During one interview, a state official confided how she kept her marriage alive and well during the busiest years of her career:

It is important to make your partner a part of the social aspect of the job. The minute you separate your life and job, then you begin to forget there is some responsibility to make [*your spouse*] feel as though they are involved. (*State Appointee*)

To reiterate: Our inquiries about potential tension between public and private obligations produced findings, which both confirm but also complicate what has been previously reported. Our subjects do in fact experience anticipated challenges achieving an acceptable balance among their various roles as public officials, community leaders, role models for others, wives, mothers, daughters, partners, and friends. They struggle to meet all of their responsibilities without sacrificing more than their families, constituents, or agencies can bear. They confront competing expectations from those closest to them, and from the broader community, expectations which sometimes conflict with their own understanding of the responsibilities they have accepted.

At the same time, however, participants in our study seem less troubled by feelings of guilt about these conflicts, and more confident in their abilities to manage everything with an acceptable degree of compromise and accommodation. They frequently involve families in public activities; use aggressive time management and scheduling techniques to avoid conflicts; rely on several support networks including parents, siblings, spouses, and friends; and on occasion, with little apparent remorse, simply decline invitations to outside events and activities.

These interviews are testament to the multiple roles women manage while serving in public office, and to the diverse strategies they have adopted to resolve tensions while preserving both family life and political status. In particular, our subjects make clear that for some, achieving balance is possible without guilt. We cannot know whether this finding reflects a new, more confident style of Latina political leadership which has actually transcended older patterns of gendered expectations—or is an artifact of our research design and interview process. In any event, we find this to be a striking divergence from previous research, and a promising avenue for future inquiry.

Photo 9.1.   Like many Latina officials, Providence Councilwoman Sabina Matos (center), frequently takes her children with her to political and community events. Here they are pictured with Rhode Island governor Gina Raimondo, walking along La Broa (Broad Street) at the Dominican Festival and Parade. Photo © 2015 Patrick Ward.

EXPECTATIONS AND STEREOTYPES

Gaining Office: Ethnic and Gender Identity as Resource and Constraint

> This department never had a Latina director. I think that made a huge impact because I bring the community factor and I am bilingual. Language is a huge asset. We are the next big thing. We are the next Irish and Polish community. (*State Appointee*)

In some ways the struggles of Irish, Polish, and other white ethnic communities during their early years of immigration are mirrored among today's Latinos. In other ways, the Latino experience is distinctive, especially for its speed, its breadth, and its racial aspects. Our earlier discussion of Rhode Island Latinas' social and economic environment makes clear that Latinas today face economic as well as political marginalization. The ascent of Latina public officials offers hope for improvement in areas where government action can affect social conditions, but only if aspirants for political office can win those offices fairly, and perform their duties effectively. We wanted to know whether our Latina subjects felt their dual identity—Hispanic, and female—was a help or a hindrance, in winning election or appointment to office.

Women of color have sometimes been cast as confronting a dual disadvantage, so that Hispanic females, for example, would suffer consequences of both sexism and racism. On the other hand, Hardy-Fanta (1997 and 2002) and Bejarano (2013) both found that Latinas perform comparatively well in electoral contests. Bejarano, in fact, has argued that women of color, particularly Latinas, enjoy a multiply *ad*vantaged position. We asked our subjects their perceptions of how dual Hispanic-female identity affected their electoral prospects, or their selection for appointed office. Our findings were more mixed here than for subjects' assessment of prior civic engagement, or the importance of role models and mentors, but in general terms the pattern was clear: On balance, our subjects felt their identities as Hispanic females—*Latinas*—were more of an advantage than a disadvantage. Our findings parallel Bejarano's. Moreover, some of our subjects felt that female gender alone was a more significant positive factor, if only because government officialdom is so overwhelmingly male.

> I think being a woman helped because it has been and is a pretty male dominated field. . . . I think my gender had more to do with it, because your first thought when you look at me is that I am African American. (*Elected Official*)

Overall, more than half of our subjects thought their gender was a positive factor in being considered for an appointment and running for office. A number of them reported a positive reception as women, because voters and appointing authorities assumed that as women, they would bring new perspectives to their public roles. One municipal board member proposed that women have an entirely different approach to problem solving, which makes them attractive candidates for public office. Women, according to her, focus more than men do on details of policy, and are more willing to foster teamwork in the community.

Many of our subjects could not separate their gender and Latino ethnic identities neatly. "Latina" identity carries a number of cultural and racial connotations in addition to gender, which may be considered positive factors during the election or appointment process. Latinas, by this reasoning, are able to identify with constituents who are women, and others who are not white, because neither group sees its interests represented by the conventional white male in public office (Fraga et al. 2006). One of our subjects recounted how being Latina affected her appointment process,

> There was just no diversity there, so both my gender as a woman and my ethnicity as a Latina, the fact that I was young and the fact that I was a not a lawyer or a judge, helped. I was a Rhode Islander who worked as a social worker and has an opinion about everything. *(State Appointee)*

According to this woman's account of her confirmation process, despite ideological differences and partisan opposition, her identity as a Latina smoothed over legislators' concerns. By approving her appointment, legislators ensured that her fellow board members would enjoy the benefits of more diversity of opinion and experience. Our subjects who ran for (and won) elective office reported that their female gender, and Latino ethnicity, gave them opportunities to connect more easily with their constituents. During canvassing, one found herself reconnecting with people she had known in childhood, including both Latino and non-Latino classmates. Bilingualism and shared experiences, she recounted, made both groups of prospective constituents feel they were gaining an accessible representative to serve their interests in public office. Latinas offer the prospect of representing two separate but closely knit identities that are very much lacking in public office.

However, a number of our subjects, both elected and appointed, noted the risk of being treated as mere "window dressing." Some who raised this caution are among the more seasoned leaders in the state, and their observations have weight; Latinas may be equipped with the knowledge and education to win office and succeed in government but as one reported, arrangements of power in the legislature, or other bodies, may be "orchestrated" to ensure that Latinas have little actual influence on political outcomes. This observation suggests that while Latinas may be desirable for the diversity they bring to the face of government, once in office their influence may be limited. One subject declared, "I think about my role as a Latina and what difference I can make. I don't accept [appointment] to just be a body." Refusing to be window dressing, and being aware of this possibility, makes it possible for Latinas to devote themselves to roles which are potentially meaningful—for them, and for the broader Latino community.

Serving in Office: High Expectations—and Even Higher Standards

In a political environment where white males predominate and minority officeholders appear in small numbers, and where a socially and economically disadvantaged Latino community expects dramatic achievements from its representatives in government, Latinas encounter serious obstacles to achieving policy and personal goals. Both elected and appointed Latinas face strong pressure from their peers in public office, as well as from their community. Peers expect them to bring new perspectives to their duties, and credibility to government institutions, while not making established officials uncomfortable, nor challenging existing arrangements of power. Constituents and communities expect them to satisfy sometimes competing demands for attention, access, policy change and, in the oldest tradition of American local politics—individual benefits for supporters, donors, and friends.

To gauge Latinas' lives in office, and describe how they experience and manage expectations, we employed questions to assess how they were received, and perceived, by peers and constituents. This set of questions brought to light two main themes that were significant for their intensity, namely, community and peer expectations and standards of performance. Seventy-five percent of our subjects reported that once in office, the expectations for them were higher and more demanding, compared to their non-Latina peers or others who formerly held their position. Our participants reported strong pressures to prove themselves "twice over" to peers and community. One official succinctly described this experience,

> In a perfect world we should all be held to the same standards, but as Latinas there are certain things we have to double-prove. *(Elected Official)*

As Latinas, our subjects reported, they are held to a higher standard than non-Latina counterparts in similar and equivalent positions, making them feel as though they need to repeatedly demonstrate their competence and their value as public servants. One source of pressure and higher expectations originates within their own peer group. Consciously, or unconsciously, colleagues in public office frequently and unabashedly question and test Latinas, seeking proof that they are in fact qualified for the elected or appointed positions they hold. Due to the fact that many of our subjects were not born in the United States, language proficiency becomes a major issue challenging them to continually demonstrate their qualifications and their understanding of topics relevant to their work.

> When they told me about the position I said, "but my accent!" Despite my accent, I study and read. . . . I have to prove myself twice over . . . because if you fail as a Latina, it's as if the whole community fails. (*Municipal Appointee*)

Many Latinas, due to their unique trajectories into public office, do not hold the same credentials as their peers. Our subjects, however, are better educated than most. Eighty-three percent have earned bachelor's degrees, and 68 percent hold master's degrees. This is an extraordinarily well-educated group of Latinas, in a state where only 3.6 percent of Latinos, and just 12.6 percent of the overall population, hold graduate or professional degrees. One subject noted that her peers will frequently ask her to repeat herself, but even more annoyingly, some will speak slowly to "make sure she understands" what they say—although she is the only member of that body to hold a master's degree! Despite our subjects' extraordinary level of preparation in regards to education, they believe their competency and capabilities in office are always open to question by colleagues.

Still, these Latinas seem intent on finding what silver linings they can; one participant described multiple experiences showing she was subject to greater scrutiny and skepticism, with respect to her qualifications and preparation, but she then recounted how being the focus of attention ironically gave her an opportunity to inject new ideas into the group discourse.

> First of all I'm the youngest, second, I'm a Latina woman. So there's definitely the opportunity to let them think of things that they wouldn't think of. I put forth a resolution and the perspective changed and they all supported it. My actions made them think, "Oh, why didn't I think of that?" (*Elected Official*)

Our subjects experience elements of their identity as both positive and negative, at the same time. This subject's youth was a detriment, because it meant she was inexperienced in the eyes of her peers. Yet in her reception as a Latina, she reported a positive response because, she said, her colleagues were looking for someone like her, "diverse," educated, and ultimately in touch with the community. Despite this potentially advantageous expectation, in the end it was her very identity as a Latina woman that made colleagues question her competency and comprehension of matters at hand.

In the end, our Latina officials found their identities as women, and as Hispanics, to be somewhat advantageous during the election/selection process, but substantially *less* advantageous in actually performing the duties of their positions. Rhode Island's political institutions seem more amenable to admitting Latinas to positions of nominal influence than to empowering them when they arrive.

ROLE MODELS FOR THE COMMUNITY

The importance of role models, as we have seen, was a significant theme in our subjects' narratives of trajectories to political leadership. While not all of their role models were political operatives, those who were empowered others through sharing political knowledge and access to influence. Our questionnaire included an item to help gauge our subjects' sense of their own leadership influence, by asking whether they acknowledged their position as a role model for other Latinas. Our subjects, today city councilors, state and municipal appointees, as well as state representatives, hold similar positions as those role models who once inspired them. Our results show that many of these women do in fact recognize, for better or worse, that they are in a position to provide the same mentoring which was so important in their own development as leaders. One subject described her intention to empower other women—and men:

> I am a very strong vocal individual, and I believe in empowering more females—and the guys as well—but I believe I am a force to be reckoned with. Are you hungry enough? Let's go get it! This is a country filled with choices and opportunities. If you want it—if you can think it, if you can dream it . . . You can go after it. *(State Representative)*

In fact, 75 percent of our subjects agreed—generally with enthusiasm—that they were, in fact, role models for other Latinas. Only one subject indicated strong reluctance, revealing that she had to grow into this responsibility, slowly overcoming her discomfort with the title, but ultimately embracing the role as one which came as a matter of course, like it or not, with any position of leadership in the Latino community.

Most of our subjects, however, accepted their responsibilities as role models, saying they felt a special obligation as a minority among largely white leaders, to use their power to set positive examples, especially to youths in the state's urban communities. Two subjects reported actively seeking mentorship opportunities, returning to their former schools to speak about their life experiences. Another described returning to her high school to speak about how she was able to defy expectations, not through luck but through hard work and effort. Another explained her hope for the future of Rhode Island's leaders, hoping to encourage youth to pursue ambitions here within the state, instead of seeking opportunities outside of Rhode Island. Another subject declared,

I hope [I'm a role model]! If not, what am I doing? I don't want to be doing this all my life. I take this opportunity to share my story; it means that you yourself can do this. I don't have a special wand. . . . I encourage being a person of willingness and taking that step forward to take up those positions. We're not there forever and politicians don't like to hear that. *(State Representative)*

This subject, like several others, saw the importance of setting an example for other Latinos, especially youth, who struggle to develop confident and positive identities in financially stressed and educationally underserved communities. Having risen from equally challenging positions themselves, these Latina leaders see themselves as living testaments to the promise of hard work and community engagement.

Not every one of our subjects saw their leadership responsibilities in this light, however. Some chose to opt out of the "role model" label completely. One said it was a "cliché" to even discuss role models. Instead, these women identified themselves as resources, particularly to youth. One, reflecting on her role as a public leader, said:

I see myself as a resource, making sure I see my role in life and as a Latina as an opportunity to open doors because many people don't have the networks and resources to help themselves . . . so instead of being a role model, I like to call people I know and say here are four or five resumes. *(State appointee)*

By providing help and resources to rising professionals, even leaders who do not consider themselves "role models" described experiences just as rewarding, and just as meaningful to their beneficiaries, as those who prefer to see themselves as role models. In the end, no matter what label they choose, these Latina leaders' positions and influence allow them to share access to otherwise inaccessible networks and opportunities.

CONCLUSION: "A FORCE TO BE RECKONED WITH"

The two thousand or so Latinas in elective office, and several thousand more who serve in senior appointive positions, represent the first cohorts of what promises to be a growing population of Hispanic women exercising power in the nation's local, state, and federal governments. Although the socio-economic distress facing Rhode Island's broader Latina population may be extreme, Latinas everywhere face marginalization in politics and society. If growing numbers of Latina officials find ways to overcome their own marginalization *within* government agencies they serve, we may see improvements in the lives of Latinas everywhere. What evidence does this study offer, to gauge whether such progress will occur?

On balance, our interviews identified a number of areas for concern, especially the condescending way Latina officials are sometimes treated by colleagues in government, the persistence of patriarchal standards and expectations, and the challenges of fundraising and mobilization among low-income constituencies—but more importantly, we identified several features of the Latina leadership experience which give cause for optimism.

First, we found that Latina leaders in Rhode Island were deeply grounded in the wide range of community-based organizations which constitute the core social capital of Latino communities. Our Latina leaders demonstrated familiarity and respect for these institutions, which promises to keep them connected to constituencies they serve. Similarly, we found a strong sense of commonality with other Latinos, even among leaders who recognized that their own educational and occupational status set them apart from the Latino population at large, and especially from the most desperate of the state's low-income Latinas with children—the very poorest of the poor in Rhode Island.

Second, we found that role models and mentors, from within the Latino community and without, have been crucial influences on Latina political leaders, and somewhat surprisingly, these mentors have sometimes been extremely well-connected "mainstream," that is, white and male, political operatives; but even more frequently, they have been family members and peers who inculcated strong values of community service and civic engagement. Again, this reality seems to suggest that for the time being at least, our Latina leaders can remain both grounded and well-connected.

Third, we found that many of our Latina leaders see themselves as role models, accepting all the responsibilities that status suggests. Even those who reject the "role model" terminology as a cliché still express commitment to serving the next generation of Latina leaders, in some tangible way, accepting that extra duty as a concurrent obligation to the formal responsibilities of their offices.

Finally, and in some ways most surprising of all, we found that while most of our participants experienced significant tension between their personal and family responsibilities on the one hand, and their public, professional duties on the other, most have found ways to manage those tensions successfully. With support from spouses, partners, family and friends, they are managing to balance competing demands on their time and attention and—unlike subjects in previous studies—many are apparently doing so with minimal feelings of guilt, shame, or personal failure.

Should our findings represent real patterns and practices among Latina leaders in Rhode Island and elsewhere, then that is very promising news indeed. Grounded and connected in constituent communities; sharing a sense of common purpose with Latinos at large; networking successfully with other Latino and non-Latino leaders and allies; taking responsibility for mentoring the next generation of leaders; and balancing the needs of families, friends, communities, and the public; if Latinas in power can continue to do all of these things, even as the needs and demands of Latino constituents grow more urgent and more complex—then Latina leaders will surely continue to be "A Force to Be Reckoned With."

NOTES

1. Data for Latino/a representation are from LatinasRepresent, a joint project of two Hispanic NGOs, Political Parity and the National Hispanic Leadership Agenda. A factsheet is available here: http://www.latinasrepresent.org/wp/wp-content/uploads/2015/02/LatinasRepresent_Factsheets.pdf.

2. Nearly 20 years earlier, Hardy-Fanta had discovered the same thing; in elections across Massachusetts, Latina women were more successful candidates than Latino men (Hardy-Fanta 1997).

3. Even for married couples with children, the racial differences in poverty rates is striking. For white couples, 3.5 percent; for Black couples, 15.7 percent, but for Latinos—32.4 percent.

4. Compared to white males, Hispanic females in Rhode Island are 8 times more likely to work in "health care support," and 5 times more likely to work in "personal care and service." White males, on the other hand, are 30 times as likely as Hispanic females to be architects or engineers, 10 times more likely to work in transportation, and 9 times more likely to work in "natural resources, construction, and maintenance." (U.S. Census Bureau; 2013 American Community Survey 1-Year Estimates, *Table B240101*). Industrial jobs, which once offered relatively high wages for immigrant men and women, no longer predominate in Rhode Island's labor market. Just 10 percent of the state's white workers are employed in manufacturing, and 16 percent of Hispanic workers.

5. Similar wage inequality can be seen for Black men and women (mean earnings of $42,301 and $35,639), and for Latino men ($39,639), compared to mean earnings for white men ($74,338). White women in Rhode Island, at $56,102, earn significantly more than all categories of minority women and men, but their earnings are still only 75 cents on the dollar compared to white men. Yet here again, Latinas suffer the greatest earnings inequality of all—earning just 45 cents to each dollar earned by white men.

6. Rhode Island is a small state, and many of the participants were known personally to one or both researchers; Affigne has been involved for many years in Latino community organizations and activities, while Gonzalez has worked as a volunteer programming assistant for Rhode Island Latino Public Radio, where she became known to many of our subjects—one of whom is married to Affigne. To minimize confidentiality concerns, Gonzalez conducted all of the interviews and anonymized all transcripts.

7. Average emphasis scores for the twelve themes ranged from a high of 2.66 (prior participation in civic activities), to a low of 1.83 (unresolved obstacles to Latina empowerment), on a three-point scale. For our interpretation of these findings, see the discussion.

TEN

Latina Differential Consciousness and Race-Gendering in Texas' Legislative Process

Patricia D. López

The Texas State Legislature is arguably the most powerful branch of government in the state. A key to examining this context lies in the ability to disentangle diverse ways of knowing. An understanding of this process reveals a glaring distinction between whose knowledge matters and whose knowledge does not in policymaking (López 2012). This knowledge hierarchy is not unique to external actors—such as civil rights organizations, educators, parents, and so forth—but is also very much present among policy elites. What you say, relative to who you are, matters. In many instances Latinas are positioned at the lower end of this knowledge hierarchy during policy debates.

To contextualize the environment in which this study takes place, a few important points about the legislature are warranted. First, the Texas State Legislature convenes in regular sessions for just 140 days beginning in January of every odd-numbered year. From the outset, this governmentality produces institutional constraints that prompt an overreliance on external and individual-centered "pockets of expertise" (Burns et al. 2008), and a space where some actors are "in the know" while others—including elected officials and their staff—are attentive, at best, or spectators, at worst (López et al. 2011). These issues of institutional capacity add further complexity to the viability of policy agendas gaining momentum. When it comes time for legislators to convene and weigh in on policy decisions, the system is designed to either obstruct the passage of legislation, or in many cases, produce piecemeal policy.

Governmentality—or the means by which the state maintains power through its process of governing (Foucault 1991)—lends itself to increased influence and authority among committee members. Aside from the Speaker of the House and Lieutenant Governor, members of the

House and Senate Education committees hold considerable power from both policy and resource allocation standpoints. These coveted seats, particularly chairmanships, tend to be long-standing among legislators. In fact, during the course of this study, the House and Senate Education committee chairs—a white male and white female, both Republican—respectively held 7- and 10-year tenures in their positions.

During the 81st, 82nd, and 83rd legislative sessions, the total number of Latinas serving in the 150-member Texas House of Representatives equaled: ten (10), six (6), and seven (7), respectively. In the case of the 31-member Senate, only two (2) Latinas held positions during the 81st session, and this number increased to just three (3) during the 82nd and 83rd sessions (Texas Legislative Reference Library 2013). With respect to statewide demographics, Latina/os constitute the majority (52 percent) of all school-aged children and youth in Texas' public school system, and nearly 60 percent of all students, and 78 percent of all Latina/o students, are low-income (TEA 2014). These figures make it nearly impossible to escape racialized and class-based undertones when discussing the state's attention to education within and outside of the legislature. These same policy debates are further colored by the epistemologies (Scheurich and Young 1997; López and Valenzuela 2014) that accompany the demographic mismatch among those making policy decisions, and those enduring the results.

THEORY OF RACE GENDERING

This chapter is a case study focused on Senator and Education Committee member Leticia Van de Putte during the 81st, 82nd, and 83rd sessions (2009, 2011, and 2013, respectively) of the Texas State Legislature. The central goals are to provide an analysis of Senator Van de Putte's agency traversing the Texas State Legislature, and what her policymaking practices tell us about the policy arena and the institution of policymaking itself. Accordingly, I draw from the theories of oppositional consciousness (Sandoval 2000) and race gendering (Hawkesworth 2003) as my points of departure.

According to Chela Sandoval (2000) differential consciousness involves the unique ability of women of color to respond to rapidly changing and politically contentious contexts. Differential consciousness posits that the multiple oppressions experienced by women of color inform their political coming-to-consciousness, which subsequently may inform a greater capacity to shift in and out of political practices in response to different configurations of power. This ability to shift and privilege one aspect of themselves over others, in context-specific ways, provides important insight for understanding Latinas' political practices in the Texas State Legislature.

Grounded in feminist notions of "gendered institutions" and the legislative experiences of African American congresswomen, race gendering represents a political process that silences, stereotypes, and challenges the epistemic authority of women of color (Hawkesworth 2003). According to Hawkesworth (2003), this framework disentangles raced and gendered dynamics within institutions that in turn call attention to practices that maintain and reproduce marginalization. Together, these frameworks help to understand more about how Latinas navigate decision-making contexts.

METHODOLOGY

This chapter draws from a longitudinal, mixed-methods study focused on the people, practices, and politics informing educational policymaking in the context of the regular, interim, and special sessions of 81st, 82nd, and 83rd Texas State Legislature (López 2012). Central to my inquiries are whose knowledge is privileged in decision-making processes and whose knowledge is not. My analysis is grounded in Chicana/Latina feminist notions of intersectionality (see Hurtado 1997; Delgado Bernal 1998), which acknowledge that persons belong to more than one social category based upon constructs such as sexuality, class, race, ethnicity, and gender, and that these categories intersect in shaping structural and political aspects of social and political life. In the case of this study, I am interested in this intersection as it relates to the experiences, exclusion, and subordination among the political actors and forms of agency that embody the construction of education policy in the context of the Texas State Legislature.

Data are comprised of numerous primary and secondary sources across various contexts, as follows: verbatim transcriptions of public legislative hearings; analysis of policy documents—that is, public reports, bill analyses, research briefs, written testimony, public forum documents, and position papers from internal (i.e., government, state agency, and legislative committees) and external entities (i.e., academic entities, interest group, formal organizations); media clippings; participant observation; "elite" and key informant interviews with researchers, practitioners, civil rights and community members, state agency staff, legislative staff, and legislators; and field notes. This study orders data chronologically. Using the qualitative software, HyperResearch, cases were developed based on time frames, or phases, that correspond with the Texas state legislature's policymaking process. All data were coded to identify themes, patterns, and corroborate findings.

Photo 10.1. Leticia San Miguel Van de Putte discussing the legislative process during the Bowen Institute for Policy Studies in Higher Education Fellows' Retreat hosted by the University of Texas Center for Education Policy. March 11, 2013. Photo Courtesy of Jaime R. Puente.

LETICIA VAN DE PUTTE

Leticia Van de Putte is a 24-year veteran of the Texas State Legislature— serving eight years in the Texas House of Representatives and sixteen in the Texas Senate—and has sat on the Senate Education Committee for twelve years, from 2003 to 2015. As a sixth-generation Latina born during the baby boom era, Senator Van de Putte is a San Antonio native, a region that constitutes the tip of the South Texas borderlands.

Senator Van de Putte captured national media attention during the in-famous 2013 "people's filibuster" when she joined numerous colleagues in defense of women's reproductive rights and proclaimed the following before the Senate chamber:

> *"At what point must a female senator raise her hand or her voice to be recognized over the male colleagues in the room?"* (Texas Senate 2013a)

Amplifying the rallying chants of hundreds of advocates occupying the Senate gallery, Van de Putte's words placed a spotlight on the historical exclusion of women and people of color that continues to permeate the

Texas State Legislature. This act of agency also captures one of the many ways that she inserts herself in the political process.

As bilingual and bicultural practicing pharmacist and small business owner, Senator Van de Putte's ascent into politics and leadership in education issues includes an upbringing influenced by the political career of her godfather, former Senator Joe Bernal (see Navarro 2008 for elaboration). As a former state legislator and State Board of Education member, Joe Bernal remains one of Texas' most influential Latino elected officials and active participants contributing to the advancement of educational equity in Texas, most notably bilingual education. Together with the influence of her mother, who was a public school teacher, Senator Van de Putte's community cultural wealth—or the forms of capital that draw upon the knowledges that historically marginalized persons bring with them from their homes and communities—inform her larger purpose of struggle toward social and racial justice (Yasso 2005). This legacy includes a framework for maintaining a voice of authority on educational issues that are tied to her unique contributions on the Senate Education Committee, as this chapter demonstrates.

DIFFERENTIAL CONSCIOUSNESS AND ACCESSING POWER

"Never attribute to malice that which could easily be explained by stupidity."

—*Leticia Van de Putte (2008)*[1]

Education policymaking in Texas is above all a matter of business. Comprising the greatest single-item budget category for the state, education draws considerable attention in the legislative arena. Unfortunately, this dominance has less to do with Texas prioritizing education, and more to do with the state's lack of investment (i.e., spending) in numerous other areas of need. The business lobby—overwhelmingly comprised of Anglo males—is among the most influential block driving education policy in the Texas. This block often gains access through key members who are intertwined in a web of personal interests and ideological affinities (López 2012). These actors and interests often eclipse empirically based knowledge in order to keep costs low and reduce education to meet the needs of industry, at the expense of upward mobility and self-determination. State-level policymaking in Texas therefore represents a site ripe for understanding power dynamics and influences that drive education, and by extension the direction of the state.

Heading into the 81st legislative session, the House and Senate Education Committee chairs led a fully appointed fifteen-member Select Committee on Public School Accountability. This group held a total of eleven

(11) statewide hearings from February 2, 2008, to October 20, 2008 (Select Committee on Public School Accountability 2008). Alongside a small number of influential actors, the Select Committee ultimately defined the language that drove Texas' overhaul of public education, beginning a statewide debate that would largely inform the scope of education policy-making for three full sessions beginning with the 2009 passage of House Bill 3 during the 81st Legislature. Prior to the Select Committee agenda, an overhaul to public education at this scale had only occurred three other times over a 25-year timeframe: 1984, 1993, and 1995, respectively.

Regardless of Van de Putte's seniority, a history of collaborating with minority and education organizations, and carrying key legislation addressing the education of low-income and language minority students (i.e., English learners), she was not appointed to the Select Committee or included in the initial agenda-setting collective. Given that time is an important institutional constraint in Texas' legislative process, the actors whose knowledge informs agenda setting become very important aspects of policymaking. On the flip side, those actors and the forms of knowledge that are excluded are arguably placed at a disadvantage. This exclusion was the case for Senator Van de Putte heading into the 81st regular session and subsequent debates that would overwhelm the Senate and House education committees as they overhauled the state's education system.

The sole Latina on the Education Committee, Senator Van de Putte's differential consciousness allowed her to draw from both historical knowledge and diverse points of views when engaging policy debates. Knowing when and how to shift between socio-cultural and redistributive deconstructions of policy became a useful weapon during debates. This strategy was particularly off-putting to a faction of business lobbyists who comprised the Texas Governor's Business Council that did not react well when being interrogated on the fiscal-merits of hot-topic issues such as curricular tracking, high-stakes testing, and budget cuts to education—all agendas driven by influential business entities and political interests that seek to privatize education, benefit from public tax dollars, and triage students away from college and into predetermined tracks.

Student assessment (i.e., high-stakes testing) is among the top politically charged issues in Texas education. As a member of the National Assessment Governing Board (NAGB)—the body of elected and appointed officials that oversees the content and operation of the National Assessment of Educational Progress (NAEP), also known as "The Nation's Report Card"—Van de Putte and her staff gain access to top research and data that are useful in policy debates. The amount of knowledge she holds on issues related to measurement, accountability, and testing is arguably top notch among legislators. Due to the powerful testing lobby and their strong ties to key leadership, namely, Governor Rick Perry and Senate Committee Chair, Florence Shapiro, Van de Putte's Latina background became a means to racialize her expertise, and diminish her contributions to mere advocacy. For example, Van de Putte's use of evidence to support the merits of investing in bilingual instruction were often contested by English-only proponents, such as Senator Shapiro, who often positioned her agency as mere "advocacy." The act of stripping her knowledge and using the advocacy label thereby reframed Van de Putte's efforts to "lowering standards" or trying to advocate for "preferential treatment for certain students." Strategically suspending her anger (Hurtado 1996), one of Van de Putte's responses was to become among the small handful of legislators who began shifting their line of questioning from issues of validity and effects on teaching and learning to those of financial wastefulness. This tactic ended up aligning with a growing faction within the Republican Party comprised of members who held a strong disdain for costly vendor contracts and who were critical of establishment Republicans who were seen as brokers (López 2012).

As one of three Education Committee members with a business background—and the only Latina businesswoman, Senator Van de Putte was rarely met with regard or engaged as a peer among business interests. While this may not be surprising when considering that nearly all of the influential business entities are conservative Anglo males, these actors alone were not at the helm of marginalizing Latina intersectionality. The political clout of these external actors was heavily reliant on the privileged access they were afforded by the Senate Education Committee chair, Florence Shapiro. As a significant gatekeeper for legitimizing knowledge, the committee chair—in this case, Senator Shapiro—exercised her ability to determine which "experts" would be afforded invited testimonies, and which would be relegated to a timed, two-minute public testimony slot. Plainly stated, the chair sets the agenda, carries major pieces of legislation, and decides which bills will get a hearing, and those that will not.

Negotiating elite, peer-to-peer power dynamics are central strategies Latina legislators use to move forward legislation. At times this means Latina-led offices do much of the groundwork to cull data, draft the legislation, and organize a diverse constituency only to identify the "right" co-sponsor—often Anglo and sometimes male—whose co-authorship and privilege provides the symbolic legitimacy needed to move through the process. In other instances, issues of gender may not be at play but their absence does not offset marginalization. This was the case with Senator Shapiro, who took on a conduit role for conservative, hegemonic policy agendas that by extension meant that she was one of the biggest obstacles for Senator Van de Putte and her constituencies' advancement of educational equity. Shapiro's agency can in part be un-

derstood within Chicana feminist scholarship that calls attention to the
ways in which white women can be persuaded to become partners of
patriarchy as a means of acquiring power in ways that are not extended
to women of color (Hurtado 1989).

As part of Texas' overhaul of public education, a second issue of conten-
tion was curricular tracking. Just one session after the state mandated that
districts place *all* students on a college-eligible curriculum plan, attempts
to dismantle this structure and replace it with multiple curricular tracks
became a central topic for the Committee. This pushback among proponents of curricular tracking occurred at the same time that Latina/os were
becoming the majority of all school-aged students in Texas, and their
college enrollment numbers were experiencing an all-time high (THECB
2009). While the legislature was able to fend off efforts to institutionalize
curricular tracking during the 81st and 82nd legislative sessions, the issue
would reemerge again during the 83rd session, as new leadership and
members restructured both the House and Senate Education Committees.

Going into the 83rd session, changes in leadership and a budget sur-
plus provided openings for shifts in policy agendas within the Senate
Education Committee and the legislature as a whole. The Committee's
new chairman, Senator Dan Patrick, had little to no loyalty to many of
the external actors who held close ties to his predecessor nor did he have
an outlined policy agenda. The state's new and unfolding STAAR system, and the previous session's unprecedented budget cuts also led to
increased public scrutiny all of which played into the hands of a collaborative legislator like Senator Van de Putte. Taking a proactive approach,
Senator Van de Putte's office began drafting legislation during the interim
and organizing constituents around policy solutions in order to get ahead
of the curricular tracking agenda and statewide momentum to end high-
stakes testing occurring in Texas. Much of her strategy involved working
with her staff to bring together diverse communities and mediate tensions
earlier rather than later. This process also involved identifying factions
within the business sector that would step in as a counter voice against
the long-standing lobby that no longer had the same foothold in the committee due to a changing of the guard.

As the session progressed, Van de Putte found herself at the center of
the anti-tracking agenda and author of a game-changing amendment to
House Bill 5—the step-sibling to House Bill 3 of the 81st session, and the
final iteration of Texas' public education overhaul. The "Van de Putte
Amendment" sought to retain the state's college-eligible curriculum for
high school students, and by extension eligibility for automatic college
admissions under the state's Top Ten Percent Plan. Often diminished to
a fight on whether or not to maintain Algebra II as a high school expec-

tation, the mainstream media and legislature's reductive characterization of the Van de Putte amendment ignored how the language would block a back-door attempt to curb the number of students who would be eligible for automatic admissions into higher education (López 2013)—a highly political issue that was becoming increasingly difficult to address in the wake of an ongoing court battle regarding higher education admissions (*Fisher v. University of Texas* 2013). From a resource-allocation standpoint, the Van de Putte amendment would also restore statutory expectations that would leave no room for the state to appeal (yet again) the adequacy claims outlined in the school finance decision. Proponents, including "progressive" Anglo organizations, either stood silent or spoke out against the amendment. In some cases these groups' opposition was related to a disassociation with curricular tracking as a lived experience, and in other instances it was related to ideological contempt toward standards-based education. Sadly, the latter framing—which is arguably a relic of privilege—forged added factions among out-numbered members of the Democratic Party.

In response to mounting public attention related to the Van de Putte Amendment and key minority and civil-rights organizations who worked on the language, nearly all Senate Democrats were receiving calls from constituents wanting to know where they stood on the tracking issue. This wake-up call that the public is watching led members of the Senate Democratic Caucus to take pause and reconvene to better understand the issue they were about to vote on. This pause to become an educated voter highlights how Senator Van de Putte's collective agency lifted anonymity and created a context where legislators across party lines were forced to make transparent their position for or against a system that would set college-eligibility as the expectation for all students. Also at play were tensions among certain Senate Democrats who questioned the intention of the Van de Putte amendment once they discovered that the language had Governor Rick Perry's support. Sadly these initial reactions tried to characterize Senator Van de Putte as carrying Republican leadership's water and disregarded the time Van de Putte put into partnering with Chairman Trey Martinez Fisher of the Mexican American Legislative Caucus (MALC) and lobbying the Governor's office to ensure that the language was not stripped if the bill ended up in the hands of a conference committee.

Near the end of the day on Friday, May 3, 2013, House Bill 5 made its way to the full Senate and was eventually postponed for a vote. After an awkward stall on the floor that allowed time for Senate Democrats to hash out differences, Lieutenant Governor Dewhurst called the chamber back to order and stumbled through the announcement to postpone the vote on HB 5, and the controversial Van de Putte amendment:

It was my intention to bring up HB 5 right now. We've been meeting on HB 5 for hours and have made a lot of progress but there are still members who have not had a chance to be briefed on HB 5, and you have asked that you be given time for more of a briefing on House Bill 5. So based upon that, I am going to wait. It is my intention to bring up House Bill 5 and pass it on Monday. Alright? (Texas Senate 2013b).

LATINA HUSTLE IN TEXAS' LEGISLATIVE PROCESS

The case of Leticia San Miguel Van de Putte reveals two important aspects related to how Latinas navigate the legislative process. First, race-gendering in the legislative process places added burdens on Latinas in order for them to advance policy agendas and accomplish the same goals as other members. Second, these same circumstances inform the practices that Latinas use in order to engage the process, which in turn may inspire new strategies that are conducive to the current conditions of the policy arena.

Race-gendering in Texas' legislative process places added burdens on Latinas as they work to advance their agendas. This climate translates into a context where Latinas are saddled with having to perform double or triple the work in order to accomplish the same ends, such as spending considerable amounts of time negotiating peer-to-peer power dynamics, particularly when they fall on opposite sides of an issue. Latinas' knowledge contributions often face scrutiny during policy debates and negotiations—by elite and external actors, alike—that question, and at times diminish, the merits of their input. In some instances, the process of race-gendering strips away strengths that may afford them an equal footing in policy debates, such as the case of business interests disregarding Senator Van de Putte's expertise as a businesswoman, or her anti-testing arguments being reduced to mere advocacy. In the fast-paced structure of the Texas State Legislature where you're in a race against the clock, these added constraints can have a cumulative effect that can quickly deplete the resources of a legislator's office, thereby making it difficult to engage in other issues occurring during the session.

As Latina legislators navigate the race-gendered gauntlet, their differential consciousness (Sandoval 2000) affords them the ability to develop new strategies for engaging the process. Knowing when to privilege one aspect of her identity and building alliances are two such strategies that Senator Van de Putte used to move her agenda forward. In the case of the HB 5 debate and the Van de Putte Amendment, her Latina identity and history of working with minority communities provided access to Latino and African American constituencies that was not available to other committee members. This extended to strategies to similarly work with Latino leadership, namely, Chairman Martinez Fisher, who brought the weight of the Mexican American Legislative Caucus (MALC) in support of the Van de Putte Amendment.

Finally, Van de Putte demonstrates how institutional memory can also be a strategy in policy debates among Latina legislators. While committee members are shown to hold added privileges that allow them to inform the direction of policy, power is not evenly distributed among all members. These race-gendered dynamics of the committee meant that Senator Van de Putte often had to suspend her anger and find different points of entry in policy debates. Leveraging her long-standing presence on the committee, Van de Putte was able to use institutional memory as a strategy, particularly when it came to blocking policies shown to be detrimental to historically marginalized communities. After twelve years of service on the Senate Education Committee, she was versed on the players and agendas that cycled through session after session. It also helped that she had little to no turnover among her staff, particularly her General Council, who similarly had developed a wealth of institutional memory. Institutional memory as a strategy allowed Senator Van de Putte to call out contradictions, and in some instances draw out political interests' true intents of actors' agendas. This strategy can guide political actors into a corner, where their attempts to wiggle their out way of the tight situation ends up airing out more dirty laundry than conventional cross examination. This strategy further places the burden of legitimization on the shoulders of the actor, as opposed to the interrogator.

Latinas have been shown to approach politics with community-oriented motivations (García and Marquez 2001), employ collaborative strategies when holding leadership positions (Hardy-Fanta 1993), and focus on substantive policies and issues of greatest interest to working class communities, such as education, healthcare, and job opportunities (Fraga et al. 2005). These qualities, which are exemplified in Senator Van de Putte, call into question the larger impacts of race-gendering in Texas' legislative process with regard to obstructing certain kinds of policies, as well as its treatment of the larger populace in policymaking. Given that the Texas State Legislature, and legislatures in most states, show no signs of relinquishing power—particularly in contexts where populations are growing increasingly diverse—it is crucial that scholarship disentangle what's really occurring in these policymaking bodies. Additionally, it is important that efforts to increase the presence of Latinas in state legislatures are informed by research that critically analyzes the institution into which they seek to enter.

NOTE

1. Epigraph quotation from López, P. D. (2012). *The Process of Becoming: The Political Construction of Texas' Lone STAAR System of Accountability and College Readiness.* University of Texas at Austin: Dissertation.

Conclusion

This edited volume focuses on Latinas as political actors in an ever-changing American political landscape. Latinas have been understudied and underrepresented as political actors in the study of American politics as well as Latino politics. Since the publication of Carol Hardy-Fanta's 1993 seminal work, *Latina Politics Latino Politics: Gender, Culture, and Political Participation in Boston*, to the current volume, a lot has changed for Latinas as political actors at the federal and state levels. We have attempted to capture those changes with contributions from various experts inside and outside the field of political science using both quantitative and qualitative analyses.

These chapters chart the changes that Latinas have faced and incorporated as political actors as they meander to elected office. In general, when women are discussed in political books or articles, Latina political actors are often overlooked or only briefly mentioned. In this volume, we discuss the progress made as well as the challenges remaining for Latina women.

Latinas in American Politics: Changing and Embracing Political Tradition rests on the argument that Latinas are changing political traditions by entering the political sphere and bringing a new voice to the table. Latina candidates force voters to consider women with cultural differences and experiences and accept them as part of the norm, which also included Latina women changing familial structures by leaving the domestic sphere and entering the political arena. Latinas embrace political tradition by taking traditional positions and running similar campaigns to other candidates. We argue that Latinas entering politics and being political is traditional—it is *how* they participate that causes change.

Why study Latinas in American politics? Does it matter whether legislatures and executives include minorities such as Latina women? If you are concerned about cultivating a healthy democracy, the answer is "yes" (Cohen 2002). The first reason that ethnic and gender diversity is important is because vibrant and stable democracies derive, in part, from perceptions and experience of legitimacy. If a society is to be successful and healthy, all points of view and full ranges of talent must be available for public decision-making. Second, it is also vital for Latinas to have full access to the public sphere because of their different life experiences from men and women of all ethnic backgrounds. Since our society continues to operate with divisions of labor in the public sphere, Latina women and men tend to have different backgrounds and points of references. Finally, it is important for Latina women to be included among our public officials for symbolic reasons. If children grow up seeing Latina, African American, or Asian women in the political sphere, they will choose from a more diverse array of options as they decide how to shape adult lives. Political ambition, particularly among minority girls, increases in a world in which minority women routinely run for all levels of national office.

Recently, within women-and-politics circles, the question of whether gender does matter in politics has risen. Although for most scholars, the obvious answer is affirmative, recent work has highlighted that these effects may be waning. While scholars such as Lawless and Hayes (2013) and Brooks (2013) find the effects of media coverage, gender, and candidate perception diminishing, the examination of intersectionality has not been fully developed. As the fields of race and politics and women and politics continue to grow, the need for scholars to combine such research becomes apparent. More work must explore how the media covers Latinas as candidates, how voters react to this coverage and most importantly, what has caused this group to be successful at electing women in local and state politics but has yet to successfully elect a Senate candidate. Although the question, "Does gender matter?" seems to elicit a simple response, the answer is anything but simple. In short, gender does matter, but how it matters is the more pressing question. The convergence of race and gender politics provides an avenue to explore in the role these components play, how an ever-changing American electorate interprets these candidates and elected officials, and in the work they carry out.

Part one of this volume focused on Latinas on the national level. First, García discusses the different attitudes of Latinas across generations. This analysis of Latino and Latina political behaviors and attitudes helps to determine why this group participates in politics, why they vote, and what demographic information most influences their decisions. We then turn to Monforti and Gershon's study examining the softening effect race has on the gender of political candidates. Cargile, Merolla, and Schroedel further explore Latinas in a campaign setting by looking at how stereotypes affect electability. Wilson and Urbano look at legislative behavior of Latinas compared with their counterparts. This chapter examines how this budding group of legislators practices descriptive representation. Lastly, Hernandez examines the effects of social media and how Latinas are using this tool to overcome smaller budgets to reach out to potential voters.

Part two examines Latina political behavior on the state level. José Marichal's chapter discusses how Latina legislators use Twitter to keep constituents informed. Marin Hellwege and Sierra explore the election of the nation's first Latina governor, Susana Martinez. The authors examine her election and reelection, and comparatively analyze Martinez to Congresswoman Michelle Lujan Grisham. Sharon Navarro looks at the historic candidacy of Leticia Van De Putte for Lieutenant Governor of Texas. Navarro examines how television ads thwarted Van De Putte's ability to use her identity in an attempt to win the election. Lizeth Gonzalez and Tony Affigne explore political challenges and future prospects of Latina candidates in Rhode Island, a state not normally associated with Latino politics. Lastly, Patricia López discusses race-gendering and intersectionality within the Texas State Senate during the 81st, 82nd, and 83rd legislatures.

We began this volume with a forward by Carol Hardy-Fanta in which she states, "I've seen changes in one of the most important groups in American politics today, Latina women." This volume attempts to encapsulate this change and provide direction for future research. Will there be a year for the Latina as the 1992 election cycle was dubbed the year of the woman? The answer is that every election cycle is the year of the Latina, as these pioneering women continue to embrace and change American political culture.

Appendixes

CHAPTER 1

Appendix A

Table A 1.1.

Sample Group	Sampled	Survey Completed	Survey Rate
White 18–34	426	269	63.1%
White 35+	896	713	79.6%
African American 18–34	473	233	49.3%
African American 35+	969	612	63.2%
Asian 18–34	132	101	76.5%
Asian 35+	387	320	82.7%
Hispanic 18–34 (English Version)	466	254	54.5%
Hispanic 35+ (English Version)	620	265	42.7%
Hispanic 18–34 (Spanish Version)	555	178	32.1%
Hispanic 35+ (Spanish Version)	609	236	38.8%
Total	5,593	3,181	56.9%

Appendix B

Okay, now we want to talk a bit about your role in politics. Please indicate whether you strongly agree, agree, disagree, or strongly disagree with the following statements. Everyone should answer these questions regardless of your formal citizenship status.

42. I believe that by participating in politics I can make a difference. Would you say you . . .
43. I have the skills and knowledge necessary to participate in politics. Do you . . .
44. The leaders in government care very little about people like me. Do you . . .
45. The government is pretty much run by a few big interests looking out for themselves and their friends. Would you say you . . .

Strongly agree 1
Agree 2
Neither agree nor disagree 3
Disagree 4
Strongly disagree 5

47. How much of the time do you think you can trust the government in Washington to do the right thing?

Almost always. 1
Frequently 2
About half the time. 3
Once in a while 4
Almost never 5

48. How much do you agree or disagree with the following statements about the government and American society:
    a. In the United States, everyone has an equal chance to succeed.
    b. Generally the American legal system treats all groups equally.
    c. In the American economic system, everyone has a fair chance.
    d. I believe in the fundamentals of our political system like the Constitution.

Strongly agree 1
Agree. 2
Neither agree nor disagree 3
Disagree 4
Strongly disagree 5

CHAPTER 2 APPENDIX

Table A 2.1. Respondent Characteristics

School 1

Race and Ethnicity	20% White	3% African American	76% Latino	4% Asian American	2% Native American	.004% Middle Eastern
Gender	53% Female	46% Male				
Party Attachment	10% Strong Republican	12% Weak Republican	34% Independent	21% Weak Democrat	24% Strong Democrat	
Average Age	22 years old					

N = 225

School 2

Race and Ethnicity	27% White	45% African American	13% Latino	19% Asian American	2% Native American	2% Middle Eastern
Gender	70% Female	30% Male				
Party Attachment	4% Strong Republican	9% Weak Republican	29% Independent	33% Weak Democrat	25% Strong Democrat	
Average Age	25 years old					

N=468

Variable Measures

- **Voter Support:** Which of the following candidates [candidate 1 or candidate 2] is more likely to receive your vote? 1= vote for Latina candidate; 0= vote for opponent.
- **Subject Race/Ethnicity:** Which racial or ethnic group best describes you? Binary variables were created for *African American* (1=African American, 0=other), *White* (1= white, 0=others), *Latino* (1=Latino, 0=other), *and Asian* (1=Asian, 0=other) subjects.
- **Female:** What is your gender? 1=Female, 0=other
- **Age:** What year were you born?
- **Political Interest:** Some people don't pay much attention to politics. How about you? Would you say that you are very interested, somewhat interested, or not interested at all in politics and government? (Not at all interested=1, somewhat interested=2, very interested=3).
- **Political Knowledge:** Knowledge is based on a four-point scale based on whether respondents correctly answered three questions asking about presidential term limits, which branch of government is responsible for deciding whether laws are constitutional, and who the speaker of the house is (0=no knowledge, 1=low knowledge, 2=moderate knowledge, 3=high knowledge).
- **Party Attachment:** Generally speaking, do you usually think of yourself as a Republican, a Democrat, an Independent, or what? 1= Republican, 2= Independent, 3=Democrat.
- **Democrat:** Generally speaking, do you usually think of yourself as a Republican, a Democrat, an Independent, or what? (1=Democrat, 0=other).
- **Ideology:** Generally speaking, in politics, do you consider yourself as conservative, liberal, middle of the road? (1=conservative, 2=independent, 3=liberal).
- **Conservative:** Generally speaking, in politics, do you consider yourself as conservative, liberal, middle of the road? (1=conservative, 0=other).
- **Opponent Characteristics**: Binary variables were created for *Latino* (1=Latino opponent, 0=other), *Latina* (1=Latina opponent, 0=other), *African American male* (1=African American male opponent, 0=other), *African American female* (1=African American female opponent, 0=other), *White male* (1=White male opponent, 0=other) *and White female* (1=White female opponent, 0=other) opponents.
- **School:** 0=School 1, 1= School 2.
- **Issue Competence:** Based on what you know about the candidates, how well do you think (the Latina candidate) would handle [Education/the Economy/Immigration]? (0=Not well at all, 1=not very well, 2=somewhat well, 3=very well).

CHAPTER 3 APPENDIX

Table A 3.1. Mean on Female Identified Traits across Experimental Conditions

	Male	*White*	*Female*	*Latino*	*Latina*
Warm	2.189	2.436	2.501	2.734	2.605
	(0.050)	(0.055)	(0.049)	(0.044)	(0.054)
Compassionate	2.172	2.416	2.589	2.796	2.579
	(0.051)	(0.056)	(0.048)	(0.045)	(0.054)
People Skills	2.770	2.677	2.862	2.795	2.545
	(0.056)	(0.058)	(0.047)	(0.046)	(0.056)
Administrative Skills	2.462	2.686	2.811	2.638	2.499
	(0.059)	(0.058)	(0.050)	(0.049)	(0.056)
Able to Compromise	2.094	2.409	2.704	2.597	2.450
	(0.056)	(0.057)	(0.051)	(0.052)	(0.058)
Democratic	2.227	2.376	2.622	2.829	2.734
	(0.054)	(0.058)	(0.054)	(0.052)	(0.062)
Trustworthy	2.026	2.376	2.588	2.636	2.499
	(0.058)	(0.059)	(0.056)	(0.053)	(0.059)

Table A 3.2. P-value on Difference in Means Tests on Female-identified Traits between Experimental Conditions

	Male v. White	*Male v. Female*	*Male v. Latino*	*Male v. Latina*
Warm	0.001	0.000	0.000	0.000
Compassionate	0.001	0.000	0.000	0.000
People Skills	0.248	0.208	0.729	0.005
Administrative	0.007	0.000	0.022	0.648
Compromise	0.000	0.000	0.000	0.000
Democratic	0.061	0.000	0.000	0.000
Trustworthy	0.000	0.000	0.000	0.000
Feminine Factor	0.000	0.000	0.000	0.000
	White v. Female	*White v. Latino*	*White v. Latina*
Warm	0.375	0.000	0.029
Compassionate	0.019	0.000	0.037
People Skills	0.013	0.110	0.101
Administrative	0.107	0.527	0.021
Compromise	0.000	0.016	0.618
Democratic	0.002	0.000	0.139
Trustworthy	0.009	0.001	0.139
Feminine Factor	0.004	0.000	0.055

(continued)

Table A 3.2. (continued)

	Female v. Latino	Female v. Latina	Latino v. Latina
Warm	0.000	0.157	0.063
Compassionate	0.002	0.888	0.002
People Skills	0.309	0.000	0.001
Administrative	0.015	0.000	0.001
Compromise	0.142	0.001	0.061
Democratic	0.006	0.170	0.240
Trustworthy	0.527	0.274	0.084
Feminine Factor	0.167	0.366	0.028

Table A 3.3. Mean on Male-Identified Traits across Experimental Conditions

	Male	White	Female	Latino	Latina
Assertive	2.906	2.775	2.903	2.845	2.616
	(0.054)	(0.053)	(0.048)	(0.046)	(0.057)
Aggressive	2.919	2.712	2.707	2.749	2.619
	(0.056)	(0.057)	(0.052)	(0.050)	(0.062)
Ambitious	3.194	3.049	3.039	2.943	2.804
	(0.057)	(0.060)	(0.048)	(0.050)	(0.056)
Strong Leader	2.384	2.575	2.683	2.702	2.466
	(0.058)	(0.058)	(0.055)	(0.051)	(0.059)

Table A 3.4. P-value on Difference in Means Tests on Male Conditions Identified Traits between Experimental

	Male v. White	Male v. Female	Male v. Latino	Male v. Latina
Assertive	0.084	0.970	0.396	0.000
Aggressive	0.010	0.005	0.023	0.000
Ambitious	0.080	0.037	0.001	0.000
Strong Leader	0.020	0.000	0.022	0.324
Masculine Factor	0.000	0.000	0.000	0.000

	White v. Female	White v. Latino	White v. Latina
Assertive	0.073	0.314	0.043
Aggressive	0.943	0.634	0.270
Ambitious	0.894	0.173	0.004
Strong Leader	0.182	0.104	0.186
Masculine Factor	0.893	0.089	0.000

	Female v. Latino	Female v. Latina	Latino v. Latina
Assertive	0.387	0.000	0.002
Aggressive	0.561	0.279	0.104
Ambitious	0.164	0.002	0.074
Strong Leader	0.801	0.007	0.003
Masculine Factor	0.110	0.000	0.016

Table A 3.5.   Mean on Issue Competencies across Experimental Conditions

	Male	*White*	*Female*	*Latino*	*Latina*
Education	3.690	3.940	4.610	4.107	3.930
	(0.089)	(0.100)	(0.080)	(0.084)	(0.096)
Assisting the Poor	3.248	3.453	4.495	4.293	4.279
	(0.098)	(0.104)	(0.081)	(0.090)	(0.099)
Reproductive Health	3.112	3.604	4.476	3.392	3.827
	(0.100)	(0.101)	(0.093)	(0.091)	(0.105)
Health Care	3.173	3.644	4.352	3.993	3.807
	(0.099)	(0.104)	(0.093)	(0.088)	(0.101)
Foreign Affairs	4.190	4.337	3.570	3.317	3.170
	(0.091)	(0.102)	(0.089)	(0.090)	(0.097)
National Security	3.947	4.078	4.162	3.860	3.582
	(0.088)	(0.101)	(0.085)	(0.087)	(0.098)
Crime and Public Safety	3.603	3.854	4.225	4.058	3.809
	(0.088)	(0.097)	(0.086)	(0.090)	(0.095)
Economy	3.437	3.876	4.281	3.869	3.625
	(0.094)	(0.102)	(0.084)	(0.089)	(0.098)
Racial Discrimination	3.536	3.639	4.373	4.229	4.176
	(0.094)	(0.099)	(0.084)	(0.099)	(0.102)
Immigration	3.266	3.559	4.083	4.029	3.833
	(0.098)	(0.104)	(0.091)	(0.106)	(0.116)

Table A 3.6.   P-value on Difference in Means Tests on Ideology and Issue Competencies between Experimental Conditions

	Male v. White	*Male v. Female*	*Male v. Latino*	*Male v. Latina*
Education	0.061	0.000	0.001	0.067
Assisting the Poor	0.151	0.000	0.000	0.000
Reproductive Health	0.001	0.000	0.000	0.000
Health Care	0.001	0.000	0.000	0.000
Feminine Issues	0.005	0.000	0.000	0.000
Foreign Affairs	0.280	0.000	0.000	0.000
National Security	0.330	0.080	0.482	0.066
Crime	0.054	0.000	0.000	0.1111
Economy	0.002	0.000	0.001	0.166
Masculine Issues	0.209	0.000	0.121	0.590
Racial Discrimination	0.451	0.000	0.000	0.000
Immigration	0.041	0.000	0.000	0.000
Minority Issues	0.135	0.000	0.000	0.000

(*continued*)

Table A 3.6. (*continued*)

	White v. Female	White v. Latino	White v. Latina
Education	0.000	0.200	0.941
Assisting the Poor	0.000	0.000	0.000
Reproductive Health	0.000	0.024	0.127
Health Care	0.000	0.011	0.264
Feminine Issues	0.000	0.001	0.028
Foreign Affairs	0.000	0.000	0.000
National Security	0.523	0.102	0.000
Crime	0.004	0.123	0.735
Economy	0.002	0.961	0.075
Masculine Issues	0.047	0.853	0.091
Racial Discrimination	0.000	0.000	0.000
Immigration	0.000	0.002	0.078
Race Issues	0.000	0.000	0.004
	Female v. Latino	Female v. Latina	Latino v. Latina
Education	0.000	0.000	0.164
Assisting the Poor	0.095	0.092	0.919
Reproductive Health	0.000	0.000	0.541
Health Care	0.005	0.000	0.166
Feminine Issues	0.000	0.000	0.348
Foreign Affairs	0.045	0.002	0.270
National Security	0.013	0.000	0.034
Crime	0.179	0.001	0.057
Economy	0.001	0.000	0.065
Masculine Issues	0.053	0.000	0.046
Racial Discrimination	0.268	0.137	0.708
Immigration	0.698	0.089	0.211
Race Issues	0.430	0.091	0.388

CHAPTER 8 APPENDIX

TV Advertisement Coding Sheet

1. Does the ad contain any policy/issue statements?
   If yes, go to question 2. If not, go to question 3.
2. How are the policy/issues discussed in the ad?

   a. The policy/issue is phrased so that it requires the viewer to know the status quo of the issue or policy in order to have an opinion on the issue (e.g., candidate × favors an increase in minimum wage, candidate × supports prayer in school).
   b. The policy/issue is explained or described in the ad, so the viewer knows the content from the text in the ad (e.g., natural gas is safe, effective, and more efficient than electricity).
   c. The policy/issue is one that the viewer would immediately be familiar with and thus it would be considered a "simple" policy message (e.g., candidate × is pro-life, believes in safe schools).
   d. The policy/issue is stated in a way that would benefit everyone. The policy/issue is stated in a normative, positive way (e.g., candidate × is fighting for smaller class sizes, clean schools, better education, protecting Medicare, reduced crime, cutting unemployment, increased jobs).

3. Does the ad make references to specific bills or pieces of legislation (e.g., HR 463, The Sarbanes-Oxley Act, The Patients' Bill of Rights)?
4. The ad discusses the favored candidate's personal qualities.
5. The ad discusses the opposing candidate's personal qualities.
6. Latino in the ad, no speaking role.
6a. Latino in the ad, speaking role.
6b. Language spoken in by Latino.
6c. Is music played in background?
7. African American in the ad, no speaking role.
7a. African American in the ad, speaking role.
8. Asian American in the ad, no speaking role.
8a. Asian American in the ad, speaking role.
9. Rural images/farmers in the ad, no speaking role.
9a. Rural images/farmers in the ad, speaking role.
10. Someone carrying a gun in the ad.
10a. Ethnicity of person carrying gun.
11. Ad mentions the American dream.

12. Senior citizen in the ad, no speaking role.
12a. Senior citizen in the ad, speaking role.
12b. Ethnicity of disabled.
12c. Language of disabled individual.
13. Disabled individual in the ad, no speaking role.
13a. Disabled individual in the ad, speaking role.
13b. Ethnicity of disabled.
13c. Language of disabled individual (if speaking).
14. Military images/anything related to war in the ad.
15. Students (in a classroom setting) featured in the ad, no speaking role.
15a. Students (in a classroom setting) featured in the ad, speaking role.
15b. Ethnicity of students in classroom.
15c. Is a teacher shown in the ad?
15d. Language of teacher.
15e. Ethnicity of teacher.
16. Blue-collar workers in the ad (e.g., construction workers, factory workers, maintenance workers) no speaking role.
16a. Ethnicity of workers.
16b. Language of workers.
17. Sports images in the ad (e.g., children playing soccer).
17a. Any symbols associated with a country (country jersey, etc.).
18. Children in the ad.
18a. Ethnicity of children.
18b. Do children speak? Language?
19. A woman in the ad, no speaking.
19a. A woman in the ad, speaking.
19b. Language the woman is speaking.
19c. Ethnicity of woman.
20. Language of ad.
21. Are there subtitles? In what language?
22. Tone of the ad (happy, sad, somber).

Examples of issues/policies: taxes, deficit/surplus/budget/debt, minimum wage, other economic references, suicide, gun control, other references to social issues, attendance record, crime, drugs, death penalty, order, ideology, education, lottery for education, child care, other child-related issues, personal values, defense, veterans, foreign policy, Bosnia, other defense foreign policy, special interests, environment, immigration, health care, social security, Medicare, welfare, civil rights/race relations, campaign finance reform, government ethics, tobacco, affirmative action, gambling, farming, business, employment/jobs, poverty, trade/NAFTA, political record, abortion, homosexuality, moral values.

Candidate/Party: Name of Ad:

Tone: 1 = Positive, 2 = Comparative, 3 = Strictly Attack

Type of criticism (for comparative and attack ads only):

7-point scale where 1= strictly issue-based criticism and 7= strictly attack

Mention opponent by name: 0=no, 1=yes

Mention candidate party: 0=no, 1=yes

Mention opponent party: 0=no, 1=yes

Use of ideological labels: 0=no, 1=yes

Focus on language: 0=English, 1= Spanish, 2 = use of English captions with Spanish spoken, 3 = use of Spanish captions with English spoken.

Focus on groups (socioeconomic or interest groups): 0 = no discussion of groups or group-based appeals, 1 = some discussion of groups or group-based appeals, 2 = heavy emphasis on groups or group-based appeals.

Focus on Parties: 0 = no discussion of parties or party-based appeals, 1 = some discussion of parties or party-based appeals, 2 = heavy emphasis on parties or party-based appeals.

Focus on ideology: 0 = no discussion of ideology or the role of government, 1 = some discussion of ideology or the role of government, 2 = heavy emphasis on ideology or the role of government.

Focus on Values: [not including references to personal ethics] 0 = No discussion of shared/cultural values, 2 = heavy emphasis on shared/cultural values.

Focus on Personal Qualities: 0 = No discussion of the personal qualities of the candidates, 1 = some discussion of the personal qualities of the candidate, 2 = heavy emphasis on personal qualities of the candidate.

Invoke leadership: 0 = Ad is not framed in terms of leadership/leadership not invoked, 1= ad is framed in terms of leadership/leadership is invoked.

Mention Record of Candidates: 0 = No mention of a candidate's experience or record in office, 1 = mention either or both candidates' experience or records in office.

Primary/Secondary/Tertiary Issue: [list of several general and specific issue categories; codes given only for those categories used in the text] 10 = Crime, 35 = Jobs/unemployment.

White/Black/Asian/Hispanic Visuals: Count of the number of people (other than the candidates) of each racial group who appear in the ad.

Skin Color of Individuals: 0 = White (light skin), 1= Dark

Children/Elderly Visuals: Count of the number of people (other than the candidates) of each age group who appear in the ad.

Male/Female Visuals: Count of the number of people (other than the candidates) of each sex who appear in the ad.

Family Visuals: Count of the number of family units (defined as two or more related individuals belonging to at least two different generations) that appear in the ad.

Mention Biography: 0 = No mention of the personal history/biography of the candidate, 1 = Mentions the personal history/biography of the candidate.

Sponsor Appears: 0 = Sponsor does not appear in ad, 1= Sponsor appears in the ad.

Opponent Appears: 0 = Opponent does not appear in ad, 1= Opponent does appear in the ad.

Military Visuals: 0 = No images of military personnel/veterans, 1= Images of military personnel/veterans

Drugs Visuals: 0 = No images of illegal drugs, 1= Images of illegal drugs.

Symbolic Images: [list three most prominent] 1 = American flag, 2 = White House, 3 = US Capitol Building, 4 = Supreme Court Building, 5 = Statue of Liberty, 6 = Military memorials, 7 = Other national monuments, 8 = Likeness of US Constitution, 9= Likeness of Declaration of Independence, 10 = State Capitol building or monument, 11 = State Flag, 12 = Military awards/citations/insignia, 13 = Eagle, 30 = Foreign monument or flag, 50 = Other widely recognized symbol not listed above, 999 = No specific symbols.

Visual Scenes: [list three most prominent types of scenes portrayed in visual imagery] 1 = Children playing, 2 = Family togetherness, 3 = Wedding, 4 = Graduation ceremony, 5 = Parents with newborn baby, 6 = Beautiful neighborhood, 7 = Picturesque landscapes, 8 = People hard and happy at work, 9 = Children happy and learning in school/full classroom, 10 = Violent criminal acts, 11 = Nonviolent criminal acts (including drug use), 12 = Crime scenes, 13 = Jails or prisons, 14 = Immigrants crossing the border/border checkpoints, 15 = Empty classrooms or schools, 16 = Empty playgrounds, 17 = Abandoned or rundown buildings, 18 = Devastated or barren landscapes, 19 = Pollution/sewage, 20 = Burning cross, 30 = Foreign military ships/planes/tanks/missiles, 33 = Nuclear explosion, 40 = Nursing home/assisted care of elderly, 41 = Sick patients in hospital, 42 = Sick/starving/malnourished children, 43 = Homeless people, 44 = Victims of a disaster, 45 = Students struggling to learn (having difficulty), 46 = People struggling to pay bills or buy essential goods, 47 = Workers being laid off or struggling to find work, 48 = People with disabilities struggling, 50 = Office of a political official, 51 = Interior of a legislative chamber, 999=None of these visual scenes.

Cite Source of Evidence: [either in narration or text on screen] 0 = No sources are cited for factual claims, 1 = Cites sources for factual claims.

Music: 1 = Ad contains uplifting/sweet/sentimental/patriotic music and major chords, 2 = Ad contains tense/somber music and minor chords, 3 = Balance of uplifting and tense, 999=No music.

Sound Effects: 1 = Ad contains positive sound effects (e.g., laughter, cheers, applause), 2 = Ad contains negative sound effects (e.g., screams, sirens, crying), 3 = Mix of positive and negative sound effects or neutral sound effects, 999=No sound effects.

Dominant Color: 1 = Black and white, 2 = Dark or gray colors, 3 = Ordinary or muted colors, 4 = bright colors ("colorful"), 5 = Mix of color schemes and none is dominant.

Emotional Appeal: 0 = No appeal to viewer emotions, 1=Appeal to viewer emotions.

Logical Appeal: 0 = No appeal to logic (i.e., logical arguments/inferences from evidence), 1=Appeal to logic.

Dominant Appeal: 0 = Emotional appeal dominant, 1 = Logical appeal dominant, 2 = Neither or other appeal dominant.

Amusement/Humor Appeal: 0 = No attempt to elicit amusement (appeal to humor), 1 = Some appeal to amusement/humor, 2 = Strong appeal to amusement/humor.

Fear Appeal: 0 = No attempt to elicit fear/anxiety, 1= Some appeal to fear/anxiety, 2 = Strong appeal to fear anxiety.

Enthusiasm Appeal: 0 = No attempt to elicit enthusiasm/hope/joy, 1 = Some appeal to enthusiasm/hope/joy, 2 = Strong appeal to enthusiasm/hope/joy.

Pride Appeal: 0 = No attempt to elicit pride (i.e., satisfaction in what's been accomplished or who we are), 1= Some appeal to pride, 2 = Strong appeal to pride.

Compassion Appeal: 0 = No attempt to elicit compassion/sympathy, 1= Some appeal to compassion/sympathy, 2=Strong appeal to compassion/sympathy.

Sex of Narrator: 0 = Male voice, 1 = Female Voice, 2 = Cannot tell sex of narrator, 5 = Both male and female voices, 999 = No narration.

Pace of Video Editing/Sequencing: 0 = Single continuous shot, 1 = Low number/frequency of cuts from one scene to next (i.e., a couple of cuts), 2 = Moderate number/frequency of cuts (i.e., several cuts), 3 = High number/frequency of cuts (i.e., rapid cuts throughout ad).

Dominant Style/Format of Ad: 0=Talking head, 1=Person on the street, 2=Just the facts (i.e., mostly text, tables, and graphs), 3 = Cartoon/animation, 4 = Imagery and voiceover, 9 = Other style or mix of styles.

CHAPTER 9 APPENDIX

Appendix A: Questionnaire

As you know, this interview will be used to write a chapter for a book about Latinas in politics in the United States. With your history and accomplishments, we believe your experiences would be very valuable to our study. The questions have been carefully written to protect your anonymity. Your answers will be confidential, and your name will not be connected to your words. If at any time during this interview you do not wish to answer a question, please feel free to let me know and we will move on to the next question.

[Personal Background, Identity, and Civic Engagement]

I really want to start at the beginning, because I imagine your story begins well before you became a public figure in Rhode Island. So I'm going to start with a few background questions.

1. "Families [of Hispanic or Latino] origin or background in the United States come from many different countries. From which country do you trace your Latino heritage?" *[LNS 13]*
2. "Where were you born?" *[LNS 15]*
3. "Have you always lived in Rhode Island? What places have you lived since coming to the United States?"
4. "What is your race? Are you White, Black, American Indian, Asian, Native Hawaiian/Pacific Islander, some other race, or more than one? *[LNS 53]*
5. "[Hispanics or Latinos] can be described based on skin tone or complexion shades. Using a scale from 1 to 5 where 1 represents very dark and 5 represents being very light, where would you place yourself on that scale? *[LNS 55, E13,16]*
6. "What is your highest level of formal education completed? *[LNS 37]*
7. "Did you participate in civic activities? If so, can you tell me what kinds of activities you were involved in? *[LNS 26]*
8. "Before you became a public official, did you ever try to get government officials to pay attention to something that concerned you, either by calling, writing a letter, or going to a meeting? *[LNS 29]*
9. "When you did this, were you working through existing groups or organizations to bring people together? *[LNS 28]*
   a. If yes, could you tell me a bit more about this group?
10. Many Latinas report that role models have been important to their careers. Were there other women or men, who influenced you or encouraged you to take on leadership roles in the community? *[Políticas I-8]*

[Current Position and Experiences]

1. What is your current leadership position now?
   a. Can you briefly describe a typical day?
2. Thinking about the election/appointment process, do you think being a woman helped or hindered your chances of success?
3. Thinking about the election/appointment process, do you think your particular identity as a Latina woman influenced the election/appointment process and chances of success?
4. Once in office, do you believe your identity as a woman has had any effect on how you were received or perceived by your peers in politics?
5. Once in office, do you believe being a Latina has had any effect on how you were received or perceived by your peers?
6. Do you believe all female public officials are held to the same standards, or do Latinas face different expectations as leaders? *[Políticas III-6]*
   a. Can you explain what these different expectations have been?
7. Women with demanding careers have varying experiences balancing their personal relationships, with family and loved ones, and professional lives. How would you describe this balance in your life?
8. Do you ever feel tensions between society's expectations of what it means to be a Latina and your own expectation of what it means to be a leader?

[Reflections on Leadership Roles in Social and Political Context]

9. As a Latina who achieved a position of influence, do you see yourself as a role model for other Latinas? Why or why not?
10. Would you say you personally have a lot in common with other Latinos in Rhode Island and nationwide? *[LNS 130]*
    a. Strongly agree
    b. Agree
    c. Disagree
    d. Strongly disagree
11. Would you describe your supporters as mainly Latinos or do they represent a wider range of ethnicities?
12. Do you think the political environment has changed in recent years to make leadership/political roles more, or less, accessible for Latinas?
13. What are the biggest obstacles for Latinas in politics in RI? *[Políticas I-5]*
14. What are the biggest obstacles for Latinas in the nation as a whole?

Bibliography

"A Profile of Latino Elected Officials in the United States and their Progress Since 1996." *NALEO Fact Sheet 2007.* http://www.naleo.org/downloads/NALEO FactSheet07.pdf, accessed on 8/5/13.

Aberbach, Joel, and Jack Walker. 1973. *Race in the City.* Boston: Little Brown.

Abrahamson, Mark, Alexandra Alpert, Yazmin García Trejo, Mark Overmyer-Velázquez, Werner Oyanadel, and Charles Robert Venator Santiago. 2009. *Connecticut Latinos: Evidence from the Connecticut Samples of the Latino National Survey-New England.* Storrs, CT: Roper Center for Public Opinion Research.

Abrajano, Marisa. 2010. *Campaigning to the New American Electorate: Advertising to Latino Voters.* CA: Stanford University Press.

Abrajano, Marisa, and Costas Panagopoulos. 2011. "Does Language Matter? The Impact of Spanish versus English-Language GOTV Efforts on Latino Turnout." *American Politics Research* 39 (4): 643–63.

Abrajano, Marissa, and Simran Singh. 2009. "Examining the Link between Issue Attitudes and News Source: The Case of Latinos and Immigration Reform." *Political Behavior* 31: 1–30.

Agranoff, Robert. 1972. *The New Style in Election Campaigns.* Boston, Mass: Holbrook Press.

Aiken, Charles, Lawrence Bowen, Oguz Nayman, and Kenneth Sheinkopf. 1973. "Quality vs. Quantity in Televised Political Ads." *Public Opinion Quarterly* 37 (2): 209–24.

Alexander, Deborah, and Kristi Andersen. 1993. "Gender as a Factor in the Attribution of Leadership Traits." *Political Research Quarterly* 46: 527–45.

Aniza, Sarah F., and Christopher R. Berry. 2011. "The Jackie (and Jill) Robinson Effect: Why do Congresswomen Outperform Congressmen?" *American Journal of Political Science* 55(3): 478–93.

Ansolabehere, S., and S. Iyengar. 1997. *Going Negative: How Political Advertisements Shrink and Polarize the Electorate.* New York: Free Press.

Ansolabehere, S., S. Iyengar, and A. Simon. 1999. ''Replicating Experiments Using Aggregate and Survey Data: The Case of Negative Advertising and Turnout.'' *The American Political Science Review* 93 (4): 901–9.

Anzaldua, Gloria. 1987. *Borderlands/La Frontera: The New Mestiza.* CA: Aunt Lute Books.

Arendt, H. 1998. *The Human Condition.* 1958. Chicago: U of Chicago Press.

Associated Press. 2007. "Former Health Secretary Grisham Announces for Congress." *Albuquerque Journal*, October 11. Accessed March 3, 2015. http://www.abqjournal.com/news/state/apgrisham10-11-07.htm.

Atkeson, Lonna Rae, and Timothy Krebs. 2008. "Press Coverage in Mayoral Elections: Is There a Gender Bias?" *Political Research Quarterly* 61 (2): 239–53.

Austin, Sharon D., and Richard T. Middleton IV. 2004. "The Limitations of the Deracialization Concept in the 2001 Los Angeles Mayoral Election." *Political Research Quarterly* 57 (2): 283–93.

Avila, Tomas Alberto. 2007. *Rhode Island Latino Political Empowerment: The Evolution of Latino Politics 1996–2006.* Providence: Milenio Publishing.

Baca Zinn, Maxine. 1975. "Political Familism: Toward Sex Role Equality in Chicano Families." *Aztlan: International Journal of Chicano Studies Research* 6: 13–26.

———. 1980. "Gender and Ethnic Identity among Chicanos." *Frontiers* 5(2): 18–24.

Banwart, Marie Christine. 2010. "Gender and Candidate Communication: Effects of Stereotypes in the 2000 Elections." *American Behavioral Scientist* 54: 265–83.

Barreto, Matt. 2007. "Si Se Puede! Latino Candidates and the Mobilization of Latino Voters." *American Political Science Review* 101 (3): 425–42.

Barreto, Matt, Gary Segura, and Nathan Woods. 2004. "The Effects of Overlapping Majority-Minority Districts on Latino Turnout." *American Political Science Review* 98 (February): 65–75.

Bejarano, Christina E. 2013. *Latina Advantage: Gender, Race, and Political Success.* Texas: University of Texas Press.

Bejarano, Christina E. 2014b. "Latino Gender and Generation Gaps in Political Ideology." *Politics & Gender* 10: 62–88.

———. 2014a. *Latino Gender Gap in U.S. Politics.* NY: Routledge.

Bejarano, Christina E., and Anna Sampaio. 2014."Revisiting Latina/o Gender Differences in Party Support." *Latino Decisions*, November 28, athttp://www.latinodecisions.com/blog/2014/11/28/revisiting-latinao-gender-differences-in-party-support/.

Bejarano, Christina E., Sylvia Manzano, and Celeste Montoya. 2011. "Tracking the Latino Gender Gap: Gender Attitudes across Sex, Borders, and Generations." *Politics and Gender* 7: 521–49.

Belanger, Eric, and Bonnie M. Meguid. 2008. "Issue Salience, Issue Ownership, and Issue-Based Vote Choice." *Electoral Studies* 27: 477–91.

Beltrán, Cristina. 2010. *The Trouble with Unity: Latino Politics and the Creation of Identity.* New York: Oxford University Press.

———. 2013. "Crossings and Correspondences: Rethinking Intersectionality and the Category 'Latino.'" *Politics & Gender* 9 (4) (December): 479–483.

Benkler, Yochai. 2006. *The Wealth of Networks: How Social Production Transforms Markets and Freedom.* New Haven and London: Yale University Press.

Bennett, Linda L. M., and Stephen E. Bennett. 1999. "Changing Views about Gender Equality in Politics: Gradual Change and Lingering Doubts." In *Women in Politics: Outsiders or Insiders?*, edited by Lois Lovelace Duke. 3rd Ed., 30–44. Upper Saddle River, NJ: Prentice-Hall.

Bennett, W. L., & A. Segerberg. 2013. *The Logic of Connective Action: Digital Media and the Personalization of Contentious Politics.* Oxford: Cambridge University Press.

Berelson, Bernard, Paul Lazarsfeld, and William McPhee. 1954. *Voting.* Chicago, IL: The University of Chicago Press.

Bejarano, Christina E. 2013. *The Latina Advantage: Gender, Race, and Political Success.* University of Texas Press.

Bobo, Lawrence, and Franklin D. Gilliam. 1990. "Race, Sociopolitical Participation, and Black Empowerment." *American Political Science Review* 84 (02): 377–93.

Bodenhausen, Galen V., Geoffrey P. Kramer, and Karin Susser. 1994. "Happiness and Stereotypic Thinking in Social Judgment." *Journal of Personality and Social Psychology* 66 (4): 621–32.

Box Steffensmeier, Janet, Suzanna de Boef, and Tse-Min Lin. 2004. "The Dynamics of the Partisan Gender Gap." *American Political Science Review* 98 (August): 515–28.

Brader, Ted. 2005. "Striking a Responsive Chord: How Political Ads Motivate and Persuade Voters by Appealing to Emotions." *American Journal of Political Science* 49 (2): 388–405.

———. 2006. *Campaigning for the Hearts and Minds: How Emotional Appeals in Political Ads Work.* Chicago, IL: University of Chicago Press.

Brader, Ted, and B. Corrigan. 2005. "Emotional Cues and Campaign Dynamics in Political Advertising. Paper presented at the Annual Meeting of the American Political Science Association, Washington, D.C.

Bratton, Kathleen A., Kerry L. Haynie and Beth Reingold. 1999. "Agenda-Setting and Legislative Success in State Legislatures: The Effects of Gender and Race." *Journal of Politics* 61: 658–679.

Bratton, K. A. 2002. "The Effect of Legislative Diversity on Agenda Setting Evidence from Six State Legislatures." *American Politics Research* 30 (2): 115–42.

Bratton, Kathleen, Kerry Haynie, and Beth Reingold. 2006. "Agenda Setting and African American Women in State Legislatures." *Journal of Women Politics & Policy* 28: 3–4, 71–96.

Brooks, Deborah Jordan. 2013. *He Runs, She Runs: Why Gender Stereotypes Do Not Harm Women Candidates.* Princeton: Princeton University Press.

Browning, Rufus P., Dale Rogers Marshall, and David Tabb. (1984). *Protest is Not Enough: The Struggle of Blacks and Hispanics for Equality in Urban Politics.* Berkeley: University of California Press.

Bullock III. Charles S. 1984. "Racial Crossover Voting and the Election of Black Officials." *Journal of Politics* 46: 239–51.

Burden, Barry C. 2007. *The Personal Roots of Representation.* Princeton, NJ: Princeton University Press.

Burns, N., L. Evans, G. Gamm and McConnaughy, C. 2008. "Pockets of Expertise: Institutional Capacity in Twentieth-Century State Legislatures." *Studies in American Political Development* 22: 229–48.

Burns, Nancy, Kay Schlozman, and Sidney Verba. 2001. *The Private Roots of Public Action: Gender, Equality and Political Participation.* Cambridge, MA: Harvard University Press.

Burns, Peter, and James G. Gimpel. 2000. "Economic Insecurity, Prejudicial Stereotypes, and Public Opinion on Immigration Policy." *Political Science Quarterly* 115 (2): 201–25.

Burrell, Barbara. 1995. *A Woman's Place is in the House: Campaigning for Congress in the Feminist Era.* Ann Arbor: University of Michigan Press.

———. 1998. "Campaign Finance: Women's Experience in the Modern Era." In *Women and Elective Office: Past, Present and Future,* edited by Sue Thomas and Clyde Wilcox. Oxford: Oxford University Press.

Butler, D. M., and E. N. Powell. 2012. *Understanding the Party Brand.* New Haven, CT: Yale University Mimeo.

Bystrom, Dianne. 2010. "Advertising, Web Sites, and Media Coverage: Gender and Communication along the Campaign Trail." In *Gender and Elections,* edited by Susan J. Carroll and Richard L. Fox, 239–62. New York: Cambridge Press.

Bystrom, Dianne, Terry A. Robertson, Mary Christine Banwart. 2001. "Framing the FightAn Analysis of Media Coverage of Female and Male Candidates in Primary Races for Governor and U.S. Senate in 2000." *American Behavioral Scientist* 44(12): 1999–2013.

Bystrom, Dianne G., Mary Christine Banwart, Lynda Lee Kaid, and Terry A. Robertson. 2004. *Gender and Candidate Communication.* New York: Routledge.

Cain, B. E., D. R. Kiewiet, and Uhlaner, C. J. 1991. "The Acquisition of Partisanship by Latinos and Asian Americans." *American Journal of Political Science,* 35: 390–422.

"California-35 Norma Torres (D)." *National Journal.* December 2014. Accessed March 3, 2015. http://www.nationaljournal.com/almanac/2014-new-mem bers/california-35-norma-torres-d-20141031.

Callaghan, Karen, and Nayda Terkildsen. 2002. "Understanding the Role of Race in Candidate Evaluation." In *Research in Micropolitics,* edited by M. X. Delli Carpini, L. Huddy, & R.Y. Shapiro, Vol. 6. Connecticut: Jai Press, Inc.

Cameron, Charles, David Epstein, and Sharyn O'Halloran. 1996. "Do Majority-Minority Districts Maximize Substantive Black Representation in Congress?" *American Political Science Review* 90 (4): 794–812.

Cameron, Joseph. 2014. "Ex-Rep. Baca Bashes 'Bimbo' Negrete McLeod, Won't Run for Seat." *The Hill,* February 18.

Campbell, D. E., and C. Wolbrecht. 2006. "See Jane Run: Women Politicians as Role Models for Adolescents." *Journal of Politics* 68 (2): 233–47.

Cardenas, Vanessa, Julie Ajinkya, and Daniella Gibbs Leger. 2011. "Progress 2050: New Ideas for a Diverse America." *Center for American Progress.* Access at https://www.americanprogress.org/wpcontent/uploads/issues/2011/10/pdf/progress_2050.pdf

Carroll, S. J. 1994. *Women as Candidates in American Politics.* Bloomington, IN: University of Indiana Press.

———. 2001. *The Impact of Women in Public Office.* Bloomington, IN: Indiana University Press.

———. 2010. "Voting Choices: The Politics of the Gender Gap." In *Gender and Elections*, edited by Susan J. Carroll and Richard L. Fox, 117–44. New York: Cambridge.

Carroll, Susan J. and Kira Sanbonmatsu, 2013. *More Women Can Run: Gender and Pathways to the State Legislature*. New York: Oxford University Press.

Carroll, Susan J. and Richard L. Fox, eds. 2014. *Gender and Elections: Shaping the Future of American Politics, 3rd Edition*. New York: Cambridge University Press.

Carter, Prudence L., Sherrill L. Sellers, and Catherine Squires. 2002. "Reflections on Race/Ethnicity, Class and Gender Inclusive Research." *African American Research Perspectives* 8 (1): 111–24.

Casellas, Jason P. 2011. "Latinas in Legislatures: The Conditions and Strategies of Political Incorporation." *Aztlan* 36 (1): 171–90.

Castells, M. 2011. *The Rise of the Network Society: The Information Age: Economy, Society, and Culture*. Vol. 1. Hoboken, NJ: John Wiley & Sons.

Center for American Women and Politics. 1991."Findings at a Glance: Impact of Women in Public Office." Center for American Women and Politics, Eagleton Institute of Politics, Rutgers, The State University of New Jersey. http://www.cawp.rutgers.edu/research/impact-women-public-officials.

Center for American Women and Politics. 2015. "Women in Elected Office 2015." Eagleton Institute of Politics. New Brunswick.

Chi, F., Yang, N., and et al. 2010. "Twitter in Congress: Outreach vs Transparency." *Social Sciences* 1: 1–20.

Childs, Sarah, and Mona Lena Krook. 2009. "Analysing Women's Substantive Representation: From Critical Mass to Critical Actors." *Government and Opposition* 44 (2): 125–45.

Ciszek, Erica. 2013. "Advocacy and Amplification. Nonprofit Outreach and Empowerment Through Participatory Media." *Public Relations Journal* 7(2): 187–213.

Clark, Cal, and Janet Clark. 1986. "Models of Gender and Political Participation in the United States." *Women and Politics* 6 (1): 5–25.

Clark, Champ. 2013. "Gov. Susana Martinez: Caring for Her Sister." *People Magazine*. Accessed at http://www.people.com/people/archive/article/0.20721515,00.html

Clausing, Jeri; Associated Press. 2011. "New Mexico Gov. Susana Martinez Confirms that Grandparents were Undocumented." *Fox News Latino*. Accessed at http://latino.foxnews.com/latino/politics/2011/09/09/new-mexico-gov-susana-martinez-confirms-that-grandparents-were-undocumented/.

Clawson, Rosalee A., and John A. Clark. 2003. "The Attitudinal Structure of African American Women Party Activists: The Impact of Race, Gender, and Religion." *Political Research Quarterly* 56: 211–21.

Clayton, Dewey. 2003. "African American Women and Their Quest for Congress." *Journal of Black Studies* 33 (3): 354–88.

Clinton, Joshua, and John S. Lapinski. 2004. "'Targeted Advertising' and Voter Turnout: An Experimental Study of the 2000 Presidential Election." *Journal of Politics* 66: 69–96.

Cohen, Cathy J. 2002. "A Portrait of Continuing Marginality: The Study of Women of Color in American Politics." In *Women and American Politics: New*

Questions, New Directions, edited by Susan J. Carroll. 109–214. New York: Oxford University Press.

Cohen, Cathy J. and Dawson, Michael. 2008. "Mobilization, Change and Political and Civic Engagement Project Survey." *Mobilization, Change and Political and Civic Engagement Project.* Chicago, IL. Data set accessed [March 2015] at http://www.2008andbeyond.com/.

Cohen, Cathy J., Kathleen B. Jones, and Joan C. Tronto. 1997. *Women Transforming Politics: An Alternative Reader.* New York: New York University Press.

Coleman, Michael. 2015. "Lujan Grisham to Launch Caregiver's Caucus in DC." *Albuquerque Journal.* Access at http://www.abqjournal.com/547416/abqnews seeker/lujan-grisham-to-launch-caregivers-caucus-in-dc.html.

Connaughton, S. L., and Jarvis, S. E. 2004. "Invitations For Partisan Identification: Attempts to Court Latino Voters Through Televised Latino-Oriented Political Advertisements, 1984–2000." *Journal of Communication* 54(1): 38–54.

Conover, Pamela, and Stanley Feldman. 1989. "Candidate Perception In an Ambiguous World: Campaigns, Cues, and Inference Professes." *The American Journal of Political Science* 33: 912–39.

Crenshaw, Kimberlé. 1989. "Demarginalizing the Intersection of Race and Sex." *University of Chicago Legal Forum* 39: 139–67.

Crenshaw, Kimberle. 1997. "Beyond Racism and Misogyny." In *Women Transforming Politics,* edited by Cathy Cohen, Kathy Jones, and Joan Tronto. New York: New York University Press.

Cruz, Jose E. 2004. "Latinos in Office." In *Latino Americans and Political Participation,* edited by Sharon Navarro and Armando Xavier Mejia. ABC-CILO: Santa Barbara, CA

Davila, Arlene M. 2008. *Latino Spin.* NY: New York University Press.

Dawson, Michael. 1994. *Behind the Mule: Race and Class in African-American Politics.* Princeton, NJ: Princeton University Press.

de la Garza, Rodolfo O., and Louis DeSipio. 2006. "Reshaping the Tub: The Limits of the VRA for Latino Electoral Politics." In *The Future of the Voting Rights Act,* edited by David L. Epstein, Richard H. Pildes, Rodolfo O. de la Garza, and Sharyn O'Halloran. New York: Russell Sage Foundation.

DeFrancesco Soto, Victoria, and Jennifer Merolla. 2008. "Spanish Language Political Advertising and Latino Voters." In *New Race Politics: Understanding Minority and Immigrant Politics,* edited by Jane Junn and Kerry Haynie, 114–29. Cambridge University Press, New York.

Delgado Bernal, D. 1998. "Using a Chicana Feminist Epistemology in Educational Research." *Harvard Educational Review* 68 (4): 555–82.

DeSipio, Louis. 1996. *Counting on the Latino Vote: Latinos as a New Electorate.* Charlottesville, VA: The University Press of Virginia.

Dodson, D. L., and S. J. Carroll. 1991. *Reshaping the Agenda: Women in State Legislatures: Report.* Center for the American Woman and Politics (CAWP), Eagleton Institute of Politics, Rutgers, the State University of New Jersey.

Dolan, Kathleen. 1998. "Voting for Women in the 'Year of the Woman.'" *American Journal of Political Science* 42(1) (Jan): 272–93.

———. 2008. "Women as Candidates in American Politics: The Continuing Impact of Sex and Gender." In *Political Women and American Democracy,* edited by Christina Wolbrecht, Karen Beckwith, and Lisa Baldez. Oxford: Cambridge University Press.

———. 2013. "Candidate Evaluations, and Voting for Women Candidates: What Really Matters?" *Political Research Quarterly* 67 (1): 96–107.

Dolan, Kathleen and Timothy Lynch. 2014. "Making the Connection? Attitudes About Women in Politics and Voting for Women Candidates." *Politics, Groups, and Identities* 3(1) (December): 1–22.

Druckman, James. 2004. "Political Preference Formation: Competition, Deliberation, and the (Ir)relevance of Framing Effects." *American Political Science Review* 98 (4): 671–86.

Duerst-Lahti, Georgia. 2002. "Knowing Congress as a Gendered Institution: Manliness and the Implications of Women in Congress." In *Women Transforming Congress*, edited by Cindy Simon Rosenthal, 20–49. Norman, OK: University of Oklahoma.

———. 2009. "Presidential Elections: Gendered Space and the Case of 2008." In *Gender and Elections: Shaping the Future of American Politics*, 2nd Edition, edited by Susan J. Carroll and Richard L. Fox, 13–43. New York: Cambridge University Press.

Duggan, M. and A. Smith. 2013. "Social Media Update 2013." *Pew Internet and American Life Project.*

Dunbar, R. I. 1992. "Neocortex Size as a Constraint on Group Size in Primates." *Journal of Human Evolution* 22 (6): 469–493.

Ennis, Sharon R., Merarys Rios-Vargas, and Nora G. Albert. "The Hispanic Population: 2010." *2010 Census Briefs.* http://www.census.gov/prod/cen2010/briefs/c2010br-04.pdf, accessed, August 5, 2013.

Entman, Robert M. 1993. "Framing: Toward a Clarification of a Fractured Paradigm." *Journal of Communication* 43: 51–58.

Erskine, Hazel. 1971. "The Polls: Women's Role." *Public Opinion Quarterly* 35 (June): 275–90.

Escobar-Lemmon, M. C., and M. M. Taylor-Robinson. 2014. *Representation: The Case of Women.* Oxford: Oxford University Press.

Eshbaugh-Soha, Matthew. 2014. "The Tone of Spanish-Language Presidential News Coverage." *Social Science Quarterly* 95 (5) (December): 1278–94.

Espiritu, Yen Le. 1992. *Asian American Panethnicity: Bridging Institutions and Identities.* Philadelphia, PA: Temple University Press.

Fenno, R. F. 1978. *Home Style: House Members in Their Districts.* Upper Saddle River, NJ: Pearson College Division.

Fenton, Natalie, and Veronica Barassi. 2011. "Alternative Media and Social Networking Sites: The Politics of Individuation and Political Participation." *The Communication Review* 14 (3): 179–196.

Fiber, Pamela, and Richard Fox. 2005. "A Tougher Road for Women? Assessing the Role of Gender in Congressional Elections." In *Gender and American Politics: Women, Men, and the Political Process*, 2nd Edition, edited by Sue Tolleson-Rinehart and Jyl Josephson. Armonk, NY: M. E. Sharpe.

Finkel, Steven E., and John G. Geer. 1998. "A Spot Check: Casting Doubt on the Demobilizing Effect of Attack Advertising." *American Journal of Political Science* 42 (2): 573–95.

Fisher v. University of Texas, 570 U.S. 2013.

Fletcher, Michael. 2009. "Solis Confirmed as Labor Secretary." *The Washington Post*, February. Accessed March 3, 2015. http://voices.washingtonpost.com/44/2009/02/24/solis_cleared_for_senate_confi.html.

Ford, Lynne. 2010. *Women and Politics: The Pursuit of Equality*. KY: Wadsworth Publishing.

Foucault, M. 1991. "Governmentality." In *The Foucault Effect: Studies in Governmentality*, edited by G. Burchell, C. Gordon & P. Miller. Chicago, IL: University of Chicago Press.

Fox, Richard, and Jennifer Lawless. 2011. "Gendered Perceptions and Political Candidacies: A Central Barrier to Women's Equality in Electoral Politics." *American Journal of Political Science* 55 (1) (January): 59–73.

Fox, Richard, and Eric Ran Smith. 1998. "The Role of Candidate Sex in Voter Decision Making." *Political Psychology* 19 (2): 405–19.

Fox, Richard, and Zoe M. Oxley. 2003. "Gender Stereotyping in State Executive Elections: Candidate Selection and Success." *Journal of Politics* 65 (3): 833–50.

Fraga, Luis Ricardo and Sharon A. Navarro. 2007. "Latinas in Latino Politics." In *Latino Politics: Identity, Mobilization, and Representation*, edited by Rodolfo Espino, David L. Leal, and Kenneth J. Meier, 177–194. Charlottesville: University of Virginia Press.

Fraga, Luis R., John García, Rodney Hero, Michael Jones-Correa, Valerie Martinez-Ebers, and Gary Segura. 2006. "*Su Casa* Es *Nuestra Casa*: Latino Politics Research and the Development of American Political Science." *American Political Science Review* 100 (4): 515–21.

Fraga, Luis R., John García, Rodney E. Hero, Michael Jones-Correa, Valerie Martinez-Ebers, and Gary Segura. 2010. *Latino Lives in America: Making it Home.* Philadelphia: Temple University Press.

Fraga, Luis Ricardo, L. Lopez, V. Martinez-Ebers, and R. Ramirez. 2006. "Gender and Ethnicity: Patterns of Electoral Success and Legislative Advocacy among Latina and Latino State Officials in Four States." *Intersectionality and Politics: Recent Research on Gender, Race, and Political Representation in the United States*, edited by Carol Hardy-Fanta, 121–45. New York: The Haworth Press.

———. 2007. "Gender and Ethnicity: Patterns of Electoral Success and Legislative Advocacy Among Latina and Latino State Officials in Four States." *Journal of Women, Politics & Policy* 28 (3–4): 121–45.

Fraga, Luis Ricardo, V. Martinez-Ebers, R. Ramirez, and L. Lopez. 2001. "Gender and Ethnicity: The Political Incorporation of Latina and Latino State Legislators." Paper presented at the annual meeting of the American Political Science Association, San Francisco, California, August 30–September 2

Fraga, L. R., V. Martínez-Ebers, L. López, and R. Ramírez. 2005. *Strategic Intersectionality: Gender, Ethnicity, and Political Incorporation*. Berkeley, CA: University of California.

Fraga, Luis Ricardo, Valerie Martinez-Ebers, Linda Lopez, and Ricardo Ramirez. 2008. "Representing Gender and Ethnicity: Strategic Intersectionality." In *Legislative Women: Getting Elected, Getting Ahead*, edited by Beth Reingold, 157–74. Boulder, CO: Lynne Rienner Publishers.

Freedman, Paul, and Kenneth Goldstein. 1999. "Measuring Media Exposure and the Effects of Negative Campaign Ads." *American Journal of Political Science* 43: 1189–1208.

Fridkin, Kim, Patrick J. Kenney, and Gina Serignese Woodall. 2009. "Bad for Men, Better for Women: The Impact of Stereotypes during Negative Campaigns." *Political Behavior* 31 (1): 53–77.

Gainous, Jason, and Kevin Wagner. 2014. *Tweeting to Power: The Social Media Revolution in American Politics.* U.K.: Oxford University Press.

García Bedolla, Lisa. 2005. *Fluid Borders: Latino Power, Identity and Politics in Los Angeles.* Berkeley, CA: The University of California Press.

García Bedolla, Lisa. 2007. "Intersections of Inequality: Understanding Marginalization and Privilege in the Post-Civil Rights Era." *Politics and Gender* 3(2): 232–48.

García Bedolla, Lisa, Jessica L. Lavariega Monforti, and Adrian D. Pantoja. 2007. "A Second Look: Is There a Latina/o Gender Gap?" *Journal of Women, Politics and Policy* 28 (3): 147–74.

García Bedolla, Lisa, Katherine Tate, and Janelle Wong. 2014. "Indelible Effects: The Impact of Women of Color in the U.S. Congress." In *Women and Elective Office: Past, Present, and Future,* 3rd Editions, edited by Sue Thomas and Clyde Wilcox. Oxford University Press.

García, F. Chris, Paul L. Hain, Gilbert K. St. Clair, and Kim Seckler, eds. 2006. *Governing New Mexico.* Albuquerque, NM: University Press.

García, Chris and Gabriel Sanchez. 2007. *Hispanics and the U.S. Political System.* NY: Routledge.

García, John A. 2015. "Latinos, Partisanship, and Electoral Engagement." In *Polarized Politics: The Impact of Divisiveness in the U.S. Political System,* edited by William Crotty. Boulder, CO; Lynne Reinner Publishers.

———. 2011. *Latino Politics in America: Community, Culture, and Interests.* 2nd Edition. Lanham, MD: Rowman & Littlefield Publishers, Inc.

García, Sonia R., and Marisela Marquez. 2001. "Motivational and Attitudinal Factors Amongst Latinas in U.S. Electoral Politics." *NWSA Journal* 13 (2): 112–22.

García, Sonia R., Valerie Martinez-Ebers, Irasema Coronado, Sharon A. Navarro, and Patricia Jaramillo. 2008. *Politicas: Latina Public Officials in Texas.* Austin, Texas: University of Texas Press.

Gay, Claudine, and Katherine Tate. 1998. "Doubly Bound: The Impact of Gender and Race on the Politics of Black Women." *Political Psychology* 19 (1): 169–84.

Gershon, Sarah Allen. 2012. "Media Coverage of Minority Congresswomen and Voter Evaluations: Evidence from an Online Experimental Survey." *Political Research Quarterly* 66 (3): 702–14.

Ghavami, N., and L. A. Peplau. 2012. "An Intersectional Analysis of Gender and Ethnic Stereotypes: Testing Three Hypotheses." *Psychology of Women Quarterly* 37: 113–27.

Githens, Marianne and Jewel L. Prestage. 1977. *A Portrait of Marginality: The Political Behavior of the American Woman.* New York: David McKay Company.

Glaser, B., and A. Strauss. 1967. *The Discovery Grounded Theory: Strategies for Qualitative Inquiry.* Chicago: Aldine Publishing Company.

Goers, Stacey. 2013. "Lujan Grisham's Long-Term Goals Are in Focus." *Roll Call.* Access at http://www.rollcall.com/news/lujan_grishams_long_term_goals_are_in_focus-226994-1.html.

Gonzales, Felicia. 2008. "Hispanic Women in the United States, 2007." *Pew Hispanic Center.* http://pewhispanic.org/files/factsheets/42.pdf (accessed March 10, 2011).

Grabe, M. E. and Bucy, E. P. 2009. *Image Bite Politics News and the Visual Framing of Elections*. Oxford, London: Oxford University Press.

Guinier, L. 1989. "Keeping the Faith: Black Voters in the Post-Reagan Era." *Harvard. CR-CLL Rev.* 24: 393.

Guo, C. and G. D. Saxton. 2014. "Speaking and Being Heard: How Nonprofit Advocacy Organizations Gain Attention on Social Media." *Academy of Management Proceedings* 1: 16174.

Gutierrez, Ramon A. 1993. "Community, Patriarchy and Individualism: The Politics of Chicano History and the Dream of Equity." *American Quarterly* 45 (1): 44–72.

Hamilton, Charles. 1977. "De-racialization: Examination of a Political Strategy." *First World* (March–April): 3–5.

Hancock, Ange-Marie. 2007a. "Intersectionality as a Normative and Empirical Paradigm." *Politics & Gender* 3 (2): 248–54.

———. 2007b. *The Politics of Disgust: The Public Identity of the Welfare Queen*. New York: New York University Press.

———. 2007c. "When Multiplication Doesn't Equal Quick Addition: Examining Intersectionality as a Research Paradigm." *Perspectives on Politics* 5 (1): 63–79.

Hardy-Fanta, Carol. 1991. "Latina Women, Latino Men, and Political Participation in Boston: *La Chispa Que Prende*." PhD dissertation, Brandeis University.

———. 1993. *Latina Politics, Latino Politics: Gender, Culture and Political Participation in Boston*. Philadelphia: Temple University Press.

———. 1995. "Latina Women and Political Leadership: Implications for Latino Community Empowerment." *New England Journal of Public Policy* (Spring/Summer): 221–35.

———. 1997. *Latino Electoral Campaigns in Massachusetts: The Impact of Gender*. Center for Women in Politics and Public Policy and the Mauricio Gastón Institute for Latino Community Development and Public Policy.

Hardy-Fanta, Carol. 1997. *Latino Electoral Campaigns in Massachusetts: The Impact of Gender*. Boston: Center for Women in Politics and Public Policy.

Hardy-Fanta, Carol, ed. 2007. *Intersectionality and Politics: Recent Research on Gender, Race, and Political Representation in the United States*. London: The Haworth Press Inc.

Hardy-Fanta, Carol. 2002. "Latina Women and Political Leadership." In *Latino Politics in Massachusetts: Struggles, Strategies, and Prospects*, edited by Hardy-Fanta and Jeffrey Gerson. New York: Routledge.

Hardy-Fanta, Carol, and Jeffrey Gerson. 2002. *Latino Politics in Massachusetts: Struggles, Strategies, and Prospects*. New York: Routledge.

Hardy-Fanta, Carol, Pei-te Lien, Dianne Pinderhughes, and Christine Marie Sierra. 2016 (Summer 2016). *Contested Transformation: Race, Gender, and Political Leadership in Twenty-First Century America*. Cambridge, NY: Cambridge University Press.

———. 2006. "Gender, race, and descriptive representation in the United States: Findings from the gender and multicultural leadership project." *Journal of Women, Politics & Policy* 28, (3/4): 7–41.

Hardy-Fanta, Carol, Pei-te Lien, Dianne M. Pinderhughes, and Christine Marie Sierra. 2007. "Gender, Race, and Descriptive Representation in the United States: Findings from the Gender and Multicultural Leadership Project." *Journal of Women, Politics & Policy* 28, (3–4): 7–41.

Hardy-Fanta, Carol, Pei-te Lien, Dianne Pinderhughes, and Christine M. Sierra. Summer 2016. *Gender and Multi-cultural Leadership Project.* Book Manuscript.

Hardy-Fanta, Carol, Christine Sierra, Pei-te Lien, Dianne Pinderhughes, and Wartyna Davis. 2005. "Race, Gender, and Descriptive Representation: An Exploratory View of Multicultural Elected Leadership in the United States." Paper presented at the 2005 Annual Meeting of the American Political Science Association, September 1–4, Washington, DC.

Harris, Vincent, "Debriefing 2014 in Texas," Speech given at the Annette Strauss Institute, University of Texas at Austin, November 5, 2014.

Hawkesworth, M. 1994. "Policy Studies within a Feminist Frame. *Policy Sciences: An International Journal Devoted to the Improvement of Policy Making* 27 (2–3): 97–118.

———. 2003. "Congressional Enactments of Race-Gender: Toward a Theory of Race-Gendered Institutions." *American Political Science Review* 97(4): 529–50.

Hayes, Danny. 2005. "Candidate Qualities Through a Partisan Lens: A Theory of trait Ownership." *American Journal of Political Science* 49: 908–23.

———. 2011. "When Gender and Party Collide: Stereotyping in Candidate Trait Attribution." *Politics & Gender* 7 (2): 133–65.

Hayes, Danny, and Jennifer Lawless. 2015. "A Non-Gendered Lens? Media, Voters, and Female Candidates in Contemporary Congressional Elections." *Perspectives on Politics* 13 (1): 95-118.

Helco, Hugh. 1978. "Issue Networks and the Executive Establishment." In *The New American Politcal System*, edited by Antony King. Washington, DC: American Enterprise Institute.

Hernandez, Samantha L. *LatinaStyle: Latina Campaign Tactics and Minimizing Threat.* Dissertation. Arizona State University. 2017.

Hero, Rodney. 1992. *Latinos and the U.S. Political System: Two-tiered Pluralism.* Philadelphia: Temple University Press.

Herrnson, Paul S., J. Celeste Lay, and Atiya Kai Stokes. 2003. "Women Running 'as Women': Candidate Gender, Campaign Issues and Voter-Targeting Strategies." *Journal of Politics* 65 (1): 244–55.

Herrnson, Paul S., and Patterson, Kelly D. 2000. "Agenda Setting and Campaign Advertising in Congressional Elections." In *Crowded Airwaves: Campaign Advertising in Elections*, edited by James A. Thurber, Candice Nelson, and David Dulio, 96–112. Washington, D.: Brookings Institute.

Hinojosa, Magda. 2010. "'She's Not My Type of Blonde': Media Coverage of Irene Saez's Presidential Bid in Rainbow Murray." In *Cracking the Highest Glass Ceiling: A Global Comparison of Women's Campaigns for Executive Office*, edited by Rainbow Murray and Pippa Norris, 31–47. Santa Barbara, California: Praeger.

"Hispanic Domestic Violence Statistics: Nearly Two-Thirds of Women Know an Abuse Victim, Allstate Foundation Survey Reports." *Latin Times,* September 18, 2014. Accessed June 4, 2015. http://www.latintimes.com/hispanic-domestic-violence-statistics-nearly-two-thirds-women-know-abuse-victim-allstate-262497.

"Hispanic Political Leadership Facts," *National Association of Latino Elected and Appointed Officials* at http://www.naleo.org/directory.html.

Hood, M. V., III., and I. L. Morris. 1997. "Amigo o Enemigo? Context, Attitudes, and Anglo Public Opinion Toward Immigration." *Social Science Quarterly* 78: 309–23.

Hood, M. V., III., I. L. Morris, and Shirkey, K. A. 1997. "'! Quedate o Vente!': Uncovering the Determinants of Hispanic Public Opinion Toward Immigration." *Political Research Quarterly* 50: 627–47.

Howell, S.E., and W. P. McLean. 2001. "Performance and Race in Evaluating Black Mayors." *Public Opinion Quarterly* 65: 321–43.

Hu-DeHart, Evelyn, Matt García, Cynthia García Coll, José Itzigsohn, Marion Orr, Tony Affigne, and Jorge Elorza. 2008. *Rhode Island Latinos—Debunking Myths & Uncovering Truths: Evidence from the New England Latino Survey.* Providence: Center for the Study of Race and Ethnicity in America.

Huber, Gregory A., and Kevin Arceneaux. 2006. *Uncovering the Persuasive Effects of Presidential Advertising.* New Haven, Conn: Yale University Press.

Huddy, L., S. Feldman, and Cassese, E. 2007. "On the Distinct Political Effects of Anxiety and Anger." In *The Affect Effect: Dynamics of Emotion in Political Thinking and Behavior,* edited by W. R. Neuman, G. E., Marcus, M. Mackuen, & A. N. Crigler, 202–30. Chicago, IL: Chicago University Press.

Huddy, Leonie and Teresa Capelos. 2002. "Gender Stereotyping and Candidate Evaluation." In *The Social Psychology of Politics,* edited by V. C. Ottati, R. S. Tindall, J. Edwards, F. B. Bryant, L. Heath, D. C. O'Connell, Y. Suarez-Balcazar, and E. Posavac. New York: Kluwer Academic Press.

Huddy, Leonie, and Nayda Terkildsen. 1993. "Gender Stereotypes and the Perception of Male and Female Candidates." *American Journal of Political Science* 37(1): 119–47.

Hurtado, A. 1989. "Relating to Privilege: Seduction and Rejection in the Subordination of White Women and Women of Color." *Signs* 14 (4): 833–55.

———. 1997. *The Color of Privilege: Three Blasphemies on Race and Feminism.* Ann Arbor, MI: University of Michigan Press.

———. 1996. "Strategic Suspensions: Feminists of Color Theorize the Production of Knowledge." In *Knowledge, Difference, and Power: Essays Inspired by Women's Ways of Knowing,* edited by N. Goldberger, J. Tarule, B. Clincy & M. Belenky. New York, NY: Basic Books.

Ignatiev, Noel. 1995. *How the Irish Became White.* Madison Ave. US: Routledge Press.

Inglehart, Ronald, and Pippa Norris. 2000. "The Developmental Theory of the Gender Gap: Women and Men's Voting Behavior in Global Perspective." *International Political Science Review* 21 (October): 441–63.

Itzigsohn, José. 2011. *Encountering American Faultlines: Race, Class, and the Dominican Experience in Providence.* New York: Russell Sage.

Itzigsohn, José, and Carlos Dore-Cabral. 2000. "Competing Identities? Race, Ethnicity and Panethnicity among Dominicans in the United States." *Sociological Forum* 15 (2).

Iyengar, Shanto, and Donald R. Kinder. 1987. *News, That Matters: Television and the American Opinion.* Chicago, IL: University of Chicago Press.

Jamieson, Kathleen Hall. 1992. *Dirty Politics: Deception, Distraction, and Democracy.* New York: Oxford University Press.

Jamieson, Kathleen Hall, Paul Waldman, and Susan Sherr. 2000. "Eliminating the Negative? Categories of Analysis for Political Advertisements." In *Crowded Airwaves: Campaign Advertising in Elections,* edited by James A. Thurber, Candice J. Nelson, & David J. Dulio, 44–56. Washington, DC: Brookings Institution.

Jaramillo, Patricia. *Coloring the Pipeline: Mexican American Women and the Decision to Run for Elective Office.* Western Political Science Association, 2007. Unpublished conference paper. Las Vegas, Nevada, 2007.

Jaramillo, Patricia. 2010. "Building a Theory, Measuring a Concept: Exploring Intersectionality and Latina Activism at the Individual Level." *Journal of Women, Politics and Policy* (July–Sept) 31 (3): 193–216.

Jennings, M. Kent. 2006. "The Gender Gap in Attitudes and Beliefs about the Place of Women in American Political Life: A Longitudinal Cross-Generation Analysis." *Politics & Gender* 2 (2): 193–219.

Johnson, D., H. Kabuchu, and S. V. Kayonga. 2003. "Women in Ugandan Local Government: the Impact of Affirmative Action." *Gender & Development* 11 (3): 8–18.

Jones, Bryan, and Frank Baumgartner. 2005. *The Politics of Attention: How Government Prioritizes Problems.* Chicago: University of Chicago Press.

Jones, Philips Edward. 2013. "Revisiting Stereotypes of Non-White Politicians' Ideological and Partisan Orientations." *American Politics Research* 42 (2): 283–310.

Jones-Correa, Michael. 1998. "Different Paths: Gender, Immigration and Political Participation." *International Migration Review* 32 (2): 326–49.

Just, Marion R., Ann N. Crigler, Dean E. Alger, and Timothy E. Cook. 1996. *Cross-Talk: Citizens, Candidate, and the Media in a Presidential Campaign.* Chicago. IL: University of Chicago Press.

Justus, Margaret. 2014. "Annual Independent Poll Reveals Texan's Diverse Attitudes on Key Campaign Issue." *The Texas Lyceum.* September 30.

Kahn, Kim Fridkin, and Edie N. Goldenberg. 1991. "Women Candidates in the News: An Examination of Gender Differences in U.S. Senate Campaign Coverage." *Public Opinion Quarterly* 55 (2): 180–199.

Kahn, Kim Fridkin. 1992. "Does Being Male Help? An Investigation of the Effects of Candidate Gender and Campaign Coverage on Evaluations of U.S. Senate Candidates." *Journal of Politics* 54 (2): 497–517.

Kahn, Kim F. 1993. "Gender Differences in Campaign Messages: The Political Advertisements of Men and Women Candidates for U.S. Senate." *Political Research Quarterly* 46 (3) (Sept): 481–502.

———. 1994. "Does Gender Make a Difference? An Experimental Examination of Sex Stereotypes and Press Patters in Statewide Campaigns." *American Journal of Political Science* 38 (1): 162–95.

———. 1996. *The Political Consequences of Being a Woman: How Stereotypes Influence the Conduct and Consequences of Political Campaigns.* New York: Columbia University Press.

Kahn, Kim F., and Patrick J. Kenney. 1999. *The Spectacle of U.S. Senate Campaigns.* Princeton, NJ: Princeton University Press.

Kahneman, Daniel, Paul Slovic, and Amos Tversky. 1979. "Prospect Theory of Decisions Under Risk." *Econometrica* 47 (2): 263–91.

Kam, Cindy D., Elizabeth J. Zechmeister, and Jennifer R. Wilking. 2008. "From the Gap to the Chasm: Gender and Participation among Non-Hispanic Whites and Mexican Americans." *Political Research Quarterly* 61 (2) (June): 205–18.

Kanthak, Kristin, and George A. Krause. 2012. *The Diversity Paradox: Political Parties, Legislatures and the Organizational Foundations of Representation in America.* New York: Oxford University Press.

Kaufmann, Karen M. 2003. "Cracks in the Rainbow: Group Commonality as a Basis for Latino and African-American Political Coalitions." *Political Research Quarterly* 56 (2): 199–210.

Kenski, Kate, and Erika Falk. 2004. "Of What is that Glass Ceiling Made?" *Women & Politics* 26 (2): 57–80.

Kerevel, Yann P. 2011. "The Influence of Spanish-Language Media on Latino Public Opinion and Group Consciousness." *Social Science Quarterly* 92 (2) (June): 509–33.

Kernstock, Elwyn Nicholas. 1972. "How New Migrants Behave Politically: The Puerto Ricans in Hartford, 1970." PhD dissertation, University of Connecticut.

King, David C., and Richard E. Matland. 2003. "Sex and the Grand Old Party: An Experimental Investigation of the Effect of Candidate Sex on Support for a Republican Candidate." *American Politics Research* 31(6): 595–612.

Knoll, Benjamin R., David P. Redlawsk, and Howard Sanborn. 2010. "Framing Labels and Immigration Policy Attitudes in the Iowa Caucuses: 'Trying to Out-Tancredo Tancredo.'" *Political Behavior* 33 (3): 433–54.

Koch, Jeffrey W. 2000. "Do Citizens Apply Gender Stereotypes to Infer Candidates' Ideological Orientations?" *Journal of Politics* 62 (2): 414–29.

Kofler, Shelley. 2014. "Map: Is Dan Patrick Running a 'Stealth' Campaign?" *Keranews.org* (October 29) at www.keranews.org/post/map-dan-patrick-running-stealth-campaign.

Kornblut, A. E. 2009. *Notes From the Cracked Ceiling: Hillary Clinton, Sarah Palin, and What it Will Take for a Woman to Win.* New York: Crown Publishers.

Kornbult, Anne. 2011. *Notes from the Cracked Ceiling.* NY: Broadway Books.

Koszczuck, Jackie, and H. Amy Stern. 2005. *CQ's Politics in America 2006.* Washington, DC: CQ Press.

Krasno, Jonathon and Donald Green. 2008. "Do Televised Presidential Ads Increase Voter Turnout? Evidence from a Natural Experiment." *Journal of Politics* 70 (1) (Jan): 245–61.

Larson, Stephanie Grecco. 2001. "Running as Women? A Comparison of Female and Male Pennsylvania Assembly Candidates' Campaign Brochures." *Women and Politics* 22 (2):107–24.

Lassen , D. S., and Brown , A. R. 2011. "Twitter: The Electoral Connection?" *Social Science Computer Review* 29 (4): 419–36.

"Latino Progress Report, 2015." *NALEO* Accessed at http://www.naleo.org/at_a_glance.

Lau, Richard R., and Lee Sigelman. 2000. "Effectiveness of Negative Political Advertising." In *Crowded Airwaves: Campaign Advertising in Elections,* edited by James A. Thurber, Candice J. Nelson, and David J. Dulio, 10–43. Washington, DC: Brookings Institution.

Lauderdale, Benjamin E. 2012. "Does Inattention to Political Debate Explain the Polarization Gap Between the US Congress and Public?" (PDF). Unpublished.

Lavariega Monforti, Jessica, Bryan D'Andra Orey, and Andrew J. Conroly. 2009. "The Politics of Race, Gender, Ethnicity and Representation in the Texas Legislature." *The Journal of Race and Policy* 5 (1): 35–53.

Lawless, Jennifer L. 2004. "Women, War, and Winning Elections: Gender Stereotyping in the Post-September 11th Era." *Political Research Quarterly* 57 (3): 479–90.

Lawless, Jennifer and Danny Hayes. 2013. "A Non-gendered Lens: The Absence of Stereotyping in Contemporary Congressional Elections." Paper presented at the annual meeting of the Southern Political Science Association, Orlando.

Lawless, Jennifer L., and Richard Fox. 2005. *It Takes a Candidate: Why Women Don't Run for Office.* New York: Cambridge University Press.

Lawless, Jennifer L., and Richard Fox. 2008. "Why Are Women Still Not Running for Public Office? In *Issues in Governance Studies*, 16 (May). http://www.brookings.edu/~/media/research/files/papers/2008/5/women%20lawless%20fox/05_women_lawless_fox.pdf.

Lawless, Jennifer L., and Richard Fox. 2010. *It Still Takes A Candidate: Why Women Don't Run for Office.* Cambridge University Press.

Lawrence, Regina, and Melody Rose. 2009. *Hillary Clinton's Race for the White House: Gender Politics and the Media on the Campaign Trail.* Colorado: Lynne Rienner.

Leeper, Mark Stephen. 1991. "The Impact of Prejudice on Female Candidates: An Experimental Look at Voter Inference." *American Politics Research* 19: 248–61.

Leighley, J. E. 2001. *Strength in Numbers? The Political Mobilization of Racial and Ethnic Minorities.* Princeton, NJ: Princeton University Press.

Lemus, Frank. 1973. *National Roster of Spanish Surnamed Elected Officials.* Los Angeles: Aztlan Publications.

Lien, Pei-Te. 1998. "Does the Gender Gap in Political Attitudes and Behavior Vary Across Racial Groups?" *Political Research Quarterly* 51 (December): 869–94.

Lien, Pei-te, Dianne M. Pinderhughes, Carol Hardy-Fanta, and Christine M. Sierra. 2007. "The Voting Rights Act and the Election of Nonwhite Officials." *PS: Political Science & Politics* 40(3): 489–94.

Lilleker, Darren G., and Nigel A. Jackson. 2010. "Towards a More Participatory Style of elction Campaigning: The Impact of Web 2.) on the UK 2010 General Election." *Policy and Internet* 2(3): 69–98.

Lilleker, D. G., M. Pack, and N. Jackson. 2010. "Political Parties and Web 2.0: The Liberal Democrat Perspective." *Politics* 30 (2): 105–12.

López, P. D. 2013. *Final Analysis of House Bill 5 (HB 5): Relating to Public School Accountability, Including Assessment, and Curriculum Requirements.* Austin, TX: Texas Center for Education Policy.

———. 2012. *The Process of Becoming: The Political Construction of Texas' Lone STAAR System of Accountability and College Readiness.* Unpublished Dissertation. Austin, TX: University of Texas at Austin.

López, P. D., and A. Valenzuela. 2014. "Resisting Epistemological Exclusion and Inserting La Clase Mágica into State-level Policy Discourses." In *La Clase Mágica: Generating Transworld,* edited by B. Flores, O. Vasquez & E. R. Clark. Lexington Publishers, Rowman & Littlefield Publishing Group.

López, P.D., A. Valenzuela, and E. García. 2011. "The Critical Ethnography of Public Policy: Social Justice and Community Responsibility." In *Companion to the Anthropology of Education,* edited by B.A. Levinson & M. Pollock. Hoboken, NJ: Wiley-Blackwell.

Lovejoy, K., and G. D. Saxton. 2012. "Information, Community, and Action: How Nonprofit Organizations Use Social Media." *Journal of Computer-Mediated Communication* 17 (3): 337–53.

Lupia, Arthur, and Matthew D. McCubbins. 1998. *The Democratic Dilemma: Can Citizens Learn What They Need to Know?* New York: Cambridge University Press.

MacManus, Susan A., Charles S. Bullock, and Barbara P. Grothe. 1986. "A Longitudinal Examination of Political Participation Rates of Mexican American Females." *Social Science Quarterly* 67 (3) (September): 604–12.

Madon, S., M. Guyll, K. Aboufadel, E. Montiel, A. Smith, P. Palumbo, and J. Jussim. 2001."Ethnic and National Stereotypes: The Princeton Trilogy Revisited and Revised." *Personality and Social Psychology Bulletin* 27: 996–1010.

Mansbridge, Jane. 1999. "Should Blacks Represent Blacks and Women Represent Women? A Contingent 'Yes.'" *Journal of Politics* 61 (3): 628–57.

———. 2003. "Rethinking Representation." *American Political Science Review* 97 (4): 515–28.

Manuel, Tiffany. 2006. "Envisioning the Possibilities for a Good Life: Exploring the Public Policy Implications of Intersectionality Theory." *Journal of Women, Politics, & Policy.* 28 (3/4): 173–203.

Manzano, Sylvia and Gabriel Sanchez. 2010. "Take One For the Team?: Limits of Shared Ethnicity and Candidate Preferences." *Political Research Quarterly* 63 (3): 568–80.

Marcus, G. E., W. R. Neuman, and M. MacKuen. 2000. *Affective Intelligence and Political Judgment.* Chicago, IL: University of Chicago Press.

Marcus, G. E., W. R. Neuman, M. MacKuen, J. Wolak, and L. Keele. 2006. "The Measure and Mismeasure of Emotions." In *Feeling Politics,* edited by David P. Redslawk, 31–46. New York: Palgrave MacMillan.

Marichal, J. 2013. "Profile Politics: Examining Polarization through Congressional Member Facebook Pages." In *Politics to the Extreme: American Political Institutions in the 21st Century,* edited by S. Kelly and S. Frisch. Palgrave McMillan.

Martinez, Marta V. 2014. *Latino History in Rhode Island: Nuestras Raíces.* Charleston, SC: The History Press.

Masuoka, Natalie. 2006. "Together They Become One: Examining the Predictors of Panethnic Group Consciousness among Asian Americans and Latinos." *Social Science Quarterly* 87 (5): 993–1011.

Massey, Barry, and Russell Contreras. 2011. "Susana Martinez: New Mexico Governor, Releases Evidence On Her Grandparents' Immigration Status." *Huffington Post.* Accessed at http://www.huffingtonpost.com/2011/11/14/susana-martinez-new-mexico-governor-undocumented-immigrants_n_1093251.html.

Matland, Richard, and Gary King. 2002. "Women as Candidates in Congressional Elections." In C. Rosenthal, *Women Transforming Congress,* edited by C. Rosenthal. Tulsa: University of Oklahoma Press.

Matson, Marsha, and Terri Susan Fine. 2006. "Gender, Ethnicity, and Ballot Information: Ballot Cues in Low-Information Elections." *State Politics & Policy Quarterly* 6 (1): 49–72.

McCall, L. 2005. "The Complexity of Intersectionality." *Signs: Journal of Women in Culture and Society* 30(3): 1771–1800.

McConnaughy, Corrine M., Ismail K. White, David L. Leal, and Jason P. Casellas. 2010. "A Latino on the Ballot: Explaining Coethnic Voting Among Latinos and the Response of White Americans." *The Journal of Politics* 72 (4): 1199–1211.

McDermott, Monika L. 1997. "Voting Cues in Low-Information Elections: Candidate Gender as a Social Information Variable in Contemporary United States Elections." *American Journal of Political Science* 41 (1): 270–83.

———. 1998. "Race and Gender Cues in Low-Information Elections." *Political Research Quarterly* 51: 895–918.

McDermot, V. A. 1980. "Interpersonal Communication Networks: An Approach Through the Understanding of Self Concept, Significant Others, and the Social Influence Process." *Communication Quarterly* 28: 13–25.

McIlwain, Charlton, and Stephen M. Caliendo. 2014. "Mitt Romney's Racist Appeals: How Race Was Played in the 2012 Presidential Election." *American Behavioral Scientist* 58 (9) (August): 1157–1168.

McSwane, J. David. "Patrick, Van de Putte Trade Jabs Over Their One Debate: They Differ Widely on Tax Reform, Abortion, and Immigration Policy." *Austin American Statesman,* September 30, 2014, A1.

Mead, G. H. 1934. *Mind, Self and Society: From the Standpoint of a Social Behaviorist.* Chicago, IL: University of Chicago Press.

Meeks, Lindsey. 2012. "Is She 'Man Enough'? Women Candidates, Executive Political Offices, and News Coverage." *Journal of Communication* 62: 175–93.

Melville, Margarita B., ed. 1980. *Twice a Minority: Mexican American Women.* St. Louis: The C. V. Mosby Company.

Mendelberg, Tali. 2001. *The Race Card: Campaign Strategy, Implicit Messages, and the Norm of Equality.* Princeton, NJ: Princeton University Press.

Merolla, Jennifer L. and Juana Mora. 2007. "The Gender Gap Among Latino Partisans." Conference paper prepared for the 2007 Annual Meeting of the Western Political Science Association, Las Vegas, Nevada.

Milkman, Ruth and Veronica Terriquez. 2012. "'We Are the Ones Who Are Out in Front': Women's Leadership in the Immigrant Rights Movement." *Feminist Studies* 38 (3) (Fall): 723–52.

Mirza, Heidi Safia. 2008. *Race, Gender and Educational Desire: Why Black Women Succeed and Fail.* New York: Routledge.

Moncrief, Gary, Joel Thompson, and Robert Schuhmann. 1991. "Gender, Race, and the State Legislature: A Research Note on the Double Disadvantage Hypothesis." *The Social Science Journal* 28 (4): 481–87.

Monteleone, James. 2014. "King Says Governor Lacks 'Latino Heart'." *Albuquerque Journal.* Accessed at http://www.abqjournal.com/459675/news/king-say-governor-lacks-latino-heart.html.

Montoya, Lisa J. 1996. "Latino Gender Difference in Public Opinion: Results from the Latino National Political Survey." *Hispanic Journal of Behavioral Sciences* 18 (2) (May): 255–76.

Montoya, Lisa J., Carol Hardy-Fanta, and Sonia García. 2000. "Latina Politics: Gender, Participation, and Leadership." *PS: Political Science & Politics* 33 (3): 555–61.

Murray, Rainbow. 2010. "Introduction: Gender Stereotypes and Media Coverage of Women Candidates." Cracking the Highest Glass Ceiling: A Global Comparison of Women's Campaigns for Executive Office. R. Murray. Santa Barbara, CA, Praeger: 3–27.

Nader, Ralph, and Manuel Luján, Jr. 1972. *Congress Project.* Washington D.C.: Grossman Publishers, 1972.

Nagler, Jonathan, and Jan Leighley. 1992. "Presidential Campaign Expenditures: Evidence of Allocations and Effects." *Public Choice* 73 (3) (April): 319–33.

National Directory of Latino Elected Officials. NALEO Educational Fund. Los Angeles, CA.

National Hispanic Caucus of State Legislators. 2015. "Hispanic State Legislator Information: Hispanic State Legislators at a Glance." http://www.nhcsl.org/hispanic-state-legislator-information.php.

Navarro, S. 2008. *Latina Legislator: Leticia Van de Putte and the Road to Leadership.* College Station, TX: Texas A&M University Press.

Nelson, Dale. 1979. "Ethnicity and Socioeconomic Status as Sources of Participation: The Case for Ethnic Political Culture." *American Political Science Review* 73(4): 1024–38.

Nelson, Thomas E., and Donald Kinder. 1996. "Issue Frames and Group Centrism in American Public Opinion." *The Journal of Politics* 58: 1055–78.

New Mexico Secretary of State. 2014. "Official Results: General Election, November 4, 2014." Accessed at http://electionresults.sos.state.nm.us/.

Nir, Lilach, and James N. Druckman. 2008. "Campaign Mixed-Message Flows and Timing of Vote Decision." *International Journal of Public Opinion Research* 20 (3): 326–46.

Norris, Pippa, and Ronald Inglehart. 2008. "Cracking the Marble Ceiling: Cultural barriers facing women leaders." Harvard University. http://www.hks.harvard.edu/fs/pnorris/Acrobat/Marble%20ceiling%20professional%20format.pdf.

Norrander, Barbara. 1999. "The Evolution of the Gender Gap." *Public Opinion Quarterly* 63 (February): 566–76.

Office of Congresswoman Michelle Lujan Grisham. 2015. "Biography." *U.S. House of Representatives.* Accessed at https://lujangrisham.house.gov/about/biography.

Office of the Governor Susana Martinez. 2015. "Meet Governor Susana Martinez." *State of New Mexico.* Accessed at http://www.governor.state.nm.us/Meet_Governor_Martinez.aspx.

Osborn, Tracy. 2012. *How Women Represent Women: Political Parties, Gender and Representation in the State Legislatures.* New York: Oxford University Press.

Pachon, Harry, and Louis DeSipio. 1992. "Latino elected officials in the 1990s." *PS: Political Science & Politics* 25, no. 02: 212–17.

Palfrey, Thomas R., and T. Poole Keith. 1987. "The Relationship Between Information, Ideology, and Voting Behavior." *American Journal of Political Science* 31 (3): 511–30.

Pantoja, Adrian D. and Sarah Allen Gershon. 2006. "Political Orientations and Naturalization Among Latino and Latina Immigrants." *Social Science Quarterly* 87 (5) (December): 1171–87.

Pardo, Mary. 1989. *Mexican American Women Activists.* PA: Temple University Press.

———. 1990. "Mexican American Women Grassroots Community Activists: 'Mothers of East Los Angeles.'" *Frontiers: A Journal of Women Studies* 11 (1): 1–7.

———. 1997. "Mexican American Women Grassroots Community Activists: 'Mothers of East Los Angeles.'" *Pursuing Power: Latinos and the Political System,* edited by F. Chris García. Notre Dame, Indiana: University of Notre Dame Press.

Parenti, Michael. 1967. "Ethnic Politics and the Persistence of Ethnic Identification." *American Political Science Review* 61(3): 717–26.

Passel, Jeffrey S., and D'Vera Cohn. 2008. *U.S. Population Projections: 2005–2050*. Washington D.C.: Pew Research Center.

Petersen, Kristen A., Hardy-Fanta, Carol, and Armenoff, Karla. 2005. "'As Tough As It Gets': Women in Boston Politics, 1921–2004." *Center for Women in Politics and Public Policy Publications*. Paper No. 13. http://scholarworks.umb.edu/cwppp_pubs/13.

Phillips, Anne. 2010. "What's Wrong with Essentialism?" *Distinktion: Scandinavian Journal of Social Theory* 11 (1): 47–60.

Philpot, Tasha S. and Hanes Walton, Jr. 2007. "One of Our Own: Black Female Candidates and the Voters Who Support Them." *American Journal of Political Science* 51 (1): 49–62.

Pinney, Neil, and George Serra. 1999. "The Congressional Black Caucus and Vote Cohesion: Placing the Caucus within House Voting Patterns." *Political Research Quarterly* 52 (3): 583–607.

Pitkin, H. F. 1967. *The Concept of Representation*. Berkeley, CA: University of California Press.

PODER PAC. 2011. "PoderPAC Endorses Michelle Lujan Grisham NM CD 1 (Dem Primary)."

Popkin, Samuel. 1994. *The Reason Voter: Communication and Persuasion in Presidential Campaigns*. Chicago, IL: University of Chicago Press.

Preuhs, Robert R. 2006. "The Conditional Effects of Minority Descriptive Representation: Black Legislators and Policy Influence in the American States." *The Journal of Politics* 68 (3): 585–99.

Prindeville, Diane-Michele. 2003. "'I've Seen Changes': The Political Efficacy of American Indian and Hispanic Women Leaders." *Women & Politics* 25 (1): 89–113.

Purple Purse. 2014. "Financial Abuse Survey." *Allstate Foundation*. www.purplepurse.org

Quinones-Mayo, Yolanda, and Rosa Perla Resnik. 1996. "The Impact of Machismo on Hispanic Women." *Affilia* 11 (3): 257–77.

Ramos-Zaya, Ana Y. 2001. "Racializing the "Invisible" Race: Latino Constructions of "White Culture" and Whiteness in Chicago." *Urban Anthropology and Studies of Cultural Systems and World Economic* 30 (4): 341–80.

Ramsey, Ross. 2014. "Analysis: Tuesday Aside, It was All Over in March." *Texas Tribune,* November 7.

Rauf, David Saleh. 2014."Patrick Sounds Alarm About Threat of ISIS Border; Van de Putte Slams Politics of Fear." *Houston Chronicle,* September 21, B10.

———. 2014. "Van de Putte Ad Attacks Foe." *San Antonio Express News*, September 6, A3.

Republican National Committee. 2012. "Excerpt from the 2012 Republican National Convention." Accessed at https://www.youtube.com/watch?v=yjbtxupVo6I.

Riggle, Ellen D., Victor C. Ottati, Robert S. Wyer, James Kuklinski, and Norbert Schwarz. 1992. "Bases of Political Judgments: The Role of Stereotypic and Non-stereotypic Information." *Political Behavior* 14 (1): 67–87.

Robinson, C. 2010. "Political Advertising and the Demonstration of Market Orientation." *European Journal of Marketing* 44(3/4), 451–60.

Rocca, Michael, and Gabriel Sanchez. 2008. "The Effect of Race and Ethnicity on Bill Sponsorship and Cosponsorship in Congress." *American Politics Research* 36: 130–52.

Rocha, Rene and Robert Wrinkle. 2011. "Gender, Ethnicity, and Support for Bilingual Education: Will Just Any Woman or Latino Do? A Contingent 'No.'" *Policy Studies Journal* 39 (2): 309–28.

Rosenthal, Brian M., and David Saleh Rauf. 2014. "Patrick Casts Wide Net to Lure Support—GOP Candidate Innovates in Use of Social Media." *Houston Chronicle*, November 1, 3A.

———. 2014. "Web is Way for Patrick Campaign." *San Antonio Express News*, November 2, A3.

Rosenwasser, Shirley, and Jana Seale. 1988. "Attitudes toward a Hypothetical Male or Female Presidential Candidate: A Research Note." *Political Psychology* 9 (4): 591–98.

Rosenwasser, Shirley, and Norma Dean. 1989. "Gender Role and Political Office." *Psychology of Women Quarterly* 13: 77–85.

Saint-Germain, Michelle. 1989. "Does Their Difference Make a Difference? The Impact of Women on Public Policy in the Arizona Legislature." *Social Science Quarterly* 70 (4): 956–968.

Sampaio, Anna. 2013. "Latinas and Electoral Politics: Expanding Participation and Power in State and National Elections." In *Gender and Elections: Shaping the Future of American Politics*, 3rd Edition, edited by Susan J. Carroll and Richard L. Fox. New York: Cambridge University Press.

Sanbonmatsu, Kira. 2002. "Gender Stereotypes and Vote Choice." *American Journal of Political Science* 46(1): 20–34.

Sanbonmatsu, Kira. 2006. *Where Women Run: Gender and Party in the American States*. Ann Arbor, MI: University of Michigan Press.

———. 2013. "The Candidacies of U.S. Women of Color for Statewide Executive Office." Paper presented at American Political Science Association, Washington, DC. http://papers.ssrn.com/sol3/papers.cfm?abstract_id=2300783.

Sanbonmatsu, Kira, and Kathleen Dolan. 2009. "Do Gender Stereotypes Transcend Party?" *Political Research Quarterly* 62: 485–94.

Sanchez, G. R. 2006. "The Role of Group Consciousness in Political Participation Among Latinos in the United States." *American Politics Research* 34 (3): 427–50.

Sanchez, Gabriel. 2012. "The Context of Immigration Policy in New Mexico Reflects National Trends." *Latino Decisions Blog*. Accessed at http://www.latinodecisions.com/blog/2012/10/31/the-context-of-immigration-policy-in-new-mexico-reflects-national-trends/.

Sanchez, Gabriel. 2014. "The Politics of Latino Representation in New Mexico." *Latino Decisions Blog*. Accessed at http://www.latinodecisions.com/blog/2014/09/19/the-politics-of-latino-representation-in-new-mexico/.

Sanchez, Gabriel R., and Natalie Masuoka. 2010. "Brown-Utility Heuristic? The Presence and Contributing Factors of Latino Linked Fate." *Hispanic Journal of Behavioral Sciences* 32(4): 519–31.

Sanchez, Gabriel, Jillian Medeiros, and Vickie Ybarra. 2010. "Hispanic Vote will decide next Governor of New Mexico." Accessed at http://www.latinodecisions.com/blog/2010/10/19/hispanic-vote-next-governor-new-mexico/.

Sandoval, C. 2000. *Methodology of the Oppressed*. Minneapolis, MN: University of Minnesota Press.

Sapiro, Virginia. 1981. "If US Senator Baker were a Woman: An Experimental Study of Candidate Images." *Political Psychology* 3 (1/2): 61–83.

Sapiro, Virginia. 1983. *The Political Integration of Women: Roles, Socialization, and Politics*. Urbana, IL: University of Illinois Press.

Scheurich, J. J., and M. D. Young. 1997. "Coloring Epistemologies: Are Our Research Epistemologies Racially Biased?" *Educational Researcher* 26 (4): 4–16.

Schlesinger, Mark, and Caroline Heldman. 2003. "Gender Gap or Gender Gaps? New Support for Government Action and Policies." *Journal of Politics* 63 (February): 59–92.

Schlozman, Kay Lehman, Nancy Burns, and Sidney Verba. 1999. "'What Happened at Work Today?' A Multistage Model of Gender, Employment, and Political Participation." *The Journal of Politics* 61 (1): 29–53.

Schneider, Monica C., and Angela L. Bos. 2011. "An Exploration of the Content of Stereotypes of Black Politicians." *Political Psychology* 32 (2): 205–33.

Schnur, D. 2007. "The Affect Effect in the Very Real World of Political Campaigns." In *The Affect Effect: The Dynamics of Emotion in Political Thinking and Behavior*, edited by W. R. Neuman, G.E. Marcus, A. N. Crigler, and M. MacKuen, 357–74. Chicago, IL: University of Chicago Press.

Scola, Becki. 2006. "Women of Color in State Legislatures: Gender, Race, Ethnicity and Legislative Office Holding." *Journal of Women, Politics, and Politics* 28 (3/4): 43–70.

———. 2013. *Gender, Race, and Office Holding in the United States: Representation at the Intersection*. NY: Routledge.

Sears, David O., Jack Citrin, and Rick Kosterman. 1987. "Jesse Jackson and the Southern White Electorate in 1984." In *Blacks in Southern Politics*, edited by L. W. Moreland, R. P. Steed. New York: Praeger.

Select Committee on Public School Accountability. 2008. *Final Interim Report*. Austin, TX: Texas State Legislature. Retrieved from: http://www.senate.state.tx.us/75r/Senate/commit/c835/c835.InterimReport80.pdf.

Shaw, Daron. 1999. "The Effect of TV Ads and Candidate Appearances on State-wide Presidential Vote, 1988–1996." *American Political Science Review* 93: 345–61.

Shea, Daniel M., and Michael J. Burton. 2006. *Campaign Craft: The Strategies, Tactics, and the Art of Political Campaign Management*. Westport, CT: Praeger.

Siebel Newsom, Jennifer. 2011. *Miss Representation*. San Francisco, CA: Roco Films Educational.

Sierra, Christine Marie. 2009. "Latinas and Electoral Politics: Movin' on Up." In *Gender and Elections: Shaping the Future of American Politics*, 2nd Edition, edited by Susan J. Carroll and Richard L. Fox, 144–64. London: Cambridge University Press.

Sierra, Christine M., and Adalijiza Sosa-Riddell. 1994. "Chicanas as Political Actors: Rare Literature, Complex Practice." *National Political Science Review* 4: 297–317.

Sierra, Christine Marie, and F. Chris García. 2010. "Hispanic Politics in a Battleground State: New Mexico in 2004." In *Beyond the Barrio: Latinos in the 2004 Elections*, edited by Rodolfo O. de la Garza, Louis DeSipio, and David L. Leal. Notre Dame, IN: Notre Dame University Press.

Sigelman, Carol K., Lee Sigelman, Barbara J. Walkosz, and Michael Nitz. 1995. "Black Candidates, White Voters: Understanding Racial Bias in Political Perceptions." *American Journal of Political Science* 39 (1): 243–65.

Sigelman, Lee, and Susan Welch. 1984. "Race, Gender, and Opinion Toward Black and Female Presidential Candidates." *Public Opinion Quarterly* 48 (2): 467–75.

Sigelman, Lee, and Carol K. Sigelman. 1982. "Sexism, Racism, and Ageism in Voting Behavior: An Experimental Analysis." *Social Psychology Quarterly* 45 (4) (Dec): 263–69.

Silber Mohamed, Heather. 2010. "The Boundaries of American-ness: Perceived Barriers among Latino Subgroups." Annual Meeting of the American Political Science Association, Washington, DC. September.

———. 2015. "Americana or Latina? Gender and Identity Acquisition Among Hispanics in the United States." *Politics, Groups and Identities* 3 (1): 40–58.

Simien, Evelyn M. 2007. "Doing Intersectionality Research: From Conceptual Issues to Practical Examples." *Politics and Gender* 3 (2): 264–71.

Simon, Rita J., and Jean M. Landis. 1989. "A Report: Women's and Men's Attitudes about a Woman's Place and Role." *Public Opinion Quarterly* 53 (June): 265–76.

Smooth, Wendy. 2005. "Black Women's Legislative Influence and the Fate of Progressive Policies in the Era of Devolution." In *Black and Latino/a Politics: Issues in Political Development in the United States,* edited by William E. Nelson, Jr., and Jessica Lavariega Monforti, 209–20. Miami FL: Barnhardt & Ashe Publishing.

———. 2006. "Intersectionality in Electoral Politics: A Mess Worth Making." *Politics & Gender* 2 (3): 400–14.

———. 2009. "African American Women and Electoral Politics: A Challenge to the Post-Race Rhetoric of the Obama Movement." In *Gender and Elections: Shaping the Future of American Politics,* 2nd Edition, edited by Susan J. Carroll and Richard L. Fox, 165–86. New York: Cambridge University Press.

Solorzano, Daniel G. and Dolores Delgado Bernal. 2001. "Examining Transformational Resistance Through a Critical Race and Latcrit Theory Framework." *Urban Education* 36 (3): 308–342.

Sonenshine, Raphael J., and Susan H. Pinkus. 2005. "Latino Incorporation Reaches the Urban Summit: How Antonio Villagraigosa Won the 2005 Los Angeles Mayor's Race." *PS: Political Science and Politics*: 713–25.

Sonmez, Felicia. 2012. "N.M. Gov. Susana Martinez Criticizes Romney's 'Self-Deportation' Idea." *Washington Post.* Accessed at http://www.washingtonpost.com/blogs/post-politics/post/nm-gov-susana-martinez-criticizes-romneys-self-deportation-idea/2012/05/14/gIQAl8l8OU_blog.html.

Stemler, Steve. 2001. "An Overview of Content Analysis." *Practical Assessment, Research, and Evaluation* 7(17). Available from http://edresearch.org.

Stewart, A. J., and C. McDermott. 2004. "Gender in Psychology." *Annual Review of Psychology* 55: 519–44.

Stokes, Atiya Kai. 2003. "Latino Group Consciousness and Political Participation." *American Politics Research* 31 (4): 361–678.

Stone, C. N. 1989. *Regime Politics: Governing Atlanta, 1946–1988.* Lawrence, Kansas: University Press of Kansas.

Stutz, Terrence. 2014. "Van de Putte Rips Patrick on School Cuts in First TV Ad in Lieutenant Governor's Race," *Dallas Morning News,* Accessed September 5 at http://trailblazersblog.dallasnews.com/category/democrats/page/2/.

Subervi-Velez, Federico. 2008. *The Mass Media and Latino Politics: Studies of U.S. Media Content, Campaign Strategies and Survey Research From 1984–2004.* N.Y.: Routledge Press.

Swain, Carol. 1995. *Black Faces, Black Interests.* Cambridge, MA: Harvard University Press.

Swers, M. L. 2002. *The Difference Women Make: The Policy Impact of Women in Congress.* Chicago, IL: University of Chicago Press.

Swers, Michele L., and Carin Larson. 2005. "Women in Congress: Do They Act as Advocates for Women's Issues?" In *Women and Elective Office: Past, Present, and Future,* edited by Sue Thomas and Clyde Wilcox, 110–28. NY: Oxford University Press.

Takash, Paule Cruz. 1993. "Breaking Barriers to Representation: Chicana/Latina Elected Officials in California." *Urban Anthropology and Studies of Cultural Systems and World Economic Development* 22 (3/4): 326–60.

Tate, Katherine. 2003. *Black Faces in the Mirror: African Americans and Their Representatives in the US Congress.* Princeton University Press.

Terkildsen, Nayda. 1993. "When White Voters Evaluate Black Candidates: The Processing Implications of Candidate Skin Color, Prejudice, and Self-Monitoring." *American Journal of Political Science* 37 (4) (Nov) : 1032–53.

Texas Education Agency (TEA). 2014. *Enrollment in Texas Public Schools, 2013–2014.* Austin, TX: Texas Education Agency.

Texas Higher Education Coordinating Board (THECB). 2009. Texas High School Graduates: College Enrollment Trends. Austin, TX: Texas Higher Education Coordinating Board. Retrieved from: http://www.thecb.state.tx.us/reports/PDF/2455.PDF?CFID=25660372&CFTOKEN=58855048.

Texas Legislative Reference Library. 2013. *Member Statistics and Session Snapshot.* Austin, TX: Texas State Legislature.

Texas Senate. 2013a. *Senate Chamber Hearing on Senate Bill 5.*

Texas Senate. 2013b. *Senate Chamber Hearing on House Bill 5.*

Texas Taxpayers and Student Fairness Coalition et al. v. Williams. 2014. Final Opinion.

The American National Election Studies (ANES; www.electionstudies.org). 1992-2009 Panel Study [dataset]. Stanford University and the University of Michigan.

Thomas, Sue and Susan Welch. 1991. "The Impact of Gender on Activities and Priorities of State Legislators." *The Western Political Quarterly* 44 (2) (June): 445–56.

Thomas, Susan. 1994. *How Women Legislate.* Oxford: Oxford University Press.

Thomas, Sue, and Clyde Wilcox, eds. 2014. *Women and Elective Office: Past, Present, and Future.* NY: Oxford University Press.

Tjaden, Patricia, and Nancy Thoennes. 2000. "Full Report of the Prevalence, Incidence, and Consequences of Violence Against Women." *National Institute of Justice, Office of Justice Programs, U.S. Dept. of Justice* and the *Centers for Disease Control.* Washington, DC.

Tolbert, C. J., and R. E. Hero. 1996. "Race/Ethnicity and Direct Democracy: An Analysis of California's Illegal Immigration Initiatives." *Journal of Politics* 58: 806–18.

Torres, Norma. 2016. "Biography." *Congressional Website of Congresswoman Norma Torres.* www.torres.house.gov.

Tucker, James Thomas. 2009. *The Battle Over Bilingual Ballots: Language Minorities and Political Access Under the Voting Rights Act.* VT: Ashgate Press.

Turrill, Dounia, and Glenn Enoch. 2015. "The Total Audience Report." *Nielsen Report.* New York: The Nielsen Company.

Tversky, A. and Kahneman, D. 1981. "The Framing of Decisions and the Psychology of Choice." *Science* 211: 453–458.

Uhlaner, Carole J., and F. Chris García. 2005. "Learning Which Party Fits: Experience, Ethnic Identity, and the Demographic Foundations of Latino Party Identification. "In *Diversity in Democracy: Minority Representation in the United States,*" edited by Gary M. Segura and Shaun Bowler, 72–101. Charlottesville, VA University of Virginia Press.

Ura, Alexa. 2014. "Patrick, Van de Putte Hone Their Immigration Messages." *Texas Tribune,* July 17 at www.texastribune.org/2014/07/17/lt-gov-candidates-hone-their-immigration-messages.

———. 2014. "Patrick and Van de Putte Spar Over Taxes." *Texas Tribune,* September 29, at www.texastribune.org/2014/09/29/debate-van-de-putte-and-patrick.

Valentino, N. A., V. L. Hutchings, and I. White. 2002. "Cues that Matter: How Political Ads Prime Racial Attitudes During Campaigns." *American Political Science Review* 96:75–90.

Valentino, N. A. Brader, Ted. Groenendyk, Eric W., Krysha Gregorowicz, and Vincent L. Hutchings. 2011. "Election Night's Alright for Fighting: The Role of Emotions in Political Participation." *Journal of Politics.* 73 (1): 156–170.

Valentino, N. A., M. W. Traugott, and V. Hutchings. 2002. "Group Cues and Ideological Constraint: A Replication of Political Advertising Effects Studies in the Lab and in the Field." *Political Communication* 19: 29–48.

Verba, Sidney, Nancy Burns, and Kay L. Schlozman. 1997. "Knowing and Caring About Politics: Gender and Political Engagement." *Journal of Politics* 59 (December): 1051–72.

Verba, Sidney, Kay Lehman Schlozman, and Henry E. Brady. 1995. *Voice and Equality: Civic Voluntarism in American Politics.* Cambridge, MA: Harvard University Press.

Walker, Diana. 2008. "The Incredibly Shrinking Democrats." *Time Magazine,* April 24.

Waters, Mary C. 1999. *Black Identities: West Indian Immigrant Dreams and American Realities.* New York: Russell Sage Foundation.

Weber, C. 2007. "Exploring the Role of Discrete Emotions in Political Campaigns." Paper presented at the Annual Meeting of the American Political Science Association, August.

Welch, Susan and Lee Sigelman. 1992. "A Gender Gap among Hispanics? A Comparison with Blacks and Anglos." *The Western Political Quarterly* 45 (1) (Mar.): 181–99.

West, C., and S. Fenstermaker. 1995. "Doing Difference." *Gender and Society* 9(1): 8–37.

West, Darrell. 2001. *Air Wars: Television Advertising in Election Campaigns, 1952–2000.* Washington, DC: Congressional Quarterly Press.

Wilcox, Clyde. 1994. "Why Was 1992 The 'Year of the Woman'? Explaining Women's Gains in 1992." In *The Year of the Woman: Myths and Realities,* edited by Elizabeth Adell Cook, Sue Thomas, and Clyde Wilcox, 1–24. CO: Westview Press.

Williams, Linda F. 1990. "White/Black Perceptions of the Electability of Black Political Candidates." In *Black Electoral Politics*, edited by Lucius J. Barker, Vol. 2. New Jersey: Transaction Publishers.

Winter, Nicholas J. G. 2008. *Dangerous Frames: How Ideas About Race and Gender Shape Public Opinion.* Chicago, IL: University of Chicago Press.

———. 2010. "Masculine Republicans and Feminine Democrats: Gender and Americans' Explicit and Implicit Images of the Political Parties." *Political Behavior* 32 (4): 587–618.

Wilson, William J. 1980. *The Declining Significance of Race.* Chicago: University of Chicago Press.

Wolbrecht, Christina. 2000. *The Politics of Women's Rights: Parties, Positions, and Change.* Princeton: Princeton University Press.

Wolfinger, Raymond E. 1965. "The Development and Persistence of Ethnic Voting." *American Political Science Review* 59(4): 896–908.

Wolfinger, R. E., & S. J. Rosenstone. 1980. *Who Votes?* New Haven, CT: Yale University Press.

"Women in Elective Office 2015: Overview Fact Sheet." CAWP Accessed at http://www.cawp.rutgers.edu/current-numbers.

Woodall, Gina Serignese, Kim L. Fridkin, and Jill Carle. 2010. "Sarah Palin Beauty is Beastly?: An Exploratory Content Analysis of Media Coverage." In *Cracking the Highest Glass Ceiling: A Global Comparison of Women's Campaigns for Executive Office*, 91–111. Santa Barbara, California: Praeger.

Yasso, T. J. 2005. "Whose Culture has Capital? A Critical Race Theory Discussion of Community Cultural Wealth." *Race Ethnicity in Education* 8 (1): 69–91.

Index

Abrajano, Marissa, 86
accents, 178
ACT. *See* Assisting Caregivers Today Caucus
activism, 154, *162*; Chicana, 99, 155–56, 188; civic, 164–67; community, 63, 167–68; hashtag, 98
advertisements, 137, 144–47, *146*; attack ads compared to positive, 138; campaigns and, 85–87, 136–39, 147n2; framing issues in, 138–39; priming voters in, 139; psychological effects of campaign, 86; Spanish and English, 86; television campaigns and, 135–38, 140–41, *142*, 144–45, 147n2, *205–9*
advocacy, 27, 112, 184, 186–87
Affigne, Tony, xxi–xxii, 195
African Americans. *See* Blacks; women of color
agendas, 64–65, 71–79, *73*, *78*, 114–18
Agranoff, Robert, 137
"American Dream," 84
American Indians, 24
American National Election Studies (ANES), xviii
analyses, 13, *15*, 77, *78*, 79, 90. *See also* research

ANES. *See* American National Election Studies
Anglos. *See* Whites
Ansolabehere, S., 85, 138
Arceneaux, Kevin, 86
Arendt, H., 110
Asians, 8–9, 24, 29–36, *30*, *35*, 37n12
assessments, of Latina legislator activity, 61–62
Assisting Caregivers Today Caucus (ACT), 132

Baca, Joe, 68
barriers, 128–29
Bejarano, Christina, xviii, 69, 99–100, 115–16; Latina candidates' viability and, 25–27, 32, 35–36, 149, 155, 175
Beltran, Christina, 99
Benitez-Thompson, Teresa, 104, 108, *109*
Berelson, Bernard, 138
Bernal, Joe, 185
Beutler, Jaime Herrera, 68, 92
biases, 14, 139
"big data," 112
bilingualism, 174, 187
bill sponsorships: Blacks and, 71, 72, 77, *78*; Latina legislators

tokenism, essentialism bred by, 123
tool, social media as, 83–84, 98, 100–101, 140–41
Top Ten Percent Plan, 188–89
Torres, Esteban, 66–67
Torres, Norma, 68, 75, 90, 92
trait factors, 47–51, *48–49*
trait stereotypes. *See* stereotypes
trust, 107–8
Twitter, 195; big data for research on, 112; as key element for networked representation, 108; Latina candidates and, 83, 85–87, 89–92; Latina legislators' accounts on, 101–3, *102–3*; Latina legislators on, 97–112; in legislative process, 97–99; as *micro-blogging* platform, 97–98; networked representation and followers on, 104–5, 108 *104*; ratios of followers on, *104*, 104–5; tweets per member account on, *103*, 103–4; Whites and campaign, 87
2000 Census Decennial Census, 9

Uber, 111
underrepresentation, 128–29, 131, 149–50, 193
unemployment, 151–52
University of Texas Center for Education Policy, *184*
Urbano, Juan Luis, xix, 195

values, 125–26
Van de Putte, Leticia, xxi, 195; background and leadership of, *184*, 184–85, 187; campaign candidacy of, 136, 140–41, *142*, 143–45, 147 *146*; contribution diminishment of, 186–87; education committee and, 186–87; liberalism and, 135–47; race-gendering theory research on, 182–91
"Van de Putte Amendment," 188–90
variables: binary, 34; dependent, 13–14 18–19, 16, 34–35, *35*; independent, 13, 18–19; multivariate model's binary, 34; socio-demographic, 13,

18–19; survey experiment design and, 25, *30*, 34
Velasquez, Nydia M., 66, *67*, 74–75, 79–81
virtual home style, 97–100, 106
vote choice, 34–36
voters, 4; campaign manipulation attempts and, 135–36; candidate identity and perceptions of, 24–36, *30, 33, 35*; ethno-racial identities and, xviii; examining identity role of, 32, 37n12; identification theory utilized on, 86; identity, 32–33, *33*; importance of minority, 29; Latina candidates and, 25, 28–33, *30, 33*; Latina/os registration rates of, 39, 58n2; Latinas and perceptions of, xvi; Latinas as registered, 11, *11*; liberalism assumptions made by, 33; priming advertisements for, 139; registration rates of Latina/o, 39, 58n2; support for, 25, 28–33, *30*; television campaigning and, 137–39; YouGov survey and stereotyped, xviii, 40–58
Voting Rights Act, electoral inequities and, 39, 58n2

wage inequalities, 151, *151*, 180n5
Wagner, 86–87, 91
Wheeler, Bruce, 110
Whites, 24–25; candidates, 41, 58n4; communities of ethnic, 173; intersectionality and, 114–20; Latina/o candidates comparisons to, 43–46, 58n6, 127–33; political predomination of male, 155, 169, 176–77, 185; in surveys, *30*, 31–32, 37n12; Twitter in campaigns and, 87; voting and, 4. *See also* non-Latina females
Wilson, Marie, 128
Wilson, Walter Clark, xix, 195
"window dressing," treatment, 176–77
Wisconsin Advertising Project, 136–37
women, xv; conflicting political agendas of minority, 114–18;

About the Contributors

Tony Affigne is professor and past chair of political science, and past director of Black studies, at Providence College, where he currently teaches American and comparative politics. He was co-editor of *Latino Politics en Ciencia Política* (NYU Press, 2014), author of "The Latino Voice in Political Analysis, 1970–2014" in the same volume, and author of "Minority Majority America and the Ghost of Woodrow Wilson," published in *Politics, Groups, and Identities* (September 2014). Affigne was co-founder and past president of the APSA Section on Race, Ethnicity, and Politics and the Latino Caucus in Political Science. Since 2001 he has served as executive board member for the Rhode Island Latino Civic Fund, and in 1982 was Rhode Island's first ever Latino candidate for elective office. He can be reached by email at affigne@providence.edu.

Ivy A. M. Cargile is an assistant professor at St. Norbert College in political science. She has her PhD from Claremont Graduate University located in Southern California. Broadly, her research interests center around political behavior in the context of the United States. She is interested in how the intersections of gender, race, and ethnicity influence electoral behavior. Specifically she explores why people engage the political system in the manner in which they do. As a result, she is concerned with how people are politically socialized and the effects of the process. She seeks to understand why people participate politically, and why they do not—especially when people are naturalized citizens. Consequently, she also does research on issues surrounding immigration and Latina/o politics. She has co-authored articles on the framing effects on Latino immigrants as well as the acquisition of democratic values by Latinos in the United States.

John García is currently a research professor, director of the Resource Center for Minority Data, and director of community outreach at the Inter-University Consortium for Political (Institute for Social Research-ISR) at the University of Michigan, as well as faculty associate in the Center for Political Studies. In addition, he served as interim director of the ICPSR Summer Program in Quantitative Methods—Summer, 2014. Dr. García has held a Professorship in the School of Government and Public Policy at the University of Arizona prior to this appointment for thirty-seven years. He received his PhD in government at Florida State University (1971).

His primary areas of research and teaching are: minority group politics, especially Latinos; political behavior; political mobilization, urban politics; social survey research; and public policy. He has published eleven books and over sixty articles and book chapters. He has been the recipient of over twenty grants to conduct research in his areas of interest, as well as instructor at the ICPSR Summer program spanning twenty-five years.

Sarah Allen Gershon is an associate professor of political science at Georgia State University. She received her PhD from Arizona State University in 2008. Dr. Gershon's research interests include media and politics, gender politics, and race and ethnicity. Her research has been published in several academic journals, including *Political Communication; Political Research Quarterly; the Journal of Women, Politics and Policy; Social Science Quarterly*, and *the Journal of Politics*.

Lizeth Gonzalez was born and raised in Rhode Island. She graduated from Providence College in 2015 with a BA in political science. During her college career, Lizeth immersed herself into various projects that brought her close to politics, policy, and the community through campaigning, research, and volunteer work. The daughter of two Guatemalan immigrants, Lizeth grew up merging her Hispanic culture with the new traditions found in the United States. This unique lens granted her an inside view into how Latinos are perceived and how they should perceive themselves. With this came the will and interest in studying immigration patterns in Latin America, as well as, Latino Politics in the United States.

Julia Marin Hellwege is PhD candidate in the Department of Political Science at University of New Mexico. She is co-author of "Differential Influence of the Great Recession on Political Participation among Race and Ethnic Groups," published in *Social Science Quarterly* (forthcoming) and her "Review Essay of Women in Legislative Politics," was published in *Politics, Groups, and Identities* (December 2014). Her dissertation asks how and why minority women state legislators act as surrogate representatives for constituents outside their districts. She teaches American and comparative politics at UNM and has taught courses on women in politics and political institutions. She is Project Manager for *Ready to Run NM,* a training program for women interested in public office, which was founded as part of a national network in collaboration with the Center for American Women and Politics at Rutgers University. In the fall of 2016, she will serve as an assistant professor in political science at the University of South Dakota.

Samantha L. Hernandez is a PhD student in the School of Politics and Global Studies at Arizona State University. She received a bachelor's degree in Political Science from Texas A&M University–Corpus Christi and a master's in Political Science from the University of Texas at San Antonio. Her current research interests include women in politics, Latino politics, urban politics, campaigns and elections, and research methods.

Patricia D. López is an assistant professor of leadership and policy studies at San Jose State University and an interdisciplinary scholar whose research contributes to the fields of Latina/o politics, Chicana/Latina feminist studies, and critical policy studies. Her recent five-year study examines the people and practices that embody public education reform, equity discourses, and the legislative processes in the context of the Texas State Legislature. Dr. López obtained her doctorate in Education Policy with a portfolio in Mexican American Studies from the University of Texas at Austin. Currently, she serves as the primary investigator and co-chair of the Texas Senate Hispanic Caucus and Mexican American Legislative Caucus Latina/o Education Task Force.

Jose Marichal is a professor of political science at California Lutheran University. He studies the effect of social media on politics and the impact of diversity on civic life. He is the author of *Facebook Democracy: The Architecture of Disclosure and the Threat to Civic Life,* along with a number of articles and book chapters on social media and politics.

Jennifer L. Merolla is a professor at the University of California, Riverside. She received her PhD in Political Science from Duke University in 2003. Her research focuses on how the political environment shapes individual attitudes and behavior. Her work includes the study of threat, voting behavior, parties, public opinion, race and ethnic politics, women and politics, and religion and politics. She is co-author of *Democracy at Risk: How Terrorist Threats Affect the Public,* published with the University of Chicago Press. Her work has appeared in journals such as the *Journal of Politics, Perspectives on Politics, Political Behavior,* and *Political Research Quarterly.*

Jessica Lavariega Monforti received her PhD in political science from Ohio State University in 2001. She is currently chair of the Department of Political Science at Pace University. She was an associate professor of political science and director of the Center for Survey Research at The University of Texas–Pan American. While much of her research focuses on the differential impact of public policy according to race, gender, and ethnicity, she is specifically interested in the political incorporation and representation of Latinos, immigrants, and women. Her latest research examines how major forces such as technology, the military system, and immigration policy impact and are impacted by Latino youth.

Leslie A. Navarro is currently a strategic advisor for organizations and higher education institutions on accreditation, planning, program development, and organizational culture. Dr. Navarro was president of Morton College in Chicago, Illinois. Prior to being president, she held the positions of executive vice president of administrative and academic affairs/chief financial officer and vice president of administration/chief financial officer. Dr. Navarro was a tenured associate professor and the head librarian of Austin Community College from 1999 to 2006. She earned her PhD in Educational Administration from UT–Austin in 2005.

Sharon A. Navarro was born and raised in El Paso, Texas. After receiving her bachelor's and master's degrees from the University of Texas at El Paso, she went on to receive her master's and doctorate from the University of Wisconsin at Madison. She is an associate professor of Political Science at the University of Texas at San Antonio. She co-edited *Latino Urban Agency* (2013), *Latino Americans and Political Participation (2004)*, co-authored *Politicas: Latina Public Officials in Texas (2008)*, and authored *Latina Legislator: Leticia Van De Putte and the Road to Leadership (2008)*. She has also published articles in *The Oxford Encyclopedia of Latinos and Latinas in Contemporary Politics, Law and Social Movements; Latino Studies Journal*, and *Aztlan: Journal of Chicano Studies*. She is currently the author of *Leticia Van de Putte: The Race for Texas Lieutenant Governor* (forthcoming).

Jean Reith Schroedel is a political science professor at Claremont Graduate University in California. She has written three single authored academic books, including *Is the Fetus a Person? A Comparison of Policies Across the Fifty States* that was given the Victoria Schuck Book Award by the American Political Science Association in 2001, as well as more than forty scholarly articles and book chapters. In 2009 Schroedel, co-edited two books on the impact of evangelical Christianity on democracy in America for the Russell Sage Foundation. She has spent much of the past several years studying voting rights issues and written a monograph entitled "Vote Dilution and Suppression in Indian Country" that is being published later this year in *Studies in American Political Development*. Schroedel also served as an expert witness in the recently settled *Wandering Medicine v. McCulloch* voting rights case that resulted in major changes in the administration of elections on Indian reservations in Montana and helped spark changes in several other states.

Christine Marie Sierra is professor emerita of political science at the University of New Mexico. Her expertise is in American politics with a focus on race, ethnicity, and gender. Her publications include work on Mexican American activism on immigration policy, Hispanic politics in New Mexico, and the politics of Latina women in the United States. She is a principal investigator on the Gender and Multicultural Leadership Project, a national study of elected officials of color in the United States (http://www.gmcl.org). Sierra has been a guest scholar at the Brookings Institution, the University of Arizona, and the Center for American Women and Politics at Rutgers University. As an expert in American and Latino/a politics, she appears frequently in local, national, and international media outlets.

Juan Urbano is an assistant professor of Political Science at Texas A&M University–Corpus Christi. Originally from Brownsville, TX, Dr. Urbano received his bachelor's degree from the University of Texas at Austin and a master's degree in political science from the University of Texas at San Antonio. He received his PhD from the University of Kansas in 2014. His areas of research include Latino political behavior, rural race relations, ethnic and gender political behavior, and Latino interest group behavior.

Walter Clark Wilson is an associate professor of political science at the University of Texas at San Antonio. He received his PhD at the University of Oklahoma, and was a congressional fellow at the Carl Albert Congressional Research and Studies Center and with the American Political Science Association. Dr. Wilson's research focuses on issues of legislative diversity and representation, with particular emphasis on Latino representation in Congress. His work appears in scholarly journals including *Legislative Studies Quarterly; Social Science Quarterly; Politics, Groups and Identities;* and *Polity.*